# Gender Differences
# in Public Opinion

# Gender Differences in Public Opinion

*Values and Political Consequences*

MARY-KATE LIZOTTE

TEMPLE UNIVERSITY PRESS
*Philadelphia • Rome • Tokyo*

TEMPLE UNIVERSITY PRESS
Philadelphia, Pennsylvania 19122
*tupress.temple.edu*

Library of Congress Cataloging-in-Publication Data

Names: Lizotte, Mary-Kate, 1982– author.
Title: Gender differences in public opinion : values and political
   consequences / Mary-Kate Lizotte.
Description: Philadelphia : Temple University Press, 2020. | Includes
   bibliographical references. | Summary: "Uses data from the American
   National Election Study to explore gender gaps in public opinion, the
   explanatory power of values, and the political consequences of these
   opinion differences. Each chapter discusses how the gender gap in a
   given topical area has influenced the gender gap in voting"—Provided
   by publisher.
Identifiers: LCCN 2019020031 (print) | LCCN 2019981201 (ebook) |
   ISBN 9781439916094 (paperback) | ISBN 9781439916087 (cloth) |
   ISBN 9781439916100 (ebook)
Subjects: LCSH: Political participation—Sex differences—United States. |
   Sex differences (Psychology)—Political aspects—United States. |
   Social values—United States—Public opinion. | Social values—Sex
   differences—United States. | Political psychology—United States. |
   United States—Politics and government.
Classification: LCC JK1764 .L59 2020 (print) | LCC JK1764 (ebook) |
   DDC 323/.0420810973—dc23
LC record available at https://lccn.loc.gov/2019020031
LC ebook record available at https://lccn.loc.gov/2019981201

♾ The paper used in this publication meets the requirements of the
American National Standard for Information Sciences—Permanence of
Paper for Printed Library Materials, ANSI Z39.48-1992

Printed in the United States of America

9  8  7  6  5  4  3  2  1

# Contents

# Figures and Tables

## Figures

## Tables

# Acknowledgments

I am thankful to so many individuals for their support and helpful advice. I am very grateful for the guidance and support from Leonie Huddy, who has provided such helpful feedback and encouragement over the years. I also thank my other graduate professors, including but not limited to Stanley Feldman, Howard Lavine, Milton Lodge, and Matthew Lebo. My undergraduate mentor and thesis advisor, James Carlson, has also always supported me.

I am so grateful for the invaluable support and advice of many other friends and colleagues in the discipline, including but not limited to Kira Sanbonmatsu, Kathleen A. Dolan, Zoe M. Oxley, Sue Tolleson Rinehart, Richard C. Eichenberg, Richard J. Stoll, Steven Greene, Laurel Elder, Toney E. Carey Jr., Monica C. Schneider, Angela L. Bos, Mirya R. Holman, Erin Cassese, and Heather L. Ondercin, as well as all the participants of the New Research on Gender and Political Psychology group and of the Gender and Political Psychology Writing Group.

I am grateful for the support of Augusta University and of Elna Green, dean of the Katherine Reese Pamplin College of Arts,

Humanities, and Social Sciences. In particular, I am thankful to Martha Ginn for being such a wonderful friend and colleague. I am also grateful to Dustin Avent-Holt, Kimberly Davies, and all of my department colleagues for their encouragement and assistance. Thanks also go to my colleagues at Birmingham-Southern College, where I wrote the first draft of the prospectus for this book.

My friends and family have always been supportive of me, for which I am grateful. I thank my parents, Celia and Marc, for instilling in me an interest in politics from a young age. My brother, Sean, and his family, Melanie, Blake, and Victoria, have always been there for me. So many others have supported me, including Erin Buckley, Bethany Callahan, Isabel Monteiro Caliva, Lyndsay Taylor Ronan, Kate Bargnesi, Jessika Mejia, Lily Li Griffin, Alicia Weaver, Heather Meggers-Wright, Tricia Witte, David Resha, and Greta Valenti. I thank them, as well as Jordan Lewis, for his humor, endless encouragement, and affection, and my consummate writing companion, Bandit.

Thanks also go to the American National Election Study and World Values Survey for the data. And I am incredibly thankful to the reviewers, Aaron Javsicas, and Temple University Press for their feedback and help during this process.

# Gender Differences
# in Public Opinion

# 1

# Introducing Gender Differences in Public Opinion

I am for keeping the thing going while things are stirring. Because if we wait till it is still, it will take a great while to get it going again. (Sojourner Truth, quoted in Campbell 1989, 252)

Alas, the 300 million pound Women March provides a strong argument for doing away with women's suffrage. Most of these vagina screechers didn't vote, but they mean business. Riiiiiiight. What a farce. (Dathan Paterno, quoted in Stevens 2017)

Since Obamacare and these issues have come up, the women are in my grill no matter where I go. They come up— "When is your next town hall?" And believe me, it's not to give positive input. (Rep. Dave Brat, quoted in Sganga 2017)

The sentiments of these individuals illustrate the importance of understanding gender differences in public opinion during a time when women's opinions and activism have appeared to experience a resurgence and have also received much media attention. If Sojourner Truth was correct, now is the time for continued activism and for the careful study of public opinion while women's opinions are salient and while the status quo is being questioned and challenged. The other two quotations highlight the negative reaction to women finding their political voice and to their increased political participation. Dathan Paterno resigned from his school board position after he tweeted this in response to the Women's March in 2017. His offensive and likely inaccurate comments about women marchers not having voted were highly controversial, placing him in hot water and leading to his resignation (Stevens 2017). The idea that women should lose the right to vote because of differences in opinion is a shocking and ludicrous notion, as well as fundamentally undemocratic. Finally, House representative from Virginia Dave Brat received a lot of attention for his comment about female constituents, but he was not the only member of Congress dealing with a vocal constituency. Women all over the country have been leading the push to keep the Affordable Care Act through their persistence at town hall meetings and their tenacious phone campaigns to the offices of elected officials (Sganga 2017).

It is worthwhile to understand whether the women participating in these marches or requesting town halls of their members of Congress are unique. Or if women in general differ from men in their opinions, which would mean that women marchers and women at town hall meetings are indicative of a larger phenomenon. Moreover, investigating why gender differences exist on certain political issues is also of interest and relevant, particularly during this time of increased activism among women and an upsurge in the number of women running for elected office. Although the factors that lead an individual to possess certain opinions about government and public policy are wide-ranging and multifaceted, I find that gender strongly influences these attitudes. What is more, gender differences in values, such as caring about the well-being of others, helping other people, and ensuring equal rights, are integral to understanding the origins of gender differences on an array of public policies.

There are several areas of research in American politics referred to as gender gaps. First, gender difference in vote choice, in which women are more likely than men to vote for Democratic candidates, is a gender gap (Huddy, Cassese, and Lizotte 2008a). A gender gap in vote choice emerged in the 2016 presidential election, with 54 percent of women and 41 percent of men voting for Hillary Clinton, the Democratic Party nominee (Center for American Women and Politics 2017). This equates to a 13 percentage point gap. Second, gender difference in party identification, in which women are more likely than men to identify with the Democratic Party, is a gender gap (Huddy, Cassese, and Lizotte 2008a). For example, a 9 percentage point gap in identification with the Democratic Party was found in April 2014, with 36 percent of women, compared to 27 percent of men, identifying as Democrats (Center for American Women and Politics 2014). Third, gender difference in voter turnout, in which women are more likely than men to turn out to vote, particularly in presidential elections, is a gender gap. In 2012, 63.3 percent of eligible women voted, and 59.3 percent of eligible men voted (Center for American Women and Politics 2019). Fourth, gender differences in other forms of participation, in which men are more likely to donate to and volunteer for political campaigns, are also gender gaps. Fifth, gender differences in political knowledge, interest in politics, political efficacy, and political awareness are gender gaps (Lay 2012; Lizotte and Sidman 2009; Verba, Burns, and Schlozman 1997). Compared to men, women have somewhat consistently been found to have lower levels of political knowledge by the most frequent method of measurement, as well as lower levels of awareness, interest, and efficacy (Lay 2012; Lizotte and Sidman 2009; Verba, Burns, and Schlozman 1997).

Last, gender differences in public opinion, in which women on average hold more liberal views than men on a number of issues, are gender gaps (Norrander 2008). For example, one poll finds a 21 percentage point gap on gun control, with 48 percent of women and 27 percent of men wanting major restrictions on owning guns; another poll finds a 4 percentage point gap in support of government action to reduce the wealth gap, with 54 percent of women, compared to 50 percent of men, supporting such action (Center for American Women and Politics 2012). In addition, women are more likely to support increased government spending for the poor, are more likely to support gay rights, are less likely to support the use of force, and are more likely to support a greater role for government (Carroll 2006; Center for American Women and Politics 2012; Lizotte 2017a; Norrander 2008; Sapiro 2002). Policy gaps are discussed in greater depth later in this chapter.

Gender gaps in public opinion matter. Research demonstrates that gender differences in issue positions contribute to the gender gap in voting (Chaney, Alvarez, and Nagler 1998; C. Clark and J. Clark 2009; Kaufmann and Petrocik 1999). Which issues are salient during a particular campaign also affects the size of gender differences in voting (Ondercin and Bernstein 2007). For three elections, in a statistical simulation in which men's issue preferences are given to women, there is a substantial decrease of the gender gap in vote choice (Chaney, Alvarez, and Nagler 1998). Support for government spending for the poor was more influential for women's vote than for men's vote in the 2004 election (C. Clark and J. Clark 2009). Moreover, Karen Kaufmann and John Petrocik (1999) find evidence that controlling for gender gaps on social issues and social welfare spending reduced the party identification gap to −0.2 percent from 9 percent in 1992 and to 4 percent from 14 percent in 1996. This means that during a particular election, if an issue on which there is a gender gap becomes salient, we would expect to see an electoral advantage for one political party and that party's candidates among women voters.

In a democracy, the public's opinions toward policy alternatives should matter. Individuals' preferences on government spending, actions, and regulations should influence elected officials and all other policy actors in the policy-making process. In a representative democracy, those elected and the government overall are supposed to represent the people and pursue policies that are in the people's interests. Encouragingly, the extant literature provides support that public opinion does influence policy makers. Public opinion, generally, is politically consequential. For example, shifts in opinion shape policy makers' decisions (Page and Shapiro 1983; Zaller 1992). Policy makers, presidential administrations, and other elected officials often seek public support for their policy agendas, necessitating successful public appeals. Public officials take public opinion into consideration and attempt to influence public opinion when there is opposition to their policy goals (Powlick 1991). Elections should ensure that elected officials are responsive to the people. Women are more than 50 percent of the population, making gender differences in public opinion of particular interest because women are more likely to turn out to vote than men (Center for American Women and Politics 2019). Thus, the origins of gender differences in public opinion deserve research attention.

Despite the significant influence of gender on public opinion, there is a conspicuous dearth of theoretically driven empirical research on why so many gender gaps on such varied policy areas exist. Prior work on gender and public opinion takes a more piecemeal approach. To date, the issue gap literature focuses on gender differences on individual issues rather than investigating multiple gaps. This method does not provide an overarching theory for why a number of gaps exist. My approach examines the emergence of gender differences in several policy areas, providing an overarching and broad theoretical framework for understanding the existence of many issue gaps.

This book is distinctive in four ways. First, it thoroughly investigates gender differences in public opinion through a careful analysis of public opinion on several policy areas where gender gaps emerge. Second, it provides a comprehensive explanatory approach to understanding multiple gaps in policy preferences, analyzing how value differences elucidate why many gaps emerge.

Third, I examine the political consequences of gender differences in public opinion, exploring how the different gender gaps have influenced the party identification and presidential vote choice of men and women. Fourth, the book contributes to several areas of research, including the study of public opinion, voter behavior, partisanship, women and politics, and political psychology.

In sum, this book attempts to fill the void in the literature by exploring in depth the role of gender in public opinion. I examine the factors that lead to certain positions on public policies, including opinions on governmental use of force both domestically and internationally, concern about environmental protections, attitudes regarding historically disadvantaged groups, and support for social welfare programs and spending. I seek to understand why women and men on average possess different policy positions even when taking into account other relevant factors such as education, class, race, income, and even party identification. Specifically, I investigate how values, such as egalitarianism, universalism, and benevolence, contribute to these various issue gaps. The analysis heavily relies on American National Election Study (ANES) data to lay bare these gender differences in opinion and the role of values in explaining these differences.

From a broader perspective, this research extends the understanding of public opinion on these policy areas, as well as provides evidence on the extent to which these gender gaps are the result of differences in values. This research also contributes to a better understanding of how appeals to different values can garner more support from women on public policy. I hope the analysis will advance political scientists' understanding of the gender gap and the importance of values when examining the public's attitudes toward these issues. At its core, this book is about how values influence public opinion, producing politically consequential gender differences.

In the following section, I summarize the existing literature on gender differences in public opinion. Gender gaps are present in many issue areas but do not materialize for all policies. The following section briefly discusses a number of established gaps.

Later chapters provide a more detailed discussion of each of these areas of public policy and the gender differences that exist.

## Gender Differences in Issue Positions

First, for the sake of clarity, I employ the term *gender gap* because that is the established terminology used to refer to differences in opinions, voting, and party identification between women and men (Huddy, Cassese, and Lizotte 2008a). Additionally, women's lived experiences clearly vary but are also indistinguishably affected by society's practice of assigning gender and the corresponding stereotype expectations (Kessler and McKenna 1978). Analysis of Canadian data reveals that sex approximates gender identity well for all but about a quarter of the sample (Bittner and Goodyear-Grant 2017). The theoretical approach of this book to gender differences in public opinion is nonessentialist, meaning that these gender gaps are not the result of foundational differences between men and women. The various gender gaps in policy preferences are sizeable; however, they are not large enough to indicate that all women differ from men.

### Force Issues

One of the larger gaps, on average 8–12 percentage points, emerges for international force issues; women are consistently less supportive than men of military interventions (Huddy, Cassese, and Lizotte 2008a; Norrander 2008). The gap on international force issues is particularly relevant to policy makers and political candidates in this post-9/11 era. The United States' role in the world, including in international disputes, is a vital one. Continued unrest in the Middle East, conflicts in Africa, threats of nuclear armament in North Korea, and the potential for sustained Russian aggression toward its neighbors, the United States, and Europe means that public opinion regarding foreign policy and the international use of force is of considerable interest. Hence, the gender gap on these attitudes is worthy of attention.

Prior work established a gender gap in support for intervention during World War II, Korea, Vietnam, the Gulf War, Afghanistan, and the Iraq War (Conover and Sapiro 1993; Huddy, Feldman, Taber, and Lahav 2005; Huddy, Feldman, and Cassese 2009; Shapiro and Mahajan 1986). Women report being generally less likely to favor the use of force to solve international problems (Norrander 2008). For the duration of the Cold War, researchers found that women were less favorable toward nuclear armament, and women were more anxious than men about the possibility of nuclear war (Bendyna et al. 1996; Gwartney-Gibbs and Lach 1991). In addition, analysis of data from 1980 to 2000 finds that women are less likely to support increased defense spending in comparison to men (Norrander 2008). Gender differences in foreign policy attitudes extend to perspectives on military strategies. For example, women are more favorable toward air strikes rather than strategies that include a commitment of troops on the ground (Eichenberg 2003).

A gap also exists for domestic force issues. Women are less supportive of the death penalty and more supportive of gun control (Howell and Day 2000; Whitehead and Blankenship 2000). The death penalty and gun control continue to be controversial and salient issues in American politics. Questions regarding the effectiveness and the morality of the death penalty arise each time an execution takes place. Advocates of increased regulations on the sale of guns and the banning of particular guns surface each time a mass shooting occurs. The public's opinions and the gender gaps on these issues are for that reason very important. Women are less likely than men to support the death penalty (Cochran and Sanders 2009; Kutateladze and Crossman 2009; Stack 2000; Whitehead and Blankenship 2000; for an exception to this finding, see Unnever, Cullen, and Roberts 2005). Women are also less likely to support police violence (Halim and Stiles 2001) or harsh punishment for criminals (Hurwitz and Smithey 1998).

A considerable amount of research has established a gender gap on gun control, with women more supportive of regulations than men (Celinska 2007; Erskine 1972; Haider-Markel and Joslyn 2001; Howell and Day 2000; Shapiro and Mahajan 1986; Wolpert and Gimpel 1998). Some of this research focuses on the gender gap (Howell and Day 2000; Shapiro and Mahajan 1986), while other studies include gender as a control variable (Celinska 2007; Haider-Markel and Joslyn 2001). As early as 1964, a gap of 14 percentage points on gun control issues existed (Erskine 1972). In a 1981 Gallup poll, women were more supportive of stricter gun sale laws by 19 percentage points (Shapiro and Mahajan 1986). Women are also more supportive of requiring a permit to buy a gun (Brennan, Lizotte, and McDowall 1993). Finally, prior research finds that women are more supportive of a handgun ban (Kleck, Gertz, and Bratton 2009).

## Social Welfare Issues

Similar in size to force issues, the gender gap on social welfare policies is well established. Social welfare issues can include support for various types of government spending, such as Social Security, the homeless, welfare, food stamps, childcare, and public schools (J. Clark and C. Clark 1993; C. Clark and J. Clark 1996; Cook and Wilcox 1995). Others have also included support for government provision of health insurance (J. Clark and C. Clark 1993; C. Clark and J. Clark 1996; Howell and Day 2000), support for a government-guaranteed standard of living, support for an increase in government services (J. Clark and C. Clark 1993; C. Clark and J. Clark 1996; Howell and Day 2000; Kaufmann and Petrocik 1999), support for government aid to black people or minorities (J. Clark and C. Clark 1993; C. Clark and J. Clark 1996; Cook and Wilcox 1995; Kaufmann and Petrocik 1999), and support for government spending on the poor (J. Clark and C. Clark 1993; C. Clark and J. Clark 1996; Cook and Wilcox 1995; Howell and Day 2000; Kaufmann and Petrocik 1999). These issues raise central ideological differences between left- and right-leaning Americans. First, these issues relate to questions about the size and role of government. Second, these issues prompt debates about the effectiveness of a helping hand versus self-reliance. It is crucial to understand why gender gaps are so sizeable and consistent on these issues.

Women are consistently more liberal on these issues in that they are more likely to support greater government spending on social welfare (Goertzel 1983; Howell and Day 2000; Kaufmann 2004; Kaufmann and Petrocik 1999; Schlesinger and Held-man 2001; Shapiro and Mahajan 1986; Shirazi and Biel 2005). Women are more likely to support government policies intended to provide for the general welfare and aimed at helping the less fortunate (Howell and Day 2000; Huddy, Cassese, and Lizotte 2008a; Norrander 2008). Of course, this means that by and large, men are more conservative than women on social welfare spending (Kaufmann, Petrocik, and Shaw 2008). Analysis of social welfare questions as a scale or as individual items, including support for government spending on food stamps, Social Security, the homeless, welfare, public schools, childcare, and the poor, typically reveals statistically significant gender gaps (Howell and Day 2000; Fox and Oxley 2016; Sapiro 2002). Women are also more supportive of increased government involvement in health-care policy, including being more favorable than men toward the Affordable Care Act (Howell and Day 2000; Lizotte 2016b). In other words, women are consistently more likely than men to support policies that provide for the disadvantaged.

Recently, this gap has averaged close to 10 percentage points (Norrander 2008). Gender differences on the issue of social welfare vary in size, depending on what particular aspect of social welfare is being studied. The gap ranges from 4 to 5 percentage points for issues such as government help to minorities, government-funded health insurance, and government-guaranteed jobs (J. Clark and C. Clark 1993; C. Clark and J. Clark 1996). The differences are much larger, up to 14 or 15 percentage points, for support of increased Social Security spending (J. Clark and C. Clark 1993; C. Clark and J. Clark 1996; Cook and Wilcox 1995). For the issues of spending for the poor, welfare, food stamps, and the homeless, the mean differences tend to be between 4 and 7 percentage points (Kaufmann and Petrocik 1999).

## Environmental Issues

Compared to force issues or social welfare policies, the gap on environmental issues is smaller in size (Norrander 2008). Previous research shows significant gender differences in environmental policy preferences. I would argue that environmental issues are one of the most pressing of our time. The potential for severe and widespread effects of climate change render it of paramount consequence to understand public opinion in this policy area, including the origins of gender differences. Women tend to report greater environmental concern (Mohai 1992). Gender differences emerge on the use of nuclear power and concern for environmental contamination as a result of nuclear waste disposal (Davidson and Freudenburg 1996). Women are more likely than men to express concern about pollution (Blocker and Eckberg 1997). There is a gender gap on climate change attitudes, with women more likely to express concern (Bord and O'Connor 1997). For example, women are significantly more likely to agree that climate change will result in coastal flooding as the result of sea levels rising, will cause droughts, and will result in an increase in natural disasters such as hurricanes (Bord and O'Connor 1997). In more recent data, the results are similar, with a 5 percentage point gap on believing that the effects of global warming have already begun, an 8 percentage point gap on believing that human behavior is causing global warming, and a 6 percentage point gap on agreeing that most scientists believe global warming is occurring (McCright 2010).

## Equal Rights

Last, gaps on equal rights are among the smallest gaps (Huddy, Cassese, and Lizotte 2008a; Norrander 2008). With respect to equal rights, the size of the gap depends on the group about whose rights are being asked. First, there are gender differences on support for gay rights. Although marriage equality is now the law of the land, the LGBTQ community is seeking other rights, such as employment rights, making this an area of continued importance to policy makers and pollsters. Women are more supportive of gay adoption rights, the right to serve in the military, and employment protections (Brewer 2003; Herek 2002a; Stoutenborough, Haider-Markel, and Allen 2006; Wilcox and Wolpert 2000). Men have more negative and hostile attitudes than women toward the LGBTQ community (Herek 1988; LaMar and Kite 1998; Mata, Ghavami, and Wittig 2010). Women are more likely to support equal rights and same-sex marriage (Haider-Markel and Joslyn 2008; Olson, Cadge, and Harrison 2006). Similarly, a gender gap in attitudes toward civil unions persists (Haider-Markel and Joslyn 2008; Olson, Cadge, and Harrison 2006).

Overall, the results with regard to gender differences in racial attitudes and race-related policy positions indicate a moderately consistent gap. The ongoing Black Lives Matter movement highlights the relevance and importance of understanding public opinion and gender differences on race-related policies. Women are more supportive of fair treatment in job practices for black people, including preferential hiring and promotion, are more favorable toward a greater government role in school integration, and are more positive toward affirmative action (Howell and Day 2000; Hughes and Tuch 2003). For example, Michael Hughes and Steven Tuch (2003), using the American National Election Study and the General Social Survey data, find that white women are significantly less likely than white men to report being against living in a racially mixed neighborhood, but these researchers fail to find gender differences for attitudes toward segregated neighborhoods or for feelings of closeness to black people. Susan Howell and Christine Day (2000) found women to be more liberal in their racial attitudes, which included perceptions of black people as trustworthy, intelligent, and hardworking.

In general, the magnitude of differences varies depending on the questions asked. Kaufmann and Petrocik (1999) found a 4–5 percentage point mean difference, with women more supportive of spending on programs to help black people. Others also find that a difference of 4 percent exists on spending for blacks (C. Clark and J. Clark 1996). For support of affirmative action, in terms of jobs, the difference varies from 4 percent to 6 percent, while support for education quotas results in a 7–9 percent difference (J. Clark and C. Clark 1993; C. Clark and J. Clark 1996; Cook and Wilcox 1995).

Gender differences also appear, though small, on the issue of equal rights for women. This issue is often considered alongside other policy questions referred to as women's issues. Generally, few gender differences exist in public opinion on women's issues. Depending on the issues, some gender differences are consistent, while others are not. With the Women's March following the inauguration of Donald Trump, it is possible that the women's movement is experiencing a resurgence and/or entering a new stage. Accordingly, the public's preferences on these issues, including whether a gender gap exists, are of substantial interest.

The term *women's issues* is fraught with a lack of clarity. Researchers have proposed different definitions, including issues that have a particular and more direct effect on women, such as equal rights and affirmative action policies. Men and women do not appear to consistently differ on their attitudes toward women's rights, such as support for the Equal Rights Amendment (ERA; Mansbridge 1985). Specifically, only a small public opinion gap of 3.7 percent exists in support for the Equal Rights Amendment, and positions on the ERA were not the driving force behind the gender gap in voting (Mansbridge 1985). For affirmative action policies directed at helping women attain better jobs and admission into institutions of higher education, there are sizeable gender differences of more than 10 percentage points (Steuernagel, Ahern, and Conway 1997). In sum, with respect to equal rights, gender differences tend to be small and do not always reach statistical significance (Chaney et al. 1998; Huddy, Cassese, and Lizotte 2008a; Mansbridge 1985; Shapiro and Mahajan 1986), but there are exceptions.

Other issues that may be categorized as women's issues, such as sexual harassment and abortion, have been understudied or have not been found to produce a large gender gap. Women are more likely to state that sexual harassment is an important issue, with a difference of 13 percent (C. Clark and J. Clark 1996; Cook and Wilcox 1995). Abortion attitudes provide another example of the absence of anticipated gender differences. There are few gender differences in support for legalized abortion in the United States (C. Clark and J. Clark 1996; Cook, Jelen, and Wilcox 1992; Cook and Wilcox 1995; Scott 1989; Strickler and Danigelis 2002). And when differences emerge, men are sometimes more supportive than women of reproductive rights by a few percentage points (J. Clark and C. Clark 1993; Shapiro and Mahajan 1986), although a few studies find that women are more supportive than men after controlling for religiosity (Combs and Welch 1982; Jelen and Wilcox 2005). Ultimately, on abortion, it is somewhat unclear if a gender gap exists because, depending on the other variables included in the statistical model, sometimes a small and significant gender gap appears, and sometimes one does not (Lizotte 2015). Connectedly, a large gender gap does not seem to exist on the issue of the Affordable Care Act birth control mandate, which requires all health insurance policies to cover artificial birth control (Deckman and McTague 2015).

Many researchers have argued that public opinion on women's issues does not contribute to the gender gap in voting (Gilens 1988; Lizotte 2016a; Mattei 2000). In the 2012 presidential election, though, attitudes toward the birth control mandate were more predictive of women's vote choice than men's (Deckman and McTague 2015). Therefore, not only is there a lack of consistent difference, but any differences that do exist do not always appear to contribute to the gap in voting. Because of the Women's March, however, we might see an increase in the electoral importance of these issues. Relatedly, during the #MeToo era, American society may find that issues such as sexual harassment, sexual assault, and other forms of mistreatment or violence against women will produce more sizeable and politically consequential gender gaps. In addition, the continued wave of stricter abortion regulations across several states, which was deemed the War on Women during the 2012 presidential election and continued after Justice Brett Kavanaugh's placement on the Supreme Court, may lead to greater salience and electoral consequence for reproductive rights. Because of data or space constraints, I unfortunately do not include an analysis of sexual harassment or reproductive rights in this book.

## Conclusion

As discussed at the outset of this chapter, public opinion—in particular gender differences in issue positions—is of great importance and political consequence. Now is especially a time of great interest in the gender gap in public opinion, given the Women's March, multistate teacher walkouts and protests, and women's involvement in the fight against repealing the Affordable Care Act. Women are finding their political voice in a heightened way compared to the past thirty years or so. Hence, knowing how women differ in their policy positions from men is of political and scholarly significance. During this time of increased activism, understanding the causes of the public's policy positions is of considerable interest to political parties, pundits, candidates, pollsters, and the media.

In conclusion, gender differences in public opinion emerge for several important and politically consequential policy areas. Because women consistently differ from men in their political attitudes and are recently more likely to vote, these gender differences in public opinion are of considerable interest to scholars and pollsters. Average differences in core values between men and women, particularly on pro-social values, are a largely untested explanation for these gender differences. Understanding gender differences in public support for policies will provide insight into general support for such policies, as well as an understanding of how to appeal to men and women on these matters. Moreover, these gender gaps have the potential to have important political consequences for partisanship and elections.

## Organization of the Book

In Chapter 2, I outline the theoretical underpinnings of the empirical investigations in subsequent chapters. The chapter provides an overview of existing explanations found in the literature on gender gaps in public opinion. I discuss four previously researched explanations, including feminist consciousness, professional and economically independent women, economically struggling women, and social role theory. Then I introduce a novel and, for the most part, previously untested explanation: values. Ample evidence shows that men and women differ in their value endorsements, which I contend is the reason for many of the gender gaps in public opinion. Relevantly, there are gender differences in pro-social values, including humanitarianism, universalism, benevolence, and egalitarianism. These values measure support for individuals, as well as society, ensuring equality, promoting social justice, and caring for close others.

Chapters 3, 4, 5, and 6 investigate the efficacy of the values explanation for different broad areas of public opinion where gender gaps emerge. Each of these chapters relies heavily on 1980–2012 American National Election Study Data (ANES) cumulative data.[1] The ANES is an established data set with a nationally representative sample that has been widely used in previous studies of the gender gap in issue preferences, party identification, and voting. At times, other data, including those of the 2011 World Values Survey[2] and the 2016 ANES, supplement the cumulative ANES analysis.

Chapter 3 specifically looks at domestic and international force issues. As noted previously, women are more likely than

---

1. ANES data are available at http://www.electionstudies.org.
2. World Values Survey data are available at http://www.worldvaluessurvey.org/WVSDocumentationWV6.jsp.

men to support gun control and oppose the death penalty, while men are more likely than women to support military interventions rather than diplomacy to deal with international disputes. The gender gap on force issues is one of the largest gaps, according to the extant literature. I find that differential value endorsement elucidates the existence of gender gaps on force issues. These findings provide insight for policy makers and activists interested in garnering support for force policies.

In Chapter 4, I consider the gender gap in environmental attitudes. As discussed previously, women are more likely than men to express concern about the environment and endorse greater government involvement to protect the environment. This is a timely issue, as public debates about the consequences of climate change have garnered a great deal of media attention in the United States. I find that value differences help illuminate why these gender differences in environmental attitudes exist. The pro-social values hypothesis could provide an avenue for acquiring more support for future environmental policies that have the possibility of improving the living conditions of all Americans.

Chapter 5 examines gender differences in attitudes toward various historically disadvantaged groups, including gay men and lesbians, African Americans, and women. The chapter demonstrates how women's greater endorsement of egalitarianism leads to increased support for rights for historically disadvantaged groups. For social movements, both present and future, these results suggest a pathway for increasing public support by emphasizing equality in their messaging and public appeals.

The focus of Chapter 6 is women's greater support for a social safety net. According to the literature, the gap on social welfare issues is the other largest gap besides force issues. As noted earlier, women are more likely than men to support government spending to help the less fortunate and other government programs to provide for the public's general welfare. Chapter 6 investigates how women's greater endorsement of egalitarianism results in differential support for social programs that make up the welfare state.

Chapter 7 provides a summary of the findings and their implications, including an analysis and discussion of the political consequences of these gender gaps. The chapter includes an examination of how the gender gaps in public opinion analyzed in prior chapters affect the gender gaps in party identification and presidential vote choice. In this final chapter, I also discuss how the findings underscore the central role of values in understanding public opinion. Moreover, I highlight that this research underscores the ways in which the political parties, social movements, interest groups, and political candidates can appeal to men and women through emphasizing how policies align with certain values. Finally, I suggest some avenues for future research on gender gaps in public opinion.

# 2

## Theoretical Approach

*Values as an Explanation*

I'm out here because I have a teenage son and a six-year-old daughter. I'm teaching them to be good, decent human beings who love and care about other communities and who care about the planet. (Nicholine Junge, quoted in Ufheil 2018)

I'm marching because I just believe that everyone should be equal, and I think this overall represents us coming together and the power of more than one person getting together. (Tyra, quoted in Rodriguez 2019)

These quotations exemplify the central point of this chapter. They demonstrate how values are at the heart of how people think about politics. Values such as caring for others and supporting equality influenced women to participate in the Women's March. It is not surprising that values strongly influence the way Americans view politics and decide their policy preferences. Growing up in the United States, children learn the Pledge of Allegiance and recite it daily in school. This pledge includes a reference to different values: "liberty and justice for all." From an early age, political socialization in our schools teaches us to value liberty, equality, justice, tolerance, democracy, and others. During adulthood, it is reasonable to assume that individuals would continue to rely on those values when evaluating political alternatives, including public policies. Furthermore, values are part of the broader political discourse. To be more specific, political campaigns through speeches, commercials, and slogans, as well as political party platforms, often draw on and attempt to appeal to people's politically relevant values. The objective of this chapter is to advocate for the key role of values in public opinion and as a cause of gender differences in policy preferences.

This chapter outlines the theoretical framework for the empirical chapters that follow. To start, this chapter details the various explanations for gender differences in public opinion with a particular focus on values. I begin with an examination of existing explanations for the origins of observed gender differences. These explanations are feminist identity, economic independence, economic hardship, and social role theory. I briefly discuss the conceptual underpinnings of each explanation and the empirical support to date for each. Next, I define what values are, summarize the scholarly history of the study of values, and offer an overview of values as an explanation of gender differences in public opinion. This part of the chapter focuses on pro-social values such as egalitarianism, which emphasizes equal opportunity and equal treatment for all and is a bedrock value for American citizens (McClosky and Zaller 1984). Finally, I discuss the measures of values available in the data, the measures in the data used to test the other theories for gender differences, and the analysis approach that I use in the subsequent chapters.

## Origins of Gender Differences

Research on gender differences investigates how gender matters with two different approaches: positional gender differences and structural gender differences (see Sapiro and Conover 1997 for a lengthy discussion). Positional differences describe when men and women hold different positions on the same attitude object, such as policy preferences. Research on positional gender differences focuses on finding a variable that explains the difference. This is also referred to as mediational analysis. Structural differences exist when men and women rely on different considerations in their evaluations of attitude objects. An example would be women relying on societal economic assessments, while men rely on personal economic assessments when voting (Chaney, Alvarez, and Nagler 1998; Welch and Hibbing 1992). This is also referred to as moderation.

Much of the research discussed here, in Chapter 1, and in my own analysis in subsequent chapters focuses more on positional differences and investigating whether values differences explain or mediate the gender gap in policy positions. Simply put, it has been well established that gender influences public opinion. This is thought to be a causal relationship in which gender is the reason for differences in issue positions. To understand this causal relationship more fully, scholars attempt to ascertain what statistically accounts for the observed gender differences with a mediating variable that will explain why women differ from men in some of their opinions. Consider an example to help illustrate the underlying reasoning of mediational analysis. If grade point average (GPA) predicted levels of happiness, where people with higher GPAs reported higher levels of happiness, the mediating variable might be self-esteem. Individuals with higher GPAs might gain positive increases in self-esteem, which then lead to higher levels of happiness. So public opinion researchers have tested several theories, discussed in the following sections, for why women tend to espouse more liberal policy positions on many political issues. In addition, I consider how value differences between men and women explain why women differ from men on various political issues. I discuss mediational analysis in greater detail in the final section of the chapter.

Scholars have put forth and investigated several theories for the gender gap. Here I discuss those theories that have gained a substantial amount of attention. I include some research that has focused on the gender gap in voting or gender differences in party identification, but that could also be applied to the gap in issue positions. I discuss feminist consciousness, economic circumstances, and social role theory as explanations. After discussing those theories, I discuss the values explanation. Each of the theories, including the values explanation, is included in Table 2.1 with a brief overview of their assumptions and research findings to date. At the end of the chapter, I provide information regarding gender differences on the values included in the analysis in Chapter 3 through Chapter 6.

## Feminism

The first explanation is feminism or feminist identity or consciousness. Feminist identity or feminist consciousness varies depending on the type of feminism. An established definition for feminist identity notes that most types of feminism include the following three components: (1) believing in sex or gender equality; (2) believing that historical inequality between men and women is not natural or predestined by a higher power but is socially constructed; and (3) acknowledging the shared experiences of women, which should motivate a desire for change (Cott 1987). Proponents of this explanation argue that feminist consciousness leads individuals to have a distinct perspective, causing attitudinal and policy preference differences.

There is evidence that feminist identity contributes to some of the gender gaps, including defense spending, environmental attitudes, and social welfare spending (Caughell 2016; Conover 1988; Deitch 1988; Somma and Tolleson-Rinehart 1997, but see Mansbridge 1985 for divergent findings). In support of this view, there is a correlation between feminist consciousness and support for unemployment spending, government spending on childcare, policies that promote equal opportunity for African Americans,

## TABLE 2.1. THEORIES FOR GENDER GAPS: ASSUMPTIONS AND RESULTS

| Theory | Assumptions | Issue gaps applied to | Results |
|---|---|---|---|
| Feminism | Feminist consciousness leads individuals to have a distinct way of looking at the world. | • Defense spending<br>• Foreign policy attitudes<br>• Environmental attitudes<br>• Social welfare spending<br>• Equal opportunity for African Americans | • Consistent predictor<br>• Unclear if a mediator |
| Economic circumstances (independent women) | Autonomous women develop opinions based on material interests. Professional women are more likely than men to work in the public sector and would be more likely to support policies benefiting that sector. | • Voting<br>• Party identification<br>• Social welfare attitudes<br>• Role of government<br>• Racial attitudes<br>• Gun control attitudes | • Inconsistent predictor<br>• Unclear if a mediator for voting and party identification<br>• Weak mediator for social welfare attitudes and role of government<br>• Not a mediator for racial attitudes and gun control |
| Economic circumstances (marginalized women) | Women make up a larger proportion of the economically disadvantaged, leading to support for government services. | • Voting<br>• Military interventions<br>• Social welfare attitudes<br>• Role of government<br>• Racial attitudes<br>• Gun control | • Inconsistent predictor<br>• Weak mediator for Social welfare attitudes and role of government |
| Social role theory and motherhood | Gender role socialization leads women and mothers to have greater communal traits, such as being nurturing and anticonflict, and lower agentic traits, such as being aggressive and assertive. | • Social welfare attitudes<br>• Foreign policy attitudes | • Consistent predictor<br>• Strong mediator of social welfare attitudes<br>• Weak evidence for foreign policy attitudes |
| Pro-social values | Women are more concerned than men for the well-being of others. | • Social welfare attitudes<br>• Racial attitudes<br>• Gun control attitudes<br>• Healthcare attitudes | • Consistent predictor<br>• Strong mediator |

and the use of military force (Conover 1988). Others also find support for feminism and antiwar attitudes (Caughell 2016; Conover and Sapiro 1993; Cook and Wilcox 1991). Feminist consciousness may not have a direct effect on political attitudes. For example, researchers have suggested feminist consciousness may indirectly influence political attitudes and behavior because feminist identity correlates with a greater endorsement of egalitarianism, as well as lower endorsements of traditionalism, individualism, and symbolic racism (Conover 1988; Cook and Wilcox 1991).

## Economic Circumstances

Two theories exist about how women's economic circumstances may contribute to the gap. The first is that professional and, therefore, economically independent women and/or psychologically independent women are causing the gender gap. This theory first emerged to explain the new voting gap in 1980, which happened as divorce rates and the proportion of women working outside the home were also increasing. Autonomous women may develop opinions and vote based on their own interests rather than on their husband's interests. Another aspect of this theory is that professional women are more likely than men to work in the public sector, such as in public schools and healthcare, and thus would be more likely to support the Democratic Party and policies benefitting that sector (Carroll 1988; Huddy, Cassese, and Lizotte 2008a).

From past research, it is unclear if this is a cause of the gap. With respect to the gender gap in voting, some of the work supports the theory (Carroll 1988; Manza and Brooks 1998), and others find mixed support at best (Howell and Day 2000; Huddy, Cassese, and Lizotte 2008a). According to ANES 1952–1992 data analysis, the increase over time in women's labor force participation explained the gap in presidential vote choice (Manza and Brooks 1998). Women in public sector occupations are more likely to support social welfare spending, but men in those occupations are even more supportive, which provides mixed evidence for this explanation; the gender gap on social welfare attitudes is largest among the most educated, which supports this theory (Howell and Day 2000). In an analysis of party identification and voting for the Democratic presidential nominee using individual ANES data sets from 1980 to 2004, being a professional woman or a woman with a high income was not a significant predictor of partisanship or vote choice (Huddy, Cassese, and Lizotte 2008a).

The other explanation involving economic circumstances focuses on the relative economic inequalities between women and men. This approach argues that the gender gap, in particular, policy preferences, is because of women's greater reliance on government services as a result of their economic marginalization. Women tend to compose a greater proportion of low-income individuals (Pressman 1988). This economic marginalization of women, particularly single women with dependent children, is often referred to as the "feminization of poverty" (Kimenyi and Mbaku 1995; Pressman 1988). Gender differences in issue positions, voting, and partisanship may exist because of the differential impact of certain policies on men and women. For example, reducing social services has a greater effect on women because women disproportionately receive such services (Sapiro 2002). In contrast, this would lead to less support for costly military interventions, which could take national economic resources away from social welfare programs that assist those with demonstrated need.

The evidence for this explanation is mixed. Research on the voting gender gap does not find consistent support for this explanation (Carroll 1988; Huddy, Cassese, and Lizotte 2008a). According to time-series analysis, at the aggregate level there is an association between the proportion of economically vulnerable women and the size of the gap in party identification (Box-Steffensmeier, De Boef, and Lin 2004). Some studies on support for war find income to be a significant predictor of support

(Bendyna et al. 1996; Nincic and Nincic 2002), while others do not (Wilcox, Hewitt, and Allsop 1996). Public opinion research in other areas, including racial policies and pocketbook voting, has also found only a weak relationship at best between self-interest and attitudes or self-interest and voting behavior (Sears and Funk 1990, 1991).

Interestingly, concerning these economic explanations, consistent evidence in the literature shows that women are more pessimistic in their perceptions of the economy and their personal financial situation. This finding exists whether asked for retrospective (Kaufmann and Petrocik 1999) or prospective (J. Clark and C. Clark 1993; C. Clark and J. Clark 1996; Cook and Wilcox 1995) economic evaluations. These differences range from 3 points to 15 points (J. Clark and C. Clark 1993; C. Clark and J. Clark 1996; Chaney, Alvarez, and Nagler 1998; Kaufmann and Petrocik 1999). Even when controlling for partisanship, these differences persist (Cook and Wilcox 1995). It remains unclear as to why this is the case. Work on the political effects of these differences has found that women's perceptions of their personal finances are not related to their vote choice. This research, however, has provided evidence of a correlation between men's perceptions of their personal finances and their vote choice (Chaney, Alvarez, and Nagler 1998). Other work has shown that there are political effects for women's perceptions of the national economy as a whole (Welch and Hibbing 1992). In fact, Susan Welch and John Hibbing (1992), using ANES data and controlling for partisanship, income, and educational attainment, find that men are more likely to engage in egocentric voting (that is, their personal financial situation predicts their vote choice), while women are likely to engage in sociotropic voting (that is, their perception of the overall economy predicts their vote choice).

## Social Role Theory and Motherhood

The final explanation receiving much attention in the literature, social role theory, postulates that gender differences in political attitudes and policy positions arise because of gender role socialization (Diekman and Schneider 2010; Eagly et al. 2004). Social role theory contends that physical characteristics interact with the features of the local environment to bring about a certain sex-based division of labor in a given society. This division of labor leads to particular gender roles, including socialization of gender expectations (Eagly 1987; Eagly and Koenig 2006). Gender expectations include society's expectancies regarding agentic and communal traits (Eagly and Steffen 1984; Eagly and Wood 2012). Communal traits comprise being nurturing and anticonflict, while agentic traits consist of being aggressive and assertive.

To be more specific, social role theory, a biosocial approach to gender differences, takes into consideration evolved characteristics, division of labor in society, and socialization (Wood and Eagly 2002). This theory argues for both distal and proximal causes of sex differences. Distal causes include physical characteristics, such as men's strength and women's reproductive responsibilities, as well as the features of the local environment, in particular, the reliance on foraging versus hunting. In addition, this theory posits that physical characteristics interact with the features of the local environment to produce a sex-based division of labor in many societies (Eagly and Koenig 2006). In a hunting-reliant society, for example, men would hunt as a consequence of their physical strength, while women would be the primary caregivers for children, owing to their becoming pregnant and lactating.

The sex-based division of labor would produce gender roles, which would likely include socialization of gender expectations, which are a proximal, or immediate, cause of sex differences (Eagly 1987; Eagly and Koenig 2006). Society has different expectations of men and women with respect to agentic and communal traits, anticipating that men will be more agentic and women will be more communal (Broverman et al. 1972; Eagly and Steffen 1984; Eagly and Wood 2012; Wood and Eagly 2012). Parents likely socialize their children to adhere to these beliefs about gender roles, including gender stereotypes and traits; differences in adherence to gender roles could be the result of discrepancies in socialization (i.e., gender-neutral socialization) or in differences in internalization of such expectations (Eagly 1987; Eagly and Koenig 2006). In the example of a society reliant on hunting, the division of labor, in which the majority of hunting is performed by men and most of the child-rearing is done by women, would likely lead to gender role socialization and societal expectations that men be aggressive and women be nurturing.

As would be predicted by social role theory, women are more likely to hold the liberal position on social compassion issues, including reducing income inequality, racial discrimination, the death penalty, and gun control (Eagly et al. 2004; Eagly and Diekman 2006). Also as predicted by this theory, motherhood appears to have a liberalizing effect on women's attitudes toward various issues, in particular, aid to the poor, healthcare, childcare spending, school spending, preference for greater government services, and food stamps spending (Elder and Greene 2006, 2007, 2012; Greenlee 2014; Lizotte 2017b). According to 1984–2000 ANES data and a scale of social welfare attitudes, including public school spending, women with children were more liberal on social welfare issues than women without children, while fatherhood has no significant effect on these attitudes (Elder and Greene 2006). Analysis of the 1996 ANES data shows that in response to a scale of social welfare questions, including public school and childcare spending, women with children are significantly more likely to support social welfare programs and spending. In fact, the gender gap on social welfare attitudes is not significant among those without children (Howell and Day 2000). There are exceptions to the tendency of mothers to hold liberal views, including on legalization of marijuana (Deckman 2016; Greenlee 2014). Additionally, analysis of the 2004 ANES data does not provide evidence of a mother gap on security and foreign policy issues (Elder and Greene 2007).

To summarize, much of the prior work takes a piecemeal approach, investigating one explanation with respect to a single gender gap. These existing theories in the literature for particular gender gaps on certain issues are interesting. Not all of these theories, however, have the potential to apply across issue areas to multiple gaps or have been found to substantially mediate more than one issue gap. Support is limited for each of these explanations. The values explanation is discussed in the following section at length and provides another possible explanation that has the potential to apply to all of the observed differences across issue areas.

## Values

Values offer a novel and comprehensive approach to understanding gender differences in policy preferences. Values are an explanation that could apply to the full range of gender gaps on the use of force, environmental attitudes, equal rights, the proper role of government, and the social safety net. Individuals likely rely on values, in addition to other factors, when considering public policy options. Values are often described as evaluative expressions of desirable behaviors or societal goals; values are more abstract than attitudes, allowing them to be applicable across varied attitude objects (Feldman 2003). Generally, values consist of individuals' views about how society should treat people and how people should behave. For example, people should help others, or society should treat people equally. In political science and social psychology, a good deal of evidence shows that values, including pro-social values such as egalitarianism, influence people's attitudes, including public policy preferences, ideology, presidential approval, party identification, and vote choice (Ciuk, Lupton, and Thornton 2018; Feldman 1988; Hare, Liu, and Lutpon 2018; Liberman 2014; Lupton, Smallpage, and Enders 2017; Peffley and Hurwitz 1985; Piurko, Schwartz, and Davidov 2011; Pollock, Lilie, and Vittes 1993; Schwartz, Caprara, and Vecchione 2010; Zaller 1992).

## Scholarly Background

A great deal of the work on values has focused on how individuals rank values, as Milton Rokeach (1973) studied, or how different values relate to one another and to what extent values are universally held cross-culturally, as Shalom Schwartz (1992) has studied. Research on values and their relationship to one another has argued that values ought to be universal because they originate from basic human needs (Schwartz 1992). There is evidence to support this in that the Schwartz basic structure of values, discussed in the next paragraph, has been replicated across cultures with rather high levels of consistency, indicating a wide-ranging agreement on the structure and prioritizing of values (Schwartz and Bardi 2001). It is fascinating to think that all human beings across the world share the same values, even though they might rank them differently or endorse certain values more or less than others. Alternate forms of measurement of the basic values also appear to beget similar results (Schwartz et al. 2001).

Research on the development of value types—sets of values that are conceptually linked and denote basic human motivations—has resulted in the categorization of ten value types (Schwartz 1992). For example, the values of equality, tolerance, peace, and social justice constitute the value type known as universalism (Schwartz 1992). The ten value types are power, hedonism, achievement, self-direction, stimulation, benevolence, universalism, conformity, tradition, and security. With a focus on pro-social values in this book, I emphasize and investigate two of these value types: universalism and benevolence. The universalism value type consists of an inclination toward tolerance, equality, and social justice. The benevolence value type represents a preference for the promotion of the safety and well-being of those close to oneself. The other Schwartz value types are not pro-social values and are therefore not included in the analysis.

Studies on values and value types have sought to understand to what extent values guide people's behaviors. There is evidence that Schwartz's value types are correlated with behaviors. Individuals endorsing universalism report a commitment to ensuring the equal treatment of all, and individuals endorsing benevolence report helping neighbors and keeping promises. Additionally, universalism correlates with behavior, according to peer ratings, not just self-reported behaviors (Bardi and Schwartz 2003). This research is important because it shows that values do influence individuals' behaviors.

## Gender Differences on Values

From a theoretical perspective, women appear to have a greater concern for the well-being of others, and this leads to many of the gender gaps in public opinion. It is not that men are not concerned with others' well-being, but on average women are more likely than men to have greater concern. With respect to international conflicts, the values explanation predicts that women are more likely than men to think about the toll on military families of sending troops, as well as of the innocent casualties of war. When thinking about gun control, women may think about the innocent lives that are traumatized or lost because of gun violence. The values explanation would expect that when women think about environmental regulations, they are more likely to think about the devastating effects that toxic waste, pollution, and unsafe drinking water have on families and, in particular, children. It also posits that women more so than men think about the disadvantages experienced by historically marginalized groups like women, African Americans, and members of the LGBTQ community. Women think about how this has negative economic, social, and psychological consequences for individuals from groups that do not enjoy equal rights in our society. Finally, I theorize that when women think about government funding for public schools, childcare, and programs to provide services and aid to the poor, they consider the positive impact that such funding can have, as well as think about the possibility of a child, disabled individual, or elderly person going hungry or without shelter if that spending is cut.

Existing research establishes gender differences in values. Of relevance to this project is the existence of gender differences in pro-social values such as humanitarianism, egalitarianism, universalism, and benevolence. In general, pro-social values measure support for helping others, treating people equally, promoting equal opportunity, caring for others, and ensuring social justice. To be more specific, humanitarianism measures support for helping others and for promoting human rights. Egalitarianism is a measure of support for equal rights and equal opportunity. Again, as discussed earlier, universalism is a Schwartz value type measuring support for tolerance, justice, and the well-being of all. Benevolence is another Schwartz value type discussed earlier, which measures a desire to help and protect the welfare of those close to the individual. I hypothesize that many gender gaps are the result of women's greater endorsement of pro-social values.

Previous findings indicate a reliable gender difference on pro-social values such as egalitarianism. This difference is likely because of differences in socialization and society's expectations of girls and women to be caring, selfless, and helpful. However, a detailed discussion on why gender differences in pro-social values exist is beyond the scope of this book. Many studies have found gender differences in egalitarianism, with women lending greater support for social equality than men (Feldman and Steenbergen 2001; Howell and Day 2000; Sapiro and Conover 1997). There is evidence of gender differences in Schwartz's values (Prince-Gibson and Schwartz 1998), including universalism and benevolence (Lyons, Duxbury, and Higgins 2005; Schwartz 1992; Schwartz and Rubel 2005). Overall, there are modest correlations between gender and values (Prince-Gibson and Schwartz 1998). In more recent work, there is evidence of small but statistically significant gender differences on benevolence, with women rating this as more important than men (Schwartz et al. 2001). Men and women differ in their endorsement of universalism, with women scoring higher on this value type compared to men, meaning that women have greater preferences for justice, tolerance, and equality (Lyons Duxbury, and Higgins 2005). Gender differences on pro-social values even appear to exist among male and female adolescents (Beutel and Johnson 2004; Beutel and Marini 1995). For example, there is evidence that gender differences exist among adolescents on compassion, measured as caring about the well-being of other people (Beutel and Marini 1995). More recent research also finds that female adolescents compared to male adolescents report greater concern for others' interests, indicating additional evidence of gender differences in pro-social values (Beutel and Johnson 2004).

Finally, there is extant evidence that pro-social values elucidate the gender gap on a few policy areas. Values reduce the gap on social welfare attitudes, racial attitudes, and gun control attitudes. In the 1996 ANES data, egalitarianism appears to partially mediate the gender gap on support for social welfare programs (Howell and Day 2000). Humanitarianism partially explains the gender gap in support for the Affordable Care Act (Lizotte 2016b). Egalitarianism reduces the gender gap in racial attitudes (Howell and Day 2000). Egalitarianism is a significant predictor of gun control attitudes and partially reduces that gender gap (Howell and Day 2000). This book replicates and extends these earlier findings to additional policy areas, including other force issues, the environment, and equal rights for LGBTQ and women; my analysis also includes more expansive years of data, including more recent years of data.

The pro-social values theory offers a proximate cause of gender differences in political attitudes and issue positions. The values explanation, however, is not necessarily mutually exclusive from or incompatible with the other explanations, in particular the feminist identity and social role theory explanations. For example, prior work on feminist identity has argued that feminists differ in their value orientations, which leads to differences in policy preferences (Conover 1988). With respect to social role theory, women may be socialized to be more concerned with the well-being of others as part of gender role socialization. It is possible that socialization causes value differences between men and women. Unfortunately, this is difficult to test with cross-sectional data. Future work could investigate if, as gender roles evolve, there is a reduction in the gender gap on pro-social values and policy positions. The subsequent chapters include analysis of each of these explanations to see if each helps to account for the gender gaps in public opinion, as well as to what extent each is distinct from the others. With respect to the values explanation distinctness, the correlations between all the other explanations and egalitarianism are noted below.

In summary, research to date indicates that men and women differ in their endorsement of pro-social values, such as concern for others, equality, humanitarianism, and tolerance (Beutel and Johnson 2004; Beutel and Marini 1995; Feldman and Steenbergen 2001; Howell and Day 2000; Lizotte 2016b; Lyons, Duxbury, and Higgins 2005; Prince-Gibson and Schwartz 1998; Schwartz 1992; Schwartz and Rubel 2005; Sidanius et al. 2000). Moderate differences in values would make sense as an explanation for the moderately sized gaps in policy preferences. Hence, the values explanation for public opinion gaps deserves further exploration. This brings me to the general hypothesis for analysis throughout the book: *Pro-social values will substantially account for the gender gap in policy positions across several policy areas. Women's propensity to care about the well-being of other people leads them to differ from men on a number public policy positions.*

## Mediational Analysis and Measures of Pro-social Values and Gender Differences

This section establishes that significant and sizeable gender differences exist in the data on pro-social values, which is a necessary condition for it to be a viable explanation of gender gaps in policy preferences. Throughout the analysis in the successive chapters, I test mediational hypotheses, meaning that I hypothesize that including pro-social values will reduce the size and statistical significance of the gender gap. There are four aspects to mediational analyses (Baron and Kenny 1986). First, the independent variable—in this case, gender—must be a significant predictor of the dependent variable, policy position. Second, the independent variable, gender, must be a predictor of the mediational variable, which in this book is a measure of pro-social values. Third, the mediational variable, pro-social values, must be predictive of the dependent variable without the independent variable, gender, in the model. Last, the effect of the independent variable, gender, on the dependent variable, policy position, should substantially reduce with the inclusion of the meditational variable, pro-social values.

To further illustrate mediation, here is a revisiting of the earlier hypothetical example. Perhaps a researcher finds that college students with higher grade point averages (GPAs) report higher levels of happiness. The researcher might wonder why students with higher GPAs are happier. The researcher decides to investigate if higher levels of self-esteem are statistically associated with higher GPAs and with higher levels of happiness. If there are statistical associations between GPA and self-esteem, as well as between self-esteem and happiness, the researcher might decide to run a mediational model to test self-esteem as a mediator of the relationship between GPA and happiness. If the effect of GPA goes away or substantially reduces with the inclusion of self-esteem, then there is evidence that the reason for higher levels of happiness among those with higher GPAs is because having a high GPA increases self-esteem, leading one to be happier.

In other words, with reference to the pro-social values hypothesis, mediational analyses test whether indicators of a hypothesized explanation eliminate the gender gap by reducing the statistical effect of gender. As demonstrated below, there are significant gender differences on pro-social values, satisfying the second part of mediational analyses. Women have statistically significant higher scores on egalitarianism, universalism, and benevolence compared to men. This means that pro-social values fits one of the criteria for mediation.

Throughout the book, I use the cumulative ANES 1980–2012 data set. The only measure of pro-social values included in this data is the standard measure of egalitarianism. Humanitarianism was only included in a single pilot study of the ANES and, therefore, cannot be used. Moreover, other values are not consistently included in the ANES. Individualism has been included in only one pilot study. Measures of liberty and justice are also not regularly included.

The measures to test the other explanations are also imperfect. The measure to test feminist identity is the feeling thermometer score toward feminists. The data include several feeling thermometer items; respondents are instructed to place themselves on a range from 0 to 100, very cold to very warm, toward a number of individuals and groups as a measure of how favorable or unfavorable the respondent feels toward the individuals and groups. Feminist identity has been asked in the ANES only in 1992 and 2016; the feminist feeling thermometer has been used as a substitute for feminist identity in a few prior studies (Huddy et al. 1997; Simien and Clawson 2004). To test the economic circumstances explanations, income and employment status are included. To test social role theory and motherhood, parental status is included, using an item that asks the number of children under the age of eighteen living in the household. Unfortunately, this means that parents with children over the age of eighteen or not living in their household are not captured by this measure. In addition, including all of the indicators for all of the explanations in one statistical model severely limits the number of observations; this is because the indicators for the explanations were not asked every year data was collected. Therefore, in subsequent chapters, the results of the analysis for the other explanations are discussed, but the tables displaying the results are included in the Appendix rather than in the chapters.

Egalitarianism measures support for equality, including supporting equal opportunity and equal rights for everyone. The following is the wording of the six egalitarianism items in the 1980–2012 ANES:

- Our society should do whatever is necessary to make sure everyone has an equal opportunity to succeed.
- We have gone too far in pushing equal rights in this country. (Reverse coded.)
- One of the big problems in this country is that we don't give everyone an equal chance.
- It is not really that big a problem if some people have more of a chance in life than others. (Reverse coded.)
- The country would be better off if we worried less about how equal people are. (Reverse coded.)
- If people were treated more equally in this country, we would have many fewer problems.

These six items are used to create an additive scale with a Cronbach's alpha of 0.70 and an inter-item correlation of 0.44. This indicates a moderate level of reliability for the scale. The scale ranges from 0 to 4, with higher values indicating greater endorsement of this pro-social value. There is a statistically significant gender difference in endorsement of egalitarianism. Women's mean on the scale is 2.50 (standard error [SE] 0.79) compared to men's mean of 2.38 (SE 0.82). The t-statistic for this mean difference is 11.30 ($p = 0.000$, degrees of freedom [df] 24,232), which is highly significant. This provides strong evidence that women are more likely to endorse egalitarianism compared to men. As noted previously, this is an important and necessary step for mediational analyses. For pro-social values to mediate the gender gap in policy positions, there must be a statistically significant gender gap on pro-social values. The gender gap is depicted in Figure 2.1. The bar on the left depicts the men's mean on the egalitarianism scale, while the bar on the right depicts the women's mean. The

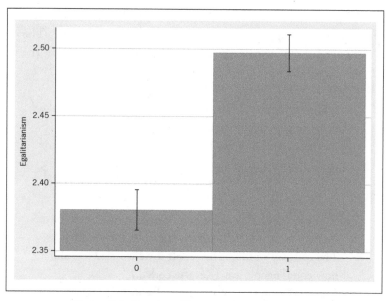

Figure 2.1. Gender differences in egalitarianism
Note: Data are from cumulative 1980–2012 ANES. On the x-axis,
1 = female; 0 = male. Egalitarianism is an additive scale of six items
ranging from 0 to 4, with higher values indicating greater endorsement
of egalitarianism.

figure includes indicators of the 95 percent confidence intervals, the standard measure of statistical significance, making it easier to see that the gap is statistically significant because the confidence intervals do not overlap.

To get a sense of the gender gap in pro-social values among subsets of men and women, I provide a breakdown of the gender differences on egalitarianism among white men and women, among black men and women, across different age cohorts, across education levels, and across income levels. Gender differences across different subgroups are displayed in Figure 2.2. In general, there is a significant gender gap among all of these subsets of men and women except black men and black women. That black men and black women do not differ in their endorsement of egalitarianism is a puzzling result. Research on African American parenting finds that an emphasis on equality is common during socialization (Thornton et al. 1990), which may explain why black men and black women do not differ on egalitarianism. Past research has also found a more egalitarian division of household labor between black men and black women, arguing that this may be because of the need to adapt to historically negative economic circumstances (Kamo and Cohen 1998).

There are considerable racial differences in endorsement of egalitarianism, and gender differences exist among whites. Among whites, the mean for women on the egalitarianism scale is 2.38 (SE 0.78), and the mean for men is 2.25 (SE 0.80). Among blacks, the gender gap is reversed. The difference between black men and black women, however, is not statistically significant, meaning that the difference between black men and black women is essentially zero. Black men have a higher mean of 3.01 (SE 0.69) compared to women at 2.97 (SE 0.70). Whites overall report lower levels of egalitarianism than blacks.

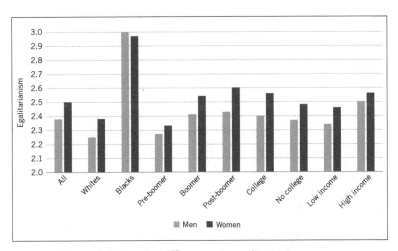

Figure 2.2. Gender differences in egalitarianism across demographic subgroups

Note: Data are from cumulative 1980–2012 ANES. Egalitarianism is an additive scale of six items ranging from 0 to 4, with higher values indicating greater endorsement of egalitarianism.

Across three different age cohorts, women are more likely to endorse egalitarianism than men. The data includes eight cohorts that I recoded into three cohorts: pre–baby boomer = born before 1942; baby boomer = born between 1943 and 1958; and post–baby boomer = born in 1959 or later. The years do not coincide perfectly with the actual baby boomer generation from the mid-1940s to the mid-1960s, but it is close, given the predetermined eight cohorts in the data set. Among pre–baby boomers, the women's mean on egalitarianism is 2.33 (SE 0.75), and the men's mean is 2.27 (SE 0.75). Among baby boomers, the women's mean is 2.54 (SE 0.81), and the men's mean is 2.41 (SE 0.86). For post–baby boomers, the women's mean is 2.60 (SE 0.77), and men's mean is 2.43 (SE 0.82).

Women also have higher means on the egalitarian scale than men across education and income levels. College-educated women have a mean of 2.56 (SE 0.89), and college-educated men have a mean of 2.40 (SE 0.91). Among those without a college degree, women have a mean of 2.48 (SE 0.75), and men have a mean of 2.37 (SE 0.78). Among those with an income below the national median, the women's mean is 2.46 (SE 0.82), and the men's mean is 2.34 (SE 0.84). Women with an income above the national median have a mean of 2.56 (SE 0.73), and men with an income above the median have a mean of 2.50 (SE 0.76). Individuals with lower incomes appear to be more egalitarian than those with higher incomes, regardless of gender.

To summarize, the gender gap on egalitarianism exists within most subgroups except for African Americans. The figure also makes evident that differences in egalitarianism between demographic subgroups are often much larger than gender differences. Given the interest after the 2016 presidential election in white women's vote choice versus black women's vote choice, as well as the differences in vote choices of college-educated white women versus non-college-educated white women, it is not surprising to find that factors besides gender have an effect on women's values. Women tend to be more egalitarian than men of the same race, birth cohort, education level, and income level. Throughout the analysis, gender differences in attitudes and policy positions across subgroups are included and discussed.

According to the birth cohort results, value differences between men and women do not appear to arise because of changes in gendered socialization. Although there are birth cohort differences in egalitarianism, the gender gap in egalitarianism is consistent over time. This is not a perfect test of whether gendered socialization influences gender differences in values. Overall, egalitarianism increases in men and women in younger birth cohorts. This appears to indicate a greater endorsement of individual and societal equality among boomers compared to the age cohort that came before them, regardless of gender; the same is true for post-boomers, who are slightly more egalitarian than boomers. The gender differences in egalitarianism, however, do not appear to reduce over time. It is possible that future work looking at more recent generations and future generations will find a reduction in the gender gap in egalitarianism. This would indicate that gendered socialization and changes in gendered socialization over time are the reason for gender differences and the reduction of gender differences in pro-social values.

For some of the chapters, I also use the 2011 World Values Survey of the United States. This survey includes a measure of Schwartz's value types, including the two pro-social values of universalism, supporting social justice, and benevolence, caring about close others. For the Schwartz value types, individuals are asked if they are similar to the person described by the item on a scale of 1 to 6, with higher values indicating more similarity.

The universalism item states: Looking after the environment is important to this person; to care for nature and save life resources. As shown in Figure 2.3, there is a sizeable and significant gender difference on universalism. The men's mean is represented by the bar on the left, and the mean for women is depicted by the bar on the right. The 95 percent confidence intervals indicate the significance of the difference between to the two bars. The women's mean is 4.14 (SE 0.4), and the men's mean is 3.94 (SE 0.04); the t-statistic is 3.63 ($p = 0.0001$, df 2,191). Women are

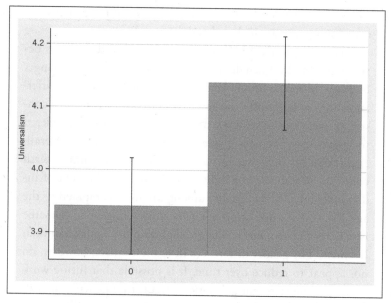

Figure 2.3. Gender differences in universalism

Note: Data are from 2011 World Values Survey (United States). On the x-axis, 1 = female; 0 = male. Higher values indicate greater universalism.

significantly more likely than men to say that they are similar to the person who cares about the environment and nature. This indicates that women are significantly more likely than men to endorse values making up the universalism value type.

The benevolence item states: It is important to this person to do something good for society. There is a significant gender difference on benevolence ($t = 4.51$, $p = 0.000$, df 2,182). The women's mean is 4.38 (SE 0.03), and the men's mean is 4.16 (SE 0.04). Figure 2.4 shows the difference. Again, the mean for women is on the right, and the mean for men is on the left. The figure depicts the gap as significant according to the 95 percent confidence intervals. Women are significantly more likely than men to endorse the benevolence value type. Women are more likely to state that they are similar to the person described in the item, believing it is important to do good for society.

To analyze certain gender gaps not included in the cumulative 1980–2012 ANES or the 2011 World Values Survey, I also include limited analysis of the 2016 ANES. These data include measures of two domestic force policy preferences, gun control and the death penalty; attitudes about climate change; and support for marriage equality, making it possible to test the pro-social values hypothesis for these gender gaps. The 2016 ANES contains the same measure of egalitarianism included in the cumulative ANES data. There is a sizeable and significant gender gap on egalitarianism in the 2016 data, with women having significantly higher overall scores on this pro-social value measure than men ($t = 6.77$, $p = 0.000$, df 3,596). The mean for women is 3.70 (SE 0.83) compared to the mean for men of 3.51 (SE 0.85)

Regarding the other explanations, there are significant gender differences in the cumulative ANES data on feminist feeling

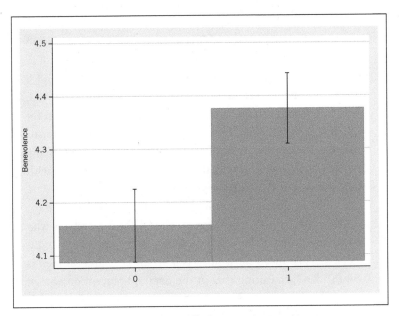

Figure 2.4. Gender differences in benevolence

Note: Data are from 2011 World Values Survey (United States). On the x-axis, 1 = female; 0 = male. Higher values indicate greater benevolence.

thermometer scores, income, employment status, and parental status. Women on average feel more warmly toward feminists ($t = 14.08$, $p = 0.000$, df 14,789). This is a single item that ranges from 0 to 97. The mean score on the feminist feeling thermometer among women is 55.72 (SE 22.58) versus among men, 50.53 (SE 22.09). The feminist feeling thermometer is moderately correlated with egalitarianism, with a Pearson's correlation of 0.35 indicating a moderate association between feeling warmly toward feminists and valuing equality.

The income measure is coded 1 for those reporting a household income below the national median and 0 otherwise. Women are more likely than men to have an income below the national median ($t = 18.65$, $p = 0.000$, df 30,013), with the women's mean 0.36 (SE 0.48) and the men's mean 0.26 (SE 0.44), indicating that 36 percent of women versus 26 percent of men in the data report a household income below the national median. There is a weak correlation between income and egalitarianism of only 0.08, indicating a weak association between having a low income and valuing equal treatment. Men are more likely than women to be currently employed outside of the home ($t = 29.21$, $p = 0.000$, df 31,319). This item is coded 1 for currently employed and 0 otherwise; homemakers are coded as not currently employed. The mean for men is 0.69 (SE 0.46) compared to the mean for women of 0.53 (SE 0.50), meaning that 69 percent of men versus 53 percent of women in the data are currently employed. Being currently employed is very weakly and negatively correlated with egalitarianism, with a Pearson's correlation of $-0.004$.

Women in the data are more likely to have children ($t = 9.61$, $p = 0.000$, df 23,997). This item is coded 1 for respondents who have children under the age of 18 living in the household and 0 otherwise. The mean for women is 0.40 (SE 49), and for men is 0.34 (SE 0.47), meaning that in the data, 40 percent of women have children compared to 34 percent of men. Motherhood is weakly correlated with egalitarianism; the Pearson's correlation is 0.07, meaning that being a mother is not strongly associated with a greater endorsement of equality.

Regarding the measures of the other explanations, the feminist feeling thermometer was not asked in as many years of the ANES survey as the egalitarianism questions. This means that the number of observations in the subsequent analysis differs for each model, depending on what explanation is being tested. Specifically, the number of observations for the feminist feeling thermometer models is considerably smaller than the number of observations in the tables including egalitarianism. Because the sample sizes differ so much, it is not entirely appropriate to compare the mediation results for the feminist feeling thermometer models and the egalitarianism models.

## Conclusion

There are several previously investigated explanations for the gender gap in public opinion and party identification. Values, a mostly uninvestigated theory, offer an excitingly comprehensive explanation that could account for the observed gender gaps in public opinion. As the quotations from participants in the Women's March included at the beginning of this chapter illustrate, values are likely at the core of how individuals think about political issues and politics. How one should treat others and how government ought to treat its citizens likely permeate the ways that individuals evaluate different political issues. In particular, concern for others and treating others well is probably one of the more important values influencing the way the public thinks about public policy.

This chapter discusses the evidence to date of gender differences in pro-social values. Past research provides plentiful evidence that men and women differ in their endorsement of pro-social values. On average, women are consistently more likely than men to score higher on measures of pro-social values. This chapter also reviews the literature demonstrating that gender differences in pro-social values help explain the gender gap on social welfare, gun control, and race-related policies. This evidence is limited to two pieces of prior work but is nonetheless quite encouraging for the values explanation. This chapter also provides evidence of a significant and sizeable gender difference in the endorsement of egalitarianism, universalism, and benevolence, which is a necessary condition for values to be a mediator of public opinion gender gaps. Chapter 3 investigates values as a reason for the gender gap on the use of force, including domestic and international force issues.

# 3

# Gender Gap on the Use of Force

"**A**s mothers, we cannot help but be concerned about the health and welfare of our husbands and children," First Lady Jacqueline Kennedy wrote, and President Kennedy stated that the Women Strike for Peace March of 1961 was made up of women "concerned as we all are about nuclear war" (quoted in Hevesi 2011). The Women Strike for Peace (WSP) organization fought for nuclear disarmament and later an end to the Vietnam War. Dagmar Wilson, founder of WSP, sought to have women strike from their jobs, including as homemakers, to demonstrate for peace in front of the White House, the Pentagon, the United Nations, and the Washington Monument on more than one occasion (Hevesi 2011).

American women's antiforce demonstrations go back much further than the Women Strike for Peace March of 1961. Women's activism and voices against the use of force have historically extended to domestic force issues as well as international force. In 1837, twenty female antislavery organizations from ten different states held the Anti-slavery Convention of American Women in New York. Suffragettes picketed the White House during

World War I and were jailed for treason for questioning a sitting president. In 1954, women again protested in front of the White House after the lynching of four black men in Georgia. In 1990, Muslim women demonstrated to bring attention to the atrocities of Saddam Hussein's régime. The Million Mom March for Gun Control was held in 2000. In 2013, three female activists started the Black Lives Matter movement in response to the Trayvon Martin shooting and acquittal of George Zimmerman; women's participation has continued after the 2014 shooting of Michael Brown.

Much has been written about gender differences in support of the use of force, particularly pertaining to support for military action and gun control. Even before the events of September 11, 2001, discussions were taking place about the proper role of the United States in international crises and when the use of military action is warranted. These debates have occurred regarding Afghanistan; Iraq; the Sudan; Syria; Russian aggression in Ukraine, Crimea, Georgia, and Chechnya; and Iran's and North Korea's nuclear programs. Hence, understanding why a consistent and sizeable gender difference emerges with respect to military action and defense spending is of continued importance. Additionally, domestic use-of-force issues are of import, given political and public debates regarding gun control, the death penalty, police brutality, and inner-city crime.

In this chapter, I investigate how differences in pro-social values help clarify why these gender differences in support of the use of force exist. Domestic issues such as gun control and the death penalty are discussed alongside international issues such as defense spending and military interventions because both involve attitudes toward the governmental use and regulation of force. Moreover, domestic force issues and international force issues, including the legitimate governmental use of force such as the death penalty and military interventions, both reflect general attitudes toward violence (see Weber 1965). First, I discuss the current literature on the gender gap on force issues, including military action and domestic force issues. Next, I provide evidence that value differences are at the core of this gender gap. The central finding of this chapter is that value differences between men and women help illuminate why a gender gap exists on these issues. I present consistent evidence that gender differences in pro-social values partially explain the gap in support for government use of force.

## Gender Differences in Support for the Use of Force in the Literature

### Gender Differences on the International Use of Force

The gender gap on the use of military force is sizeable and consistently surfaces.[1] The gender gap in support for military interventions varies in size but is often around 8 percentage points or higher (Shapiro and Mahajan 1986). Gender differences have been found with respect to many armed conflicts, including, but not limited to, World War II, the Korean War, and the Vietnam War (Brandes 1992; Shapiro and Mahajan 1986). More recently, gaps have emerged with respect to the Gulf War (Bendyna et al. 1996; Conover and Sapiro 1993) and the use of force in Afghanistan after the 9/11 terrorist attacks (Huddy et al. 2005). Gender gaps also appeared in response to the Iraq War and the War on Terrorism (Eichenberg 2003).

In addition to support for military conflicts, gender differences exist regarding the best solutions for international crises, support for nuclear arsenals, and attitudes about the proper level of defense spending (Cook and Wilcox 1991; Shapiro and Mahajan 1986; Smith 1984). Women are less likely than men to favor the use of force to solve international problems (Norrander 2008). Women were less supportive during the Cold War of the development and existence of nuclear armaments (Bendyna et al. 1996; Gwartney-Gibbs and Lach 1991). Finally, women are less likely to support a large defense budget (Norrander 2008).

---

1. Although they have been edited, the following sections are largely based on a portion of my dissertation (Lizotte 2009).

Gender differences in foreign policy attitudes go beyond support for impending or ongoing military intervention and extend to strategy preferences. Women are more likely to prefer air strikes to strategies reliant on ground troops (Eichenberg 2003). Generally, women are more likely to prefer actions that will bring about the peaceful resolution of conflict in comparison to men, who are more likely to favor military strategies causing escalation of conflict. Such differences regarding resolution versus escalation emerged in response to the Korean War, the Vietnam War, Operation Desert Shield, and Operation Desert Storm (Nincic and Nincic 2002). Relatedly, women report higher levels of concern about terrorist retaliation and escalation if military force is used (Huddy et al. 2005). Women are also less supportive of aggressive interrogation techniques or torture as a way to deal with the threat of terrorism (Lizotte 2017a).

Gender differences appear to vary in size depending on the stage of conflict. The gender gap appears to be largest before military engagement. For example, surveys conducted during the middle of a conflict do not find gender differences on support for the overall mission; rather, gender gaps materialize with respect to preferred strategies and perceptions of the intervention's goals (Wilcox, Hewitt, and Allsop 1996). This occurs because gender differences considerably diminish after a conflict begins and troops have been committed (Conover and Sapiro 1993; Bendyna et al 1996). It is not entirely clear why the gender gap varies relating to the stage of the conflict, but it may happen because of a rallying effect, which results in greater levels of overall support during a military engagement (Mueller 1973) and in response to a national crisis like the September 11 attacks (Hetherington and Nelson 2003).

Along with differences in support for interventions, there is also evidence that women are more sensitive to the loss of life during a military intervention. Gender differences exist in response to civilian and troop casualties (Crawford, Lawrence, and Lebovic 2017; Eichenberg 2003). For example, women were pessimistic about troop and civilian casualties during the Gulf War;

women compared to men appear to judge the loss of life to be unacceptable (Bendyna et al. 1996). Importantly, women appear to be more sensitive to actual casualties and not just the abstract possibility of casualties (Eichenberg 2003).

## Explanations for the Force Gap in the Literature

A great deal of research has been done on the gender gap in support of military interventions—more than on most of the gender gaps, except for perhaps support for social welfare programs and spending. Therefore, much of this research has not focused on establishing the gap, because it has already been well established. Rather, this work has largely concentrated on investigating different explanations for this gap. Thus far, there does not appear to be a strong front-runner explanation in the empirical evidence.

For example, one theory is that economic and political marginalization among women causes their higher levels of opposition to the use of force. With respect to economic marginalization, wars are expensive, often leading to a decrease in funding for domestic programs on which low-income women rely (Abell 1994). In terms of political marginalization, women have experienced a historical lack of power and alienation from politics (Gidengil 1995; Welch and Hibbing 1992). Women's marginalization in terms of political power may lead to different perspectives on international disputes (Tickner 1992). The evidence for this explanation is mixed. Income is a significant predictor of attitudes toward war, but it does not appear to mediate the gender gap (Bendyna et al. 1996; Nincic and Nincic 2002; Wilcox, Hewitt, and Allsop 1996). Results are similar for defense spending attitudes where a strong relationship between economic indicators and attitudes does not materialize (Kriesberg and Klein 1980). Recent analysis finds that if women had the same income as men, the gender gap in support for war would be reduced by 9 percentage points (Feinstein 2017). Overall, prior work does not provide overwhelming evidence for the economic and political marginalization explanation as a mediator of the gender gap. It does appear to be predictive of war attitudes but fails to remove the gender effect.

The second theory is that feminist consciousness causes women who identify as feminist to be less likely to support war. Historically, women's movements have been associated with pacifist principles (Beckwith 2002; Costain 2000), and feminism includes opposition to traditional hierarchical structures and the historical distribution of power (Brock-Utne 1985). Scholars arguing for the feminist consciousness explanation believe that because women are more likely than men to identify as feminists, this is the reason for the gender gap. Feminists are less supportive of conventional war, nuclear war, and defense spending compared to nonfeminists (Conover 1988; Cook and Wilcox 1991). Feminists are more pacifist, in general, and reported less support for the Gulf War, in particular opposition to the bombing of civilians (Conover and Sapiro 1993). The evidence to date suggests that feminist orientation does not fully explain the gender gap on foreign policy attitudes; although feminists are less militaristic, feminist identity does not fully mediate the gap (Cook and Wilcox 1991).

The third theory is that there are fundamental differences in aggression between men and women, which lead to differences in support for the international use of force. These scholars have claimed that the difference in aggression is a result of basic physiological differences—mainly that women differ in aggression because of their role in reproduction (Elshtain 1986). Studies concerned with ascertaining the degree to which aggression differences exist between the sexes have found mixed results. In a meta-analysis, there were no sex differences in indirect aggression or in circumstances of provocation, but women are more likely than men to display displaced aggression, and men are more likely to engage in direct, physical aggression (Archer 2004). Other work has also found that under provocation, women and men do not differ in terms of aggression (Bettencourt and Miller 1996). In general, the aggression explanation would make the most sense if there were a larger gap between men and women on support for the use of military force than what has been found in the past. If women, on average, are innately less aggressive, then this theory seems to predict that the majority of women should be against the use of the force. As detailed earlier, the gap is significant and sizeable but not as large as one might expect, according to this particular theory.

The fourth theory is that the role of motherhood leads to less support for war among women in comparison to men. Theoretical work, not relying on empirical data, has argued that the role of motherhood may lead women to be against the use of force to deal with international crises. This research argues that women's role as mothers leads to pacifist ways of thinking and behaving because maternal practices are characterized by nonviolent conflict management, such as compromise and reconciliation (Ruddick 1980). This theoretical work has also contended that motherhood is associated with caring and nurturing perspectives, which would presumably lead to a preference for resolving conflicts, including international disputes without the use of force (Elshtain 1985). Finally, this theory argues that maternal thinking is of a moral nature, which again should be associated with nonviolent approaches to resolving conflict (Dietz 1985). There is little empirical evidence to support this explanation (Conover and Sapiro 1993; Feinstein 2017; Jaggar 1991; Zalewski 1994). For example, mothers were not different from nonmothers on measures of militarism, fear of war, support for the Gulf War, or support for the bombing of civilians (Conover and Sapiro 1993). More recently, women with children were not more likely than nonmothers to oppose war (Feinstein 2017).

The mixed evidence from these other explanations indicates a need to explore a new and untested theory for the gender gap in support of the use of international force and defense spending. Pro-social values is a novel approach to understanding why women tend to oppose military interventions and increased defense spending. It could be that women's propensity toward being concerned about other people leads them to differ from men on questions of defense spending and the use of military force. In the next section, I discuss the existing research on gender differences in support of the domestic use of force.

## Gender Differences on Domestic Force Issues

Research to date also indicates a gender gap in support of governmental force with respect to the criminal justice system. First, women are less likely than men to support the death penalty (Cochran and Sanders 2009; Dotson and Carter 2012; Kutateladze and Crossman 2009; Lambert et al. 2009; Lehmann and Pickett 2017; Stack 2000; Whitehead and Blankenship 2000; for an exception to this finding, see Unnever, Cullen, and Roberts 2005). For example, only 65 percent of women compared to 83 percent of men said they favor the death penalty for those convicted of murder (Whitehead and Blankenship 2000). Another study found a similar gap, with 63.9 percent of women favoring the death penalty compared to 81.9 percent of men (Applegate, Cullen, and Fisher 2002). Women are also more likely to believe by 13 percentage points that an innocent person could be executed and by 7 percentage points that evidence is lacking that the death penalty deters murder (Whitehead and Blankenship 2000). Researchers have explored various explanations for this gap without successfully mediating the gap (Boots and Cochran 2011; Cochran and Sanders 2009). The gender gap in support of the death penalty is robust to the inclusion of several control variables such as ideology, authoritarianism, party identification, racial attitudes, religious identification, age, education, and income (Lehmann and Pickett 2017). Women are also less likely to support police violence (Halim and Stiles 2001) or harsh punishment for criminals (Applegate, Cullen, and Fisher 2002; Hurwitz and Smithey 1998). In addition, women are more likely than men to view the main goal of prisons to be rehabilitation rather than punishment or the protection of society (Applegate, Cullen, and Fisher 2002).

In addition to research on gender differences in support of the death penalty and punishment for criminals, there is also a robust gender gap on gun control. The considerable amount of research establishing a gender gap on gun control consistently finds that women are more supportive of stricter regulations on gun owner- ship than men (Celinska 2007; Erskine 1972; Haider-Markel and Joslyn 2001; Howell and Day 2000; Shapiro and Mahajan 1986; Wolpert and Gimpel 1998). This tends to be a rather large gender gap of more than 10 percentage points (Erskine 1972; Shapiro and Mahajan 1986). Women are more supportive of requiring a permit to buy a gun (Brennan, Lizotte, and McDowall 1993) and are even more supportive of a complete handgun ban (Kleck, Gertz, and Bratton 2009).

The gender gap in support of gun control appears to be very robust to inclusion of various control variables and other vari- ables related to gun attitudes. Women are less supportive of con- cealed carry laws controlling for various other factors, including education, age, owning a gun, party identification, and political knowledge (Haider-Markel and Joslyn 2001). The gender gap remains significant with the inclusion of attitudes toward hunt- ing, concerns about burglary, concerns about robbery, and fear of crime (Celinska 2007). Women are also less likely than men to own a gun and are less likely to view gun ownership as a means of self-protection; controlling for these factors, however, does not mediate the gender gap on gun control (Kleck, Gertz, and Brat- ton 2009).

## Recent Polling on Force Attitudes

Evidence of gender differences on force issues extends beyond the scholarly literature to include public opinion polls. Public opinion polling has found consistent and sizeable gender differences on foreign policy issues, particularly the use of force. A 1994 Gallup poll found a 19-point gender gap for the United States sending ground troops into North Korea. A 1996 CNN poll documented a 15-point gender gap on attitudes toward the presence of Ameri- can troops in Bosnia. Poll results also indicate gender differences on abstract attitudes such as preferences for diplomacy versus military force. For example, there was an 18-point gender gap in a 1994 *New York Times* poll on whether military strength or diplomacy was the preferred method to guarantee peace.

After the terrorist attacks of September 11, the gender gap was much smaller than usually found in public opinion polls. A Gallup poll conducted within one week of the attacks and released in early October 2001 found a 2-point gap, with 90 percent of men and 88 percent of women supporting a military response. This 2-point gap was misleading, however, because the gender gap on other polling questions was much larger. Women reported less support for a long military engagement by 16 percentage points, were more likely to oppose the use of ground troops by 9 percentage points, were less likely to support the draft being reinstated by 12 percentage points, and were less likely to support military retaliation by 12 percentage points if it resulted in 1,000 American troops dying. Women were 12 percentage points less likely to support a long-lasting war against terrorism, 5 percentage points less likely to support military retaliation aimed at Afghanistan, and 12 percentage points less likely to support military retaliation against Iraq (Jones 2001).

Additional public opinion polling results follow these patterns of gender differences. In a prewar survey, the Pew Research Center asked respondents about their support for military action in Iraq, finding that 76 percent of men versus 70 percent of women were in support (Pew Research Center 2002). In the same survey, women appeared more concerned about casualties. When asked if they would favor military action in Iraq even if thousands of casualties were the result, 63 percent of men versus 50 percent of women were in favor of military action (Pew Research Center 2002). Another 2002 Pew Research Center survey found a smaller gap of 12 percentage points, with 69 percent of men and 57 percent of women supporting military action in Iraq. In a 2013 survey, a 17-point gap existed on using military force in Syria (Pew Research Center 2013c) and an 18-point gap in 2014 on military action against ISIS (Pew Research Center 2014a).

Women are less favorable to the use of drone strikes as a way to fight terrorism, with 70 percent of men versus 53 percent of women approving of the Obama administration's use of drone strikes (Stokes 2013). Women are less supportive of missile strikes in Syria than men, with a 20-point gap where 68 percent of men versus 48 percent of women approve (Pew Research Center 2017). Women are also less supportive of sending ground troops to fight ISIS, with 41percent of women supporting versus 52 percent of men favoring ground troops (Pew Research Center 2015a). These polling results demonstrate that women are consistently less likely than men to support the use of military force.

Gender differences on domestic force issues have also consistently emerged in polling results. In a 2000 Gallup poll, 52 percent of men compared to 72 percent of women expressed support for stricter gun control laws. In that same survey, women were more likely to think that the availability of guns is a primary cause of gun violence, with 24 percent of women compared to 18 percent of men believing that the availability of guns causes gun violence (Gallup 2000). In a 2012 survey, 39 percent of women said it was important to protect gun rights compared to 60 percent of men (Pew Research Center 2012a). In 2015, gender gaps existed on banning assault weapons, creating a federal database of gun sales, and requiring background checks for gun show purchases, with women more likely to support each of these (Pew Research Center 2012b). The assault weapon ban garnered a 17-point gap, the database question had an 8-point gap, and the gun show item resulted in a 4-point gap. In a 2004 Gallup poll, 74 percent of men reported being in favor the death penalty compared to 62 percent of women. A 2015 Pew Research Center poll found an even larger gap, with 64 percent of men and 49 percent of women favoring the death penalty (Pew Research Center 2015b). In 2016, there was a 12-point gap, with 55 percent of men and 43 percent of women in favor (Oliphant 2016). Clearly, women differ from men in their views of gun control and the death penalty.

## Gendered Force Movements

Along with the academic studies and public opinion polls, women's antiforce attitudes are also evident when considering activism in the United States. Antiwar movements include organizations consisting of only women, such as the Women's International League for Peace and Freedom, which was founded to protest World War I; Women against Military Madness, which formed in the early 1980s; and more recently Code Pink: Women for Peace. Women Strike for Peace has focused much of its efforts on nuclear test ban treaties and nuclear disarmament. Many of these organizations focus on social justice issues, as well as opposing the use of military force. This is not intended to be an exhaustive list of such organizations. In addition, the gun control movement encompasses women-focused groups and demonstrations, including the Moms Demand Action for Gun Sense in America, which is associated with the Everytown for Gun Safety Action Fund, and the Million Mom March, which included gun control as part of its advocacy.

Comprehensive women's organizations and movements have also included force issues as part of their platforms and initiatives. For example, the Feminist Majority supports nonviolence, including banning gun ownership for domestic violence offenders. The Feminist Majority, however, supported the Afghanistan War because of the belief that it would be liberating for Afghan women and girls. The Women's Environment and Development Organization (WEDO) advocates for peace with a focus on how climate change causes resource scarcity and leads to armed conflicts. Also, the organizers of the January 2017 Women's March include in their list of principles being against police brutality and various aspects of the criminal justice system, including a desire to find alternatives to incarceration.

In sum, a good deal of evidence shows that gender differences exist on attitudes toward the use of force. Women are less likely to support the use of military force to solve international crises. Women are less likely to support increased defense spending.

Women are more likely to support regulations on gun ownership and sales. Women are also less supportive of the death penalty. All of this points to a need to understand the origins of these gender differences. In the next section, I outline the values hypothesis and conceptualization of these gender gaps on force issues. Then I delineate the analysis and findings, which offer strong support for the pro-social values hypothesis.

## Hypothesis

Recent work, not focused on gender differences, in political science provides evidence of the importance of values in understanding foreign policy preferences. Values such as militant internationalism and cooperative internationalism correlate with the Schwartz (1992) value types and predict foreign policy positions (Rathbun et al. 2016). For example, self-transcendence values, including benevolence and universalism, predict opposition to the unilateral use of military force (Goren et al. 2016). In addition, values have been shown to predict domestic force policy positions. Egalitarianism is a predictor of death penalty attitudes, with greater levels of egalitarianism leading to greater opposition toward the death penalty (Unnever and Cullen 2007). The same is true for gun control attitudes with egalitarianism predicting support for gun control (Howell and Day 2000). Thus, I hypothesize that gender differences in levels of pro-social values are causing the gender gap on force-related policies.

Theoretically, the pro-social values explanation would predict that women view force issues through a lens of caring for the well-being of others, meaning that women are against the use of force because of a tendency toward concern for others or their endorsement of pro-social values. When women think about the international use of force, they may think about innocent civilians being killed or suffering as the result of the destruction that occurs during war. In line with this theory, women may think about children being traumatized and families being devastated by military conflict. For these reasons, the values explanation would expect women to prefer diplomacy to the use of force to solve international disputes. And when women think about domestic use-of-force issues, they may think about the potential for guns to be used to kill innocent people, such as school shootings, mass shootings at movie theaters or concerts, and domestic disputes involving gun violence. Similarly, when women think about the death penalty, they may have concern about wrongly accused individuals being put to death. In other words, women see the use of force as threatening the safety, well-being, and security of others, either those living in close proximity or in other parts of the world.

## Women Less Supportive of Government Use of Force

To test the efficacy of values as an explanation for the gender gap, a gap must exist. As is the case throughout the book, I use the 1980–2012 American National Election Study (ANES) cumulative data. Significant and sizeable gender gaps appear on three force questions included in the data. I also include analysis of one item from the 2011 World Values Survey of the United States. There is a sizeable and significant gender gap on this item as well.

The first question I analyze in the cumulative ANES data is the defense-spending item. Respondents are asked, "Some people believe that we should spend much less money for defense. Others feel that defense spending should be greatly increased. Where would you place yourself on this scale or haven't you thought much about this?" Response options range from 1 = greatly decrease defense spending to 7 = greatly increase defense spending. I treat this as a continuous variable and use ordinary least squares regression, but the results do not differ when analyzed using ordered-logistic regression. As shown in Table 3.1 and column Defense 1, there is a significant gender gap on the issue of defense spending, with women less supportive of increasing spending. On this scale from 1 to 7, holding all control variables in Defense 1 column at their means, which is standard practice, the predicted probability for men is 4.13 (SE 0.01) and for women is 3.92 (SE 0.01). Generally, women are less supportive of increased defense spending than men.

The analysis includes the typical control variables found in survey research: age, race, education, income, region, church attendance, religious identification, and the political party holding the White House. In addition to gender, most of the other variables are significant, as indicated by an asterisk. Positive coefficients in the table indicate a positive relationship; for example, an increase in age is associated with greater support for increased defense spending. Negative coefficients indicate a negative relationship; for example, being female as opposed to being male is associated with lower support for increased defense spending. Older individuals, whites, frequent church attendees (i.e., more religious individuals), Catholics, Protestants, and Southerners are more likely to support increasing defense spending. Educated individuals and low-income individuals are less likely to support increased defense spending. Finally, a Republican presidential administration is associated with less support for defense spending.

Next, I provide a summary of the gender gap across different subgroups, finding that all women compared to men within the subgroups of race, age, education level, and income are less likely to support increased defense spending. The gender gap is significant across racial groups, with white women less supportive of defense spending than white men, and black women less supportive than black men. The gender gap is significant across age cohorts, with women significantly less likely to support increased defense spending than men in the pre–baby boomer, baby boomer, and post–baby boomer cohorts. The gender gap is also significant among those with and without a college degree, with women less likely to support increased defense spending. Finally, the gender gap is significant across income levels as well. Among those with

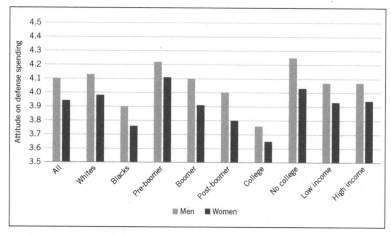

Figure 3.1. Gender differences in defense-spending attitudes across demographic subgroups

Note: Data are from cumulative 1980–2012 ANES. The scale for defense spending is from 1 = spend less to 7 = greatly increase spending.

a below-median income and among those with an above-median income, women are less likely to support increased defense spending than men. Figure 3.1 displays the gender gap within each of these demographic groups. As was the case with values in Chapter 2, the differences between demographic groups is quite interesting, in addition to the consistent gender gap across groups. For example, whites are more likely to support greater defense spending than blacks, regardless of gender.

The next question regarding force asks respondents about the hypothetical use of military force. Respondents are asked, "In the future, how willing should the United States be to use military force to solve international problems—extremely willing, very willing, somewhat willing, not very willing, or never willing?" The response options are 1 = never willing, 2 = not very willing, 3 = somewhat willing, 4 = very willing, and 5 = extremely willing. Again, I treat this as a continuous variable and use ordinary least squares regression, but the results do not differ if analyzed using ordered-logistic regression instead. As shown in the Military 1 column of Table 3.1, there is a significant gender difference, with women less likely to support the use of military force. The predicted probability holding all control variables at their mean for men is 3.17 (SE 0.02) compared to women's 3.04 (SE 0.02). Several of the control variables are also significant predictors of attitudes toward the use of force. Age and income are not significant predictors. Education, white racial identification, and a Republican presidential administration are associated with lower support for the use of military force. Church attendance, Catholic affiliation, Protestant affiliation, and living in the South are associated with greater support for the use of military force. In general, women are less supportive of the hypothetical use of military force to deal with international crises.

These gender differences exist among whites and blacks. White women are less supportive of the use of military force than white men, and the same is true of black women compared to black men. This gender gap is significant among pre– and post–baby boomers but not among baby boomers. The gender gap is also significant across education levels and income levels. College-educated women and women without a college degree are less likely to support the use of military force than men with the same education level. Among low-income and above-median-income individuals, women are less likely to support the use of military force. In Figure 3.2, each of these gender gaps is displayed. The support among men and the support among women across demographic subgroups are quite similar, with women consistently less supportive of the use of force than men of the same group.

The third dependent variable included is from the 2011 World Values Survey of the United States. This question, labeled War, asks respondents, "Do you agree or disagree with the following statement: Under some conditions, war is necessary to obtain justice." Respondents chose from two options coded 1 = agree and 0 = disagree. Because of the binary nature of the dependent variable, I use logistic regression. There is a statistically significant gender gap, as shown in the War 1 column of Table 3.1. Women are less likely than men to agree that war is necessary

## TABLE 3.1. GENDER DIFFERENCES ON FORCE ISSUES

| | Defense 1 | Defense 2 | Military 1 | Military 2 | War 1 | War 2 | Gun 1 | Gun 2 | Death 1 | Death 2 |
|---|---|---|---|---|---|---|---|---|---|---|
| Female | -0.22** | -0.18*** | -0.13*** | -0.12*** | -0.32*** | -0.29*** | 0.51*** | 0.46*** | -0.30*** | -0.22*** |
| | (0.02) | (0.02) | (0.02) | (0.02) | (0.10) | (0.11) | (0.07) | (0.08) | (0.06) | (0.07) |
| Age | 0.00*** | -0.00*** | -0.00 | -0.00 | 0.00 | 0.00 | 0.00 | 0.01** | 0.00** | 0.00** |
| | (0.00) | (0.00) | (0.00) | (0.00) | (0.00) | (0.00) | (0.02) | (0.00) | (0.00) | (0.00) |
| Education 1 = college | -0.48*** | -0.40*** | -0.18*** | -0.18*** | 0.23** | 0.24** | 0.61*** | 0.52*** | -0.85*** | -0.80*** |
| | (0.02) | (0.03) | (0.03) | (0.03) | (0.11) | (0.12) | (0.08) | (0.09) | (0.07) | (0.07) |
| Income 1 = low | -0.13*** | -0.11*** | -0.03 | -0.02 | 0.08*** | 0.08*** | -0.01*** | -0.02*** | -0.01* | -0.01* |
| | (0.02) | (0.03) | (0.03) | (0.03) | (0.03) | (0.03) | (0.00) | (0.01) | (0.00) | (0.00) |
| Race 1 = white | 0.23*** | 0.03 | -0.06** | -0.09*** | 1.10*** | 1.09*** | -0.89*** | -0.65*** | 0.61*** | 0.43*** |
| | (0.02) | (0.04) | (0.03) | (0.03) | (0.11) | (0.11) | (0.08) | (0.09) | (0.07) | (0.08) |
| Church attendance | 0.03*** | 0.03*** | 0.02** | 0.01 | 0.05** | 0.03 | -0.08*** | -0.04 | 0.05** | 0.05** |
| | (0.01) | (0.01) | (0.01) | (0.01) | (0.02) | (0.02) | (0.02) | (0.03) | (0.02) | (0.02) |
| Catholic | 0.23*** | 0.18*** | 0.11*** | 0.09** | | | 0.25*** | 0.32*** | -0.19** | -0.27*** |
| | (0.03) | (0.04) | (0.04) | (0.04) | | | (0.10) | (0.12) | (0.09) | (0.10) |

|  | | | | | | | | | | |
|---|---|---|---|---|---|---|---|---|---|---|
| Protestant | 0.30*** | 0.25*** | 0.10*** | 0.09** | | | 0.06 | 0.18 | −0.24 | −0.23 |
| | (0.03) | (0.03) | (0.04) | (0.04) | | | (0.22) | (0.25) | (0.19) | (0.21) |
| South | 0.34*** | 0.30*** | 0.09 | 0.08*** | | | −0.42*** | −0.43*** | 0.04 | 0.01 |
| | (0.02) | (0.02) | (0.03) | (0.03) | | | (0.09) | (0.11) | (0.08) | (0.09) |
| Republican president | −0.15*** | −0.18*** | −0.12*** | −0.11*** | | | | | | |
| | (0.02) | (0.02) | (0.02) | (0.02) | | | | | | |
| Egalitarianism | | −0.36*** | | −0.07*** | | | | 0.94*** | | −0.62*** |
| | | (0.01) | | (0.01) | | | | (0.05) | | (0.04) |
| Universalism | | | | | | −0.28*** | | | | |
| | | | | | | (0.05) | | | | |
| Benevolence | | | | | | 0.13*** | | | | |
| | | | | | | (0.05) | | | | |
| $R^2$ | .05 | .08 | .02 | .09 | .06 | .07 | .05 | .14 | .03 | .06 |
| $N$ | 22,443 | 18,043 | 5,253 | 14,988 | 2,143 | 2,115 | 3,774 | 3,237 | 3,991 | 3,412 |

Note: Defense and military data are from the 1980–2012 ANES; positive coefficients indicate support for increased defense spending and support for using the military. War data are from the 2011 World Values Survey; positive coefficients indicate a belief that war is justified. Gun and death data are from the 2016 ANES; positive coefficients indicate support for increased gun control and support for the death penalty.

* $p < .10$; ** $p < .05$; *** $p < .01$

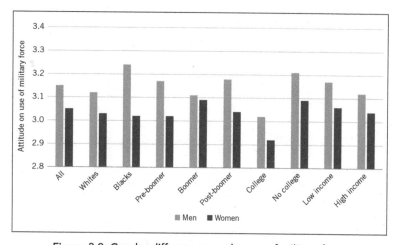

Figure 3.2. Gender differences on the use of military force

Note: Data are from cumulative 1980–2012 ANES. The scale for use of force is from 1 = never willing to use force to 5 = extremely willing to use force.

to obtain justice in some conditions. The predicted probability for men is 0.79 (SE 0.01) and for women is 0.73 (SE 0.01). These predicted probabilities are calculated holding the other variables in the War 1 column at their mean, which is standard practice when calculating predicted probabilities. Not all of the same control variables are available in the World Values Survey. I include age, education, income, race, and church attendance. All of these except for age, which is not significant, predict agreement with the statement. So college-educated individuals, higher-income individuals, whites, and people attending church more frequently are more likely to believe that war is necessary to obtain justice. Women, compared to men, are less likely to believe that war is at times crucial to bring about justice.

The 2016 ANES data include two questions about domestic force: support for gun control and support for the death penalty. The gun control question asks respondents if they believe gun control laws should be made more strict, kept the same, or be made less strict. Only a small percentage of individuals want gun control laws to be made less strict. This item is recoded so that 1 indicates a desire to make gun laws more strict and 0 includes both response options of keeping guns laws the same and making them less strict. In the table, positive coefficients indicate greater support for stricter gun laws. As expected, women are significantly more likely to support stricter gun control laws compared to men. The predicted probability for the stricter laws response option for women is 0.63 (SE 0.01) and for men is 0.51 (SE 0.01). Whites, Southerners, individuals with a low income, and frequent church attendees are less likely to support stricter gun control laws. Individuals with a college degree or higher and Catholics are more likely to support stricter gun control laws. Age and mainline Protestant identification are not predictors of gun control attitudes.

As depicted in Figure 3.3, the gender gap exists across all subgroups, with women consistently being more supportive of gun control laws than men. This gender gap is statistically significant among whites and blacks. The gender gap is significant in all age cohorts. The gender gap is also significant across education levels and income levels, with women more supportive of stricter gun

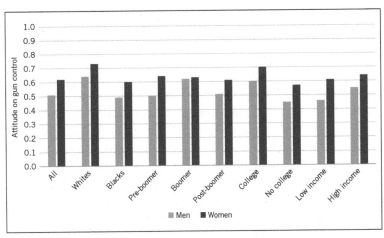

Figure 3.3. Gender differences on gun control
Note: Data are from 2016 ANES. 1 = stricter laws; 0 = laws kept same or less strict.

control laws than men, regardless of their education and income. Although the level of support for stricter gun regulations varies between different subgroups, women are consistently more supportive than men of the same race, age, education, or income group.

The death penalty question asks respondents to what degree they favor or oppose the death penalty. The response options are coded as follows: 1 = oppose strongly, 2 = oppose not strongly, 3 = favor not strongly, or 4 = favor strongly. Positive values in the table indicate greater support for the death penalty. I use ordered logistic regression, given the ordinal nature of this dependent variable. Women are significantly less likely to favor the death penalty. The predicted probability that women respond to this question with the response option of favor strongly is 0.50 (SE 0.01) and that men respond with favor strongly is 0.58 (SE 0.01). Men are more likely than women to favor the death penalty. Older individuals, whites, and individuals who attend church more frequently are more likely to favor the death penalty. Mainline Protestant identification is not a significant predictor of death penalty attitudes. Catholics, low-income individuals, and the college educated are less likely to favor the death penalty.

In terms of the gender gap across subgroups, as shown in Figure 3.4, gender differences are somewhat less consistent for death penalty support than for gun control attitudes. The gender gap on death penalty attitudes is significant among whites but not among blacks. White women are less favorable toward the death penalty compared to white men, but black men and black women share very similar views on the death penalty. Gender differences among those with a college degree and those with less than a college degree are statistically significant. Regardless of education level, women are less favorable toward the death penalty than men of the same education level. The gender gap is significant among low-income men and women as well as among high-income men and women. The gender gap between men and women of the pre-boomer age cohort is not statistically significant, but the

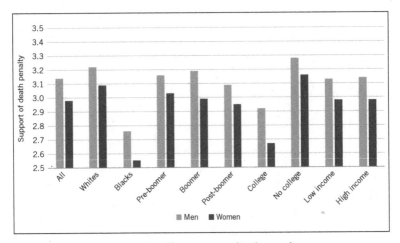

**Figure 3.4. Gender differences on death penalty support**
Note: Data are from 2016 ANES. Higher values indicate stronger support for the death penalty.

gender gaps are significant among the boomer cohort and the post-boomer cohort.

## Pro-social Values Provide Insight into Gender Differences in Use of Force

To test the explanatory power of pro-social values, I add egalitarianism to the analysis discussed previously. I find strong support for the pro-social values hypothesis that women's greater endorsement of pro-social values accounts for a significant portion of the effect of gender on force attitudes. As discussed in greater length in Chapter 2, the only measure of pro-social values included in the ANES data on a regular basis and therefore included in the cumulative file is egalitarianism. Egalitarianism measures support for equality and the belief that society should pursue equal opportunity.

First, turning to the defense-spending question, including egalitarianism in the analysis reduces the gender gap. These

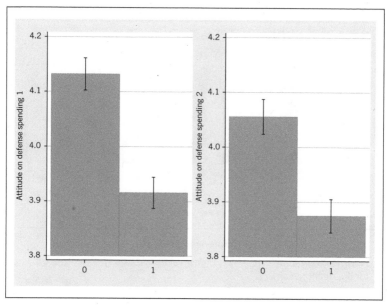

Figure 3.5. Gender differences in defense-spending attitudes

Note: Data are from cumulative 1980–2012 ANES. On the x-axis, 1 = female; 0 = male. Higher values indicate greater support for defense spending. The left graph shows the marginal effects calculated from the Defense 1 column of Table 3.1; the right graph shows the marginal effects calculated from the Defense 2 column. Marginal effects are calculated with demographic variables set at their mean.

results are displayed in the Defense 2 column of Table 3.1. When egalitarianism is included in the model, there is a reduced effect of gender on defense spending. Figure 3.5 depicts the defense-spending gender gap without egalitarianism on the left-hand side and the gender gap with egalitarianism included on the right-hand side. The left graph of Figure 3.5 clearly shows a large gap, even including the control variables at their mean, and the right graph shows a substantively smaller gap when pro-social values are included. According to mediational analyses, egalitarianism mediates 18.81 percent of the effect of gender on defense-spending attitudes. Throughout the book, I use the Hicks and Tingley (2011) medeff mediation package for Stata to calculate the percent mediated. All other necessary conditions for mediation discussed in

Chapter 2 (Baron and Kenney 1986) are also met, but are not shown for simplicity. There is a significant gender gap in egalitarianism (as shown in Chapter 2), and egalitarianism predicts spending attitudes without gender in the model. This means that the gender gap on defense-spending attitudes is partially a result of women's greater concern for the well-being of others.

The full analysis is included in the Defense 2 column of Table 3.1. The results in the table show that the same control variables continue to be significant. Older people, those that attend church frequently, Catholics, Protestants, and Southerners are more likely to support defense spending. Being college educated, having a below-median income, and Republican presidential administrations are each associated with lower support for increasing defense spending. The race identification variable is no longer significant. As hypothesized, egalitarianism is significant and is associated with lower support for increased defense spending.

Finally, the reduction of the gender effect does not appear to be an artifact of gender differences in partisanship. In analysis not shown, party identification is included in the model, using the standard 7-point item, with higher values indicating Republican identification. Egalitarianism remains a significant predictor of defense-spending attitudes with party identification in the model. Party identification is also a significant predictor, with Republicans more likely to support increased defense spending.

Referring to the use-of-military-force question, including egalitarianism in the model also reduces the size of the gender gap. Egalitarianism reduces the effect of gender. Mediational analyses indicate that egalitarianism mediates 6.97 percent of the effect of gender on attitudes toward the use of military force. The other conditions are also met for mediation, as discussed in Chapter 2. The analysis including egalitarianism is in the Military 2 column of Table 3.1. Similar to the prior results, age and income continue to not predict use-of-force attitudes. In addition, when egalitarianism is included in the model, church attendance is no longer significant. Educated individuals, whites, and a Republican administration continue to be associated with less support for the use of military force. Catholics, Protestants, and Southerners are more likely to support the use of military force. Finally, egalitarianism is predictive of lower levels of willingness to use military force. Again, I ensure that the reduction in the effect of gender when egalitarianism is included in the analysis is not just a result of gender differences in partisanship. In analysis not shown, including party identification does not remove the effect of egalitarianism, and Republicans are associated with greater willingness to use military force. This provides additional support for the values hypothesis. Gender differences in pro-social values provide insight into the gender gap on force issues.

Analysis of the third dependent variable, which measures whether war is ever necessary to obtain justice, is quite similar to the defense-spending and use-of-military-force analyses. The analysis including universalism and benevolence are displayed in the War 2 column of Table 3.1. The inclusion of universalism in the model appears to partially explain why women are less likely to think that war is necessary at times. Education and income continue to be associated with a higher likelihood of stating that war is necessary at times. Church attendance and age are not significant predictors. Universalism is a significant negative predictor, meaning that those who endorse universalism are less likely to believe that war is ever necessary. Surprisingly, benevolence is a positive predictor. Perhaps individuals concerned about close others believe that military action to protect individuals in close proximity is necessary at times. According to the mediational analyses, universalism mediates 13.62 percent of the effect of gender on attitudes toward war ever being justified. Benevolence only mediates 1.21 percent of the effect of gender. Unfortunately, although it is listed in the questionnaire, a party identification variable is not included in the data set. Therefore, I cannot report that the relationship between universalism and war attitudes is not an artifact of partisan differences. These universalism results provide support for the pro-social values hypothesis.

The results for the domestic force questions also support the pro-social values hypothesis. For the gun control question, egalitarianism partially mediates the effect of gender by 25.10 percent. There is also a reduction in the size of the gender coefficient when egalitarianism is included. Egalitarianism is associated with support for stricter gun control laws. Finally, the effect of egalitarianism remains with the inclusion of party identification. These results provide additional supportive evidence for the pro-social values hypothesis that women are less likely to support the use of domestic force out of concern for others' well-being. For the death penalty question, egalitarianism mediates 37.26 percent of the effect of gender. Again, there is a reduction in the size of the gender coefficient with the inclusion of egalitarianism. These results mean that individuals who endorse pro-social values are less likely to favor the death penalty and that pro-social value endorsement partially explains why women are on average less favorable toward the death penalty. In analysis not included in the table, the effect of egalitarianism does not change when party identification is included in the model. This strongly suggests that women are less likely to favor the death penalty partially because of their propensity to care about others.

## Testing Other Explanations of Gender Differences

In analysis displayed in Table A3.1 in the Appendix, there is also support for the other explanations of the gender gap. Individuals with more warm feelings toward feminists are less likely to support defense spending, and it mediates 24.25 percent of the gender gap. As is displayed in the Table 3.1, individuals with an income below the national medium are less supportive of increased defense spending, and income only mediates 4.95 percent of the gender gap. Being employed does not predict defense-spending attitudes and does not mediate the gender gap. Having children predicts greater support for defense spending and does not mediate the gender gap; motherhood, however, predicts lower levels of support and mediates 24.75 percent of the gender gap.

There is an important note regarding the results from the other explanations. When looking at the Appendix tables, the number of observations for each model listed in the last row of each table tends to be significantly smaller than the number of observations in the tables testing the values explanation. For example, in Table A3.1 in the column testing the feminist identity explanation as a predictor of defense-spending attitudes, there are 10, 201 observations. The second column of Table 3.1, testing the values explanation as a predictor of defense-spending attitudes, there are 18,043 observations. Therefore, it may not be appropriate to directly compare the mediation results because the sample sizes are so different. In other words, the feminist feeling thermometer was asked in fewer years leading to much fewer observations, so the mediation results should not be directly compared to that of the values explanation.

As displayed in Table A3.2 in the Appendix, there is limited support for the other explanations. Feeling warmly toward feminists predicts less support for the use of military force and mediates 5.45 percent of the gender gap. Income and being employed do not predict force attitudes and do not mediate the gap. Having children and being a mother do not predict attitudes toward the use of military force and do not mediate the gender gap.

The other explanations are also supported in connection with the gender gap on gun control and the death penalty. Feeling warmly toward feminists predicts greater support for stricter gun control laws and lower support for the death penalty; the feminist feeling thermometer mediates 35.15 percent of the gender gap on gun control and 50.38 percent of the gender gap on the death penalty. Low-income individuals are less likely to support stricter gun control, and income does not mediate the gender gap. Having a low income is associated with lower support for the death penalty and mediates 4.72 percent of the gender gap. Employment status is unrelated to gun control attitudes and does not mediate the gap. Currently employed individuals are more supportive of the death penalty, and this mediates 4.99 percent of the gender gap. Having children and being a mother do not mediate the gender gap; having children is actually associated with not wanting stricter gun control attitudes, while being a mother is not statistically significant. The effects of parenthood and motherhood are similar for death penalty attitudes; neither is a mediator. Parents are more supportive of the death penalty, while motherhood is not a significant predictor.

The results for the pro-social values explanation in comparison to these results are stronger and/or more consistent. Among the other explanations, the feminist explanation receives the most support. This suggests that the economic circumstances and motherhood explanations may not account for the gender gap on force issues. A better comparative test of the values explanation versus the feminist explanation would use the same sample, with the same number of observations, and a superior measure of feminist identity.

## Summary and Conclusion

This chapter provides support for the pro-social values hypothesis. The gender gaps in the use of force are partially accounted for by gender differences in values. Women's greater concern compared to men for others' well-being leads to lower levels of support for defense spending, lower levels of support for the use of military force, a lower likelihood of believing that war is ever necessary, greater support for gun control, and greater opposition to the death penalty. Values provide insight into why these gender gaps exist. Out of care and concern for others, women are less supportive of the international and domestic use of force.

Present global conditions and the salience of domestic force issues provide several examples of why understanding the gender gap on the use of force is so important. Iran's desire for and North Korea's existing nuclear programs pose threats to American national security. The continued threat of ISIS and other terrorist groups in the Middle East and North Africa have also led to calls for the use of military force. With respect to domestic force, gun control has become a salient issue with the high number of mass shootings since AR-15s became available for sale to the public again. In addition, recent school shootings, such as the one in Parkland, Florida, have caused increased activism among younger people against the availability of semiautomatic assault rifles to the public. Also, other domestic force issues such as the death penalty, high levels of incarceration, and police shootings of innocent individuals continue to receive news media and public attention.

Therefore, it is reasonable to believe that these issues will continue to be a chief issue in political campaigns, particularly for the presidency, but also for congressional and statewide elections. Women will likely continue to be more antiforce than men, as they have been since the time of slavery and the suffrage movement, as noted in the introduction to this chapter. Suffragists were antislavery and antiwar, while women have also organized against nuclear armament, the Vietnam War, lynching, and the gun deaths of innocent civilians. This could continue to make it difficult for pro–death penalty, antigun control, and hawkish candidates to win over female voters.

In Chapter 4, I move on to testing the pro-social values hypothesis as an explanation for gender differences of environmental policies, including environmental protections and environmental regulations. I also look at gender differences in attitudes about climate change, as well as testing pro-social values as an explanation for the gap on climate change beliefs.

# 4

# Gender Gap on Environmental Attitudes

> It will take a massive effort to move society from
> corporate domination, in which industry's rights
> to pollute and damage health and the environment
> supersede the public's right to live, work, and play in
> safety. . . . Our children's futures, and those of their
> unborn children, are at stake.
>
> —Lois Gibbs, "Learning from Love Canal"

Before Erin Brockovich, Lois Gibbs became an activist who fought for the safety and rights of homeowners and community members exposed to toxic waste in the Love Canal neighborhood of Niagara Falls in 1978. As a twenty-seven-year-old mother of two children who were experiencing multiple uncommon illnesses, Gibbs began to organize her community to protect the health and safety of her children and other families. Gibbs went on to start the Center for Health, Environment and Justice, which has helped more than two million people combat environmentally caused health threats throughout the United States (Center for Health, Environment and Justice, n.d.). Women's concern about the safety and well-being of others, as Lois Gibbs demonstrated, might be the reason for the observed gender gap on environmental policies.

The environment is an issue that has been underrepresented in the women-and-politics literature, particularly in recent years.

This is a timely issue because public debates about the consequences of climate change have garnered a great deal of media attention in the United States. Additionally, natural disasters, such as Hurricane Katrina and Hurricane Sandy, and human-made disasters, such as the oil spill in the Gulf of Mexico, have heightened awareness of the human-ecological balance. The same is likely true for the countless documentaries that chronicle the effects of climate change, such as *An Inconvenient Truth*, *Before the Flood*, and *Chasing Ice*. Of course, documentaries about other environmental issues also increase public awareness. There was even a bipartisan push for climate change awareness and action in 2008, when Newt Gingrich and Nancy Pelosi and then Pat Robertson and Al Sharpton appeared in commercials together about the need to address environmental issues. During the 2008 presidential debates, candidates Mitt Romney and Barack Obama acknowledged the need to address environmental issues. The environment did not become a hot topic during the 2016 general election, but even so, the two major party candidates, Donald Trump and Hillary Clinton, were extremely distinct in their positions. Last, the Dakota Access Pipeline issue acquired extensive social media attention in 2016.

Given contemporary media attention, partisan debates, and the increasing indications of climate change, opinions about the environment seem to be of increased importance in recent years. In this chapter, I investigate how differences in pro-social values help to clarify why these gender differences exist. First, I discuss the current literature on the gender gap in environmental attitudes. Next, I provide evidence that values differences are at the core of this gender gap. The central finding of this chapter is that value differences between men and women appear to explain the gap in environmental attitudes. There is strong evidence that the gap in support of government spending to protect the environment and the gap in support of government regulations to protect the environment are caused by gender differences in pro-social values.

## Gender Differences on Environmental Attitudes in the Literature

Previous research has shown that women and men think differently and have different concerns about environmental problems. There are significant gender differences in environmental concern, with women tending to report greater environmental concern (McCright 2010; Mohai 1992). These differences are pronounced even when controlling for various demographics (Mohai 1992) and are not mediated by ideology, party identification, knowledge about climate change, or social roles (i.e., parenthood or motherhood; McCright 2010). This indicates that the gap is yet to be fully understood because it is robust to the inclusion of several other factors. It is more than just a partisan gap caused by women being more likely to identify with the Democratic Party. It is more than just an ideological difference where women might be more likely to support an activist government that does more in general (Carroll 2006). These results also indicate that social roles, as suggested by social role theory, do not explain the gap.

Two studies find similar results, with women significantly differing from men on climate change or global warming questions, many of which are knowledge questions, not just concern questions. In the more recent study, 59 percent of women believe that global warming is occurring compared to 54 percent of men. An even larger difference exists for believing that humans are causing global warming, with 64 percent of women believing humans are the cause versus 56 percent of men. There is a gender gap on agreement that most scientists believe global warming is happening, with 66 percent of women versus 60 percent of men agreeing. In this same recent study, women express greater concern about global warming on two items. First, 35 percent of women versus 29 percent of men say that they worry a great deal about global warming. Second, 37 percent of women believe global warming will threaten their way of life, compared to 28 percent of men (McCright 2010). All of these differences are statistically significant.

In the older piece, the findings are quite analogous. Women are significantly more likely to agree that sea levels will rise, causing coastal flooding, and climate change will lead to increased drought. Similar differences exist between women and men on pollution increases, natural disaster increases, and loss of animal and plant species as the result of climate change (Blocker and Eckberg 1997).

## Explanations in the Literature for the Gender Gap in Environmental Attitudes

Three theories for the existing gender differences are prominent in this literature. To my knowledge, no one has investigated the possibility that values differences between men and women are at the root of this gender gap in environmental attitudes. First, there has been a focus on explaining gender differences as either a product of socialization or structural pressures to assume the role of nurturer. Women's heightened concern for environmental problems has been theorized to stem from women's socialization to be more compassionate and to assume the role of caregivers for children and the household. However, evidence in support of both socialization and structural hypotheses has been mixed, with many studies paying lip service to these explanations while only employing gender as a control variable (see Blocker and Eckberg 1997 for an exception).

Second, some scholars have argued that gender differences in environmental attitudes are a result of differences in knowledge. Little evidence has been found in support of this explanation (Bord and O'Connor 1997; Davidson and Freudenburg 1996; Hayes 2001). In fact, women express greater levels of climate change knowledge than do men (McCright 2010). These results were outlined above with respect to whether global warming is happening now, being caused by humans, and believed by most scientists to be happening now.

Finally, there is also work specifically linking feminism and environmental attitudes. This research, often referred to as ecofeminism, finds evidence of feminism as a predictor of environmental attitudes (Gupte 2002; Smith 2001; Somma and Tolleson-Rinehart 1997). Several theoretical explanations exist as to why feminists would have pro-environmental attitudes, including antipatriarchal dominance and exploitation of nature, female-centered and nature-focused new age religious beliefs, and women in science or environment-related careers exposed to feminism (for an extensive discussion, see Somma and Tolleson-Rinehart 1997). This research on ecofeminism, however, does not provide evidence that feminist identity is a mediator of the gender gap in environmental attitudes. The relationship between feminism and pro-environmental attitudes is significant among men and women, and feminist identity is a predictor of environmental attitudes, but it is unclear if it mediates the effect of gender (Smith 2001; Somma and Tolleson-Rinehart 1997).

## Recent Polling on Environmental Attitudes

Recent polling data follows these patterns of gender differences. In a Pew report, several gender differences emerged. In this survey, women were more likely to say that the earth is warming and were more likely to favor emission limits, oppose offshore drilling, and oppose fracking (Stokes, Wike, and Carle 2015). According to a different Pew poll in 2015, women were also more likely than men to state that climate change is a serious problem, that climate change will personally harm them, and that climate change will force people to make major changes to reduce its effects (Zainulbai 2015). All of these differences are large. For the serious problem question, 83 percent of women agreed compared to 66 percent of men; that is a 17-point gap. For the personal harm question, 69 percent of women versus 48 percent of men agreed, which is a 21-point gap. For the change question, 75 percent of women and 57 percent of men agreed, resulting in an 18-point difference (Zainulbai 2015).

Other recent polls indicate growing concern about global warming. A 2016 Gallup poll found that 64 percent of Americans categorize themselves as worried about global warming; this marks the highest percentage of concern among Americans since 2008 in the yearly poll (Saad and Jones 2016). A CBS News Poll in April 2019 found that 53 percent of Americans think global warming is causing a serious impact right now, and another 26 percent believe it will cause an impact in the future, while 15 percent do not think it will have a serious impact ("Environment" 2019). These polls do not break down the results by gender, but the findings suggest the need to understand the origins of environmental attitudes. Last, a recent polling report about the environment and climate change noted that of the 36 percent of Americans who make up the climate-engaged public because of their deep concerns about climate change, 55 percent are women (Funk and Kennedy 2016). This nicely transitions to the following section, in which I discuss how the environmental movement has been gendered in intriguing ways, including the existence of women's organizations focused solely on environmental issues.

## A Gendered Environmental Movement

In certain ways, the environmental movement has been gendered. Several organizations have an environmental focus and a woman-centered membership. Women's Voices for the Earth is an environmental organization focused on promoting a toxic chemical–free future, including toxic chemical–free cleaning products, toxin-free hair salons, and toxin-free feminine care products. This organization's messaging is about health. Women's Voices argues for a focus on women because of claims that toxic chemicals are often evaluated on the basis of their effect on men rather than the more harmful effects on women, including the reproductive health of women and girls. Second, Women for a Healthy Environment similarly focuses on women's health and the environmental factors that undermine health, including toxins, food, clean air, and clean water. This organization advocates for green cleaning in schools, safe cosmetics, increased food labeling, and bans on environmentally damaging products. The woman emphasis centers on making health choices for oneself and one's family, along with advocating for a safe and healthy future. Third, the Audubon's Women in Conservation has a mission to support environmental opportunities for women and girls, as well as educating women on issues related to the environment and conservation. In addition to emphasizing conservation efforts to protect wildlife, this organization has highlighted the importance of women in journalism providing a green perspective and women promoting and advocating for green food.

Comprehensive women's organizations and movements have also included environmental issues on their agenda. For example, the National Organization for Women discusses climate change and other environmental issues on its website. This organization argues that women are disproportionately affected by climate change and other environmental threats. The League of Women Voters includes environmental protection as one of its issue areas, on which it advocates. Women's Environment and Development Organization (WEDO) is another example of a women's organization that advocates on more than one issue area, including the environment. WEDO refers to itself as a "global women's advocacy organization for a just world that promotes and protects human rights, gender equality, and the integrity of the environment."[1] WEDO is concerned with climate change and environmental justice, among other issues. Last, the historic Women's March on January 21, 2017, included individuals with an environmental focus, such as the disproportionate impact of climate change on women globally and advocating environmental justice worldwide.

In sum, there is a good deal of evidence that gender differences exist on environmental policy preferences. Women are more likely to express concern about the environment, including health risks of toxic chemicals and the detrimental effects of climate change. Women are also more likely to report greater knowledge

---

1. See the organization's website, at https://wedo.org.

about climate change and a desire for more government action to protect the environment. Furthermore, several organizations seek to take advantage of these gender differences by having gendered messaging regarding the environment. All of this points to a need to understand the origins of these gender differences. The next section discusses the values hypothesis followed by the analysis and results, which provide support for the values hypothesis.

## Hypothesis

I hypothesize that gender differences in levels of pro-social values are causing the differences in support for environmental protection policies and environmental concern. Conceptually, women may see environmental issues through a lens of concern for others' well-being. The pro-social values explanation would contend that environmental issues such as air pollution, water pollution, and the consequences of climate change concern women because of their propensity toward concern for others or their endorsement of pro-social values. When women think about environmental issues, they might think about the potential for wildlife and human suffering. For example, when confronted with the impact of climate change, women may think about the hardships of losing one's home, of being forced to migrate because of flooding or drought, and of suffering through an increased number of natural disasters. Migration could result in a loss of one's way of life or culture and other problems, such as overcrowding and conflict. Flooding and droughts could lead to an increase in the cost of food and even the scarcity of certain foods. Furthermore, women may be more likely to think about the potential for loss of life as a result of damage to the environment. In other words, women see environmental damage as a threat to the safety and well-being of their family, friends, children, future generations, and even distant others living in other parts of the world.

Some particularly relevant findings fit with this hypothesis. Egalitarianism is an important predictor of environmental attitudes, with an increase in egalitarianism endorsement associated with higher levels of environmentalism (Carlisle and Smith 2005). When environmental problems are framed as local issues or when they are perceived as related to personal health and well-being, women have been found to exhibit greater concern for the environment (see Davidson and Freudenberg 1996 for an extensive review of this literature; Blocker and Eckberg 1997; Klineberg, McKeever, and Rothenbach 1998; Stern, Dietz, and Kalof 1993). This suggests that women are concerned for the well-being of themselves and others with respect to environmental problems. One study finds a relationship between altruism and environmental attitudes for women (Dietz, Kalof, and Stern 2002); another, using a convenient sample, finds that women are more other oriented, speculating that this leads to a gender difference in environmentalism (Zelezny, Chua, and Aldrich 2000). My analysis tests whether women's greater propensity to hold pro-social values leads to gender differences in environmental attitudes.

## Women Support Greater Spending and More Regulations to Protect the Environment

As in Chapter 3, I first want to establish that there are statistically significant gender differences on environmental policies in the cumulative ANES and 2016 ANES data sets. This chapter does not include analysis of the 2011 World Value Survey data. There are significant and sizeable gender gaps on the two questions included in the cumulative ANES data measuring environmental attitudes. There is also a significant gender gap on the 2016 ANES climate change question.

First, I address one of several spending items regularly included in the ANES data. This spending question asks respondents if government spending should be (1) decreased, (2) kept the same, or (3) increased to protect the environment. This question uses the following question stem: "If you had a say in making up the federal budget this year, for which programs would you like to see spending increased and for which would you like to see spending decreased." As shown in Figure 4.1, the gender

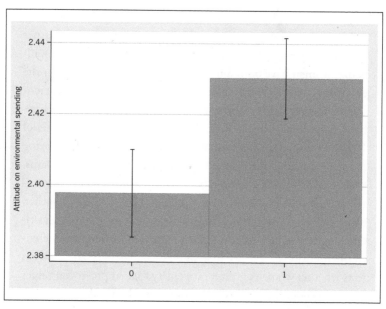

Figure 4.1. Gender differences in environmental-spending attitudes

Note: Data are from cumulative 1980–2012 ANES . On the x-axis, 1 = female; 0 = male. On the y-axis, 1 = decrease spending; 2 = maintain spending; 3 = increase spending. Marginal effects are calculated with demographic variables set at their mean.

gap is quite substantial, with women much more likely than men to support keeping government spending to protect the environment the same or increasing it. Higher values indicate greater levels of support for government spending to protect the environment. The bar for women is on the right of Figure 4.1, while the bar for men is on the left. The 95 percent confidence intervals in the bar graph indicate that this gap is statistically significant because the confidence interval lines do not overlap.

Figure 4.1 is based on analysis including the typical control variables age, race, education, income, region, church attendance, religious identification, and the political party holding the White House. The analysis is depicted in the first Spending column in Table 4.1. In addition to gender, many of the other variables are also significant in this model. Older individuals, whites, frequent church attendees (i.e., more religious individuals), Protestants, and Southerners are less likely to support government spending to protect the environment. On the other hand, college education, lower income, and years of a Republican presidency are associated with greater support for government spending. The only variable that is not significant is Catholic identification.

Turning to gender differences among different subgroups, Figure 4.2 displays the gender gaps across demographic subgroups. The gender gap is significant among whites but not among blacks. White women are more likely than white men to support increased environmental spending. The gender gap is significant only among the baby boomer generation. The gender gap on spending is significant among college-educated individuals but not among those with less than a bachelor's degree. The gap is not significant among those with an income below the median but is significant among those with an income above the median. The most stark between-group difference is the very high support for increased spending among African Americans.

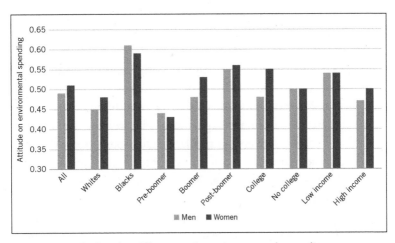

Figure 4.2. Gender differences in environmental spending across demographic subgroups

Note: Data are from cumulative 1980–2012 ANES. 1 = decrease spending; 2 = maintain spending; 3 = increase spending. Analysis controls for demographic variables are set at their mean.

The second dependent variable is a question that asks respondents to place themselves on a continuum concerning government regulations on businesses to protect the environment. The question wording is as follows: "Some people think we need much tougher government regulations on business in order to protect the environment. (Suppose these people are at one end of a scale, at point 1.) Others think that current regulations to protect the environment are already too much of a burden on business. (Suppose these people are at the other end of the scale, at point 7.) And, of course, some other people have opinions somewhere in between, at points 2, 3, 4, 5 or 6. Where would you place yourself on this scale, or haven't you thought much about this?" The environmental regulations question was only asked in 1996, 1998, and 2000; therefore, the number of observations for this analysis is much smaller compared to the previous spending question. I reverse-coded the item so 1 corresponds to the belief that regulations are already a burden and 7 corresponds to wanting tougher regulations to protect the environment. This means that higher values indicate greater support for regulations to protect the environment. This question is of particular interest because the political rhetoric including the partisan and ideological debates about environmental policy often depicts business interests or business growth in opposition to environmental regulations. This question allows respondents to take a side on that supposed conflict. As is evident in Figure 4.3, there is a sizeable gender difference on support for greater government regulations, with women more likely than men to support greater regulations to protect the environment. In the figure, the bar on the right is for women, and the bar on the left is for men. This gap is significant, as shown by the 95 percent confidence interval indicators.

As was the same for the environmental spending analysis, this depiction of the gap in Figure 4.3 includes all of the above-listed control variables. Even with these controls in the model, women are significantly more likely than men to support regulations to protect the environment. The full analysis is in the Regulations 1 column of Table 4.1. As shown in the table, other variables

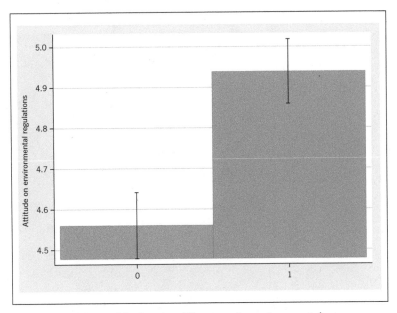

Figure 4.3. Gender differences in environmental
regulations attitudes

Note: Data are from cumulative 1980–2012 ANES. On the x-axis, 1 =
female; 0 = male. The scale for regulations is from 1 = regulations burden
on business to 7 = tougher regulations. Marginal effects are calculated with
demographic variables set at their mean.

besides gender are significant in the model. Similar to the spending results, older individuals, whites, frequent church attendees,
and Protestants are less likely to support environmental regulations. The rest of the variables, including education, Catholic
identification, and region, are not significant predictors.

Once more looking at the gender differences across demographic subgroups, Figure 4.4 displays the gender gaps on the environmental regulation question for racial, age, education, and income subgroups. Similar to the environmental-spending results,
the gender gap on support for environmental regulations is only
significant among whites and not among blacks. White women
are more likely than white men to support increased environmental regulations. Black men and black women are equally likely

TABLE 4.1. GENDER DIFFERENCES IN ENVIRONMENTAL ATTITUDES

| | Spending 1 | Spending 2 | Regulations 1 | Regulations 2 | Climate 1 | Climate 2 |
|---|---|---|---|---|---|---|
| Female | 0.07** | -0.00 | 0.38*** | 0.30*** | 0.19*** | 0.15** |
| | (0.03) | (0.03) | (0.06) | (0.06) | (0.06) | (0.07) |
| Age | -0.01*** | -0.01*** | -0.01*** | -0.01*** | -0.01*** | -0.02*** |
| | (0.01) | (0.00) | (0.00) | (0.00) | (0.00) | (0.00) |
| Education 1 = college | 0.17*** | 0.09*** | 0.01 | -0.05 | 0.44*** | 0.37*** |
| | (0.03) | (0.03 | (0.06) | (0.06) | (0.07) | (0.07) |
| Income 1 = below median | 0.22*** | 0.17*** | 0.05 | 0.00 | -0.01* | -0.01** |
| | (0.03) | (0.03) | (0.07) | (0.07) | (0.00) | (0.00) |
| Race 1 = white | -0.51*** | -0.21*** | -0.34*** | -0.12 | -0.17*** | 0.02 |
| | (0.03) | (0.03) | (0.07) | (0.07) | (0.07) | (0.08) |
| Church attendance | -0.09*** | -0.08*** | -0.09*** | -0.06*** | -0.09*** | -0.08*** |
| | (0.01) | (0.01) | (0.02) | (0.02) | (0.02) | (0.02) |

|  | (1) | (2) | (3) | (4) | (5) | (6) |
|---|---|---|---|---|---|---|
| Catholic | 0.04 | 0.11** | -0.04 | -0.01 | -0.18** | -0.11 |
|  | (0.04) | (0.04) | (0.10) | (0.01) | (0.09) | (0.10) |
| Protestant | -0.13*** | -0.10** | -0.20** | -0.15* | 0.01 | 0.07 |
|  | (0.04) | (0.04) | (0.09) | (0.09) | (0.19) | (0.20) |
| Region 1 = South | -0.09*** | -0.01 | 0.04 | -0.08 | -0.33*** | -0.31*** |
|  | (0.03) | (0.03) | (0.06) | (0.06) | (0.08) | (0.09) |
| Republican president | 0.63*** | 0.59*** | — | — | — | — |
|  | (0.03) | (0.03) |  |  |  |  |
| Egalitarianism | 0.72*** | 0.54*** |  | 0.54*** |  | 0.75*** |
|  | (0.02) | (0.03) |  | (0.03) |  | (0.04) |
| $R^2$ | .03 | .07 | .05 | .13 | .02 | .07 |
| $N$ | 22,885 | 20,501 | 3,191 | 2,971 | 4,046 | 3,461 |

Note: Spending and regulations data are from the 1980–2012 ANES; positive coefficients indicate support for spending and regulations to protect the environment. Climate data are from the 2016 ANES; positive coefficients indicate a belief that human beings are causing climate change.

* $p < .10$; ** $p < .05$; *** $p < .01$

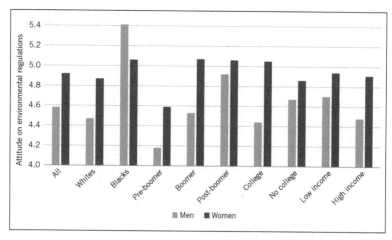

Figure 4.4. Gender differences in environmental regulations across demographic subgroups

Note: Data are from cumulative 1980–2012 ANES. The scale for regulations is from 1 = regulations burden on business to 7 = tougher regulations. Analysis controls for demographic variables are set at their mean.

to support regulations to protect the environment. The gender gap is significant among pre–baby boomers and baby boomers, and is marginally significant among post–baby boomers. The gap exists across education levels among those with and without a college degree. The gender gap is significant on regulations for both below-median and above-median income groups. Besides among blacks, for which the gap is not significant likely because of a small number of observations, the figure shows that women are consistently more supportive of greater regulations across subgroups.

For the third dependent variable, the 2016 ANES includes an item measuring whether individuals believe climate change is the result of (1) mostly natural causes, (2) about equally human activity and natural causes, or (3) mostly human activity. Higher values indicate a greater likelihood to report that climate change is the result of mostly human activity. There is a significant gender gap on this question, with women more likely than men to believe that climate change results from mostly human activity.

The predicted probability of the mostly human activity response option is 0.36 (SE 0.01) for men and 0.41 (SE 0.01) for women. That is to say, the probability that women chose the mostly human activity option is 0.05 higher than the probability that men chose this same option. Individuals with more education are also more likely to believe that climate change is the result of human activity. Older individuals, lower-income individuals, whites, frequent church attendees, Catholics, and Southerners are all less likely to believe that climate change is the result of mostly human activity.

Gender differences between subgroups are depicted in Figure 4.5. This gender gap is not consistent across different demographic subgroups. The gender gap is significant among whites, but the gap is reversed among blacks, with black men being more likely than black women to believe that climate change is the result of mostly human activity. Gender differences are not significant between those with less than a college degree. The gap is significant among the college educated. The gender gap is only significant among the baby boomer age cohort, not the older or younger

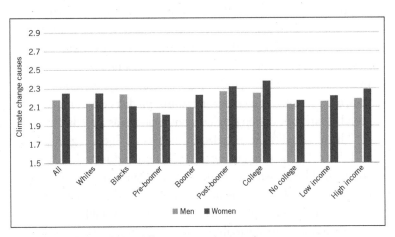

Figure 4.5. Gender differences in climate change causes across demographic subgroups

Note: Data are from 2016 ANES. 1 = mostly natural; 2 = both natural and human; 3 = mostly human.

cohorts. The gap is not significant among those with low incomes, but is statistically significant among those with high incomes.

## Pro-social Values Provide Insight into Gender Differences in Environmental Attitudes

To test the explanatory power of pro-social values, I add egalitarianism to the analysis discussed above. I find strong support for the pro-social values hypothesis that women's greater endorsement of pro-social values explains the gender gap in support of policies to protect the environment. First, turning to the spending question, including egalitarianism in the analysis reduces the gender gap to zero. In other words, when egalitarianism is accounted for, there is no longer an effect of gender on environmental spending. Figure 4.6 depicts women's and men's support for spending. Just like in the earlier figures, the left bar is for men, and the right bar is for women. As indicated by the 95 percent confidence intervals, the gap is no longer significant. This is very strong support for the pro-social values hypothesis. Including pro-social values eliminates the effect of gender on support for government spending to protect the environment. In fact, according to mediational analyses, egalitarianism mediates 80.54 percent of the effect of gender on environment-spending attitudes. All other necessary conditions for mediation (Baron and Kenney 1986) also exist but are not shown in the table; there is a significant gender gap in egalitarianism (as shown in Chapter 2), and egalitarianism predicts environmental-spending attitudes when gender is not included as a predictor.

The full analysis is included in the second Spending column of Table 4.1. The gender coefficient is zero and is no longer accompanied by an asterisk, indicating that gender is not a significant predictor of environmental-spending attitudes once egalitarianism is included in the model. The results in the table also show that the same control variables continue to be significant. Older people, whites, those who attend church frequently, and Protestants are less likely to support spending. The college-educated, low-income individuals, Catholics, and during Republican

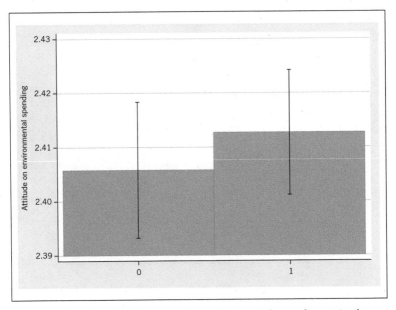

Figure 4.6. Gender differences in environmental-spending attitudes controlling for pro-social values

Note: Data are from cumulative 1980–2012 ANES. On the x-axis, 1 = female; 0 = male. On the y-axis, 1 = decrease spending; 2 = maintain spending; 3 = increase spending. Marginal effects are calculated with demographic variables set at their mean.

presidential administrations are more likely to support spending. The region variable is not significant. Moreover, the reduction of the gender effect to zero is not simply an artifact of gender differences in partisanship. In analysis not shown, party identification is included in the model. Not surprisingly, party identification is significant, with Republican identifiers less likely to support environmental spending. The effect of egalitarianism, however, is still significant, indicating that it is distinct from the effect of partisanship. Age, education, income, church attendance, Catholic identity, and Republican administration continue to be significant in this model. Once more, this is very strong support for the pro-social values hypothesis. Values illuminate why gender differences on environmental policy exist.

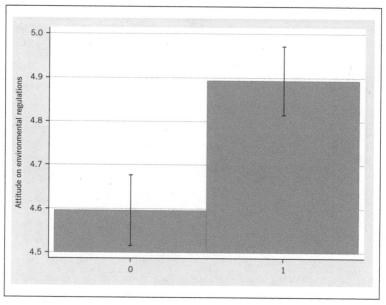

Figure 4.7. Gender differences in environmental regulations
attitudes controlling for pro-social values

Note: Data are from cumulative 1980–2012 ANES. On the x-axis, 1 =
female; 0 = male. The scale for regulations is from 1 = regulations burden
on business to 7 = tougher regulations. Marginal effects are calculated with
demographic variables set at their mean.

For the regulations question, including egalitarianism in the
model also reduces the size of the gender gap. Unlike the spending results, egalitarianism does not fully remove the effect of gender, but does considerably reduce it. Figure 4.7 shows women's
and men's support for environmental regulations. The gap is still
significant but smaller than in Figure 4.2. Mediational analyses
indicates that egalitarianism mediates 21.53 percent of the effect
of gender on attitudes toward environmental regulations. In analysis not shown, egalitarianism predicts attitudes about regulation
without gender in the model, which is necessary for mediation
to exist.

The Regulations 2 column in Table 4.1 display the coefficients for this analysis. First, note that there is a reduction in the

size of the gender coefficient. Similar to the prior results, older people, frequent church attendees, and Protestants are less likely to support regulations. Again, I ensure that the reduction in the effect of gender when egalitarianism is included in the analysis is not just a result of gender differences in partisanship. In additional analyses not included in the table, egalitarianism is still significant when party identification is included in the model. Not surprisingly, Republicans are less likely than Independents and Democrats to support government regulations to protect the environment. This provides additional evidence to support the values hypothesis. Gender differences in pro-social values provide insight into the gender gap in environmental policy attitudes.

With respect to the climate change question in the 2016 ANES, pro-social values substantially explain the gender differences. Including egalitarianism in the model reduces the size and significance of the gender variable. The mediation test reports that egalitarianism mediates 46.09 percent of the effect of gender on climate change attitudes. This provides more support for the pro-social values hypothesis. Women's climate change attitudes stem partially from their concern for others' well-being. The control variable results are very similar to the analysis that does not include pro-social values. Older individuals, frequent church attendees, and Southerners are less likely to believe that climate change is the result of mostly human activity. College-educated individuals are more likely to believe that human activity is a main cause of climate change. The effect of race and the effect of Catholic identity are no longer significant when egalitarianism is included. Last, in analysis not shown, including party identification does not alter the effect of egalitarianism.

## Testing the Feminist, Economic, and Motherhood Explanations

There is support for the other explanations as well. Feelings toward feminists predict environmental-spending attitudes and mediate 59 percent of the gender gap. Individuals with lower incomes are more supportive of this spending, and income mediates 18.11 percent of the gap. Employment status does not predict environmental-spending attitudes and does not mediate the gap. Having children and being a mother do not mediate the gender gap, with having children predicting less support for environmental spending, while being a mother is not a significant predictor. Differences in the number of observations for each analysis, in particular, the much lower sample size for the feminist feeling thermometer model, make it difficult to directly compare the mediation results for the different explanations. These results are displayed in Table A4.1 in the Appendix.

As shown in Table A4.1, the other explanations provide very limited insight as to why women differ from men on support for government regulations to protect the environment. Warm feelings toward feminists are associated with increased support and mediate 16.36 percent of the gender gap. Income and employment status do not predict regulation attitudes and do not mediate the gap. Similarly, having children and being a mother are not significant predictors of environmental regulation attitudes and are not mediators of the gender gap.

For the climate change–dependent variable, there is only support for feminism. Feeling warmly toward feminists is associated with an increase in believing that climate change is the result of human behavior, mediating 52.60 percent of the gap. Income, employment status, having children, and being a mother are not predictive of this attitude and do not mediate the gender gap. These results can be found in Table A4.2 in the Appendix.

The pro-social values explanation appears superior to the other explanations. The feminist explanation receives the most support among the other explanations. Economic circumstances and parental status do not mediate gender differences in environmental policy positions. The mediation results, although not directly comparable, suggest that values mediate a greater proportion of the gender gap on environmental attitudes than the other explanations.

## Summary and Conclusion

In a similar story to that of Lois Gibbs at the beginning of this chapter, Leanne Walters noticed several strange health issues in her family, leading her to help uncover the high lead levels in Flint, Michigan's water. A professor supplied testing kits, and with the help of neighbors, Walters collected more than eight hundred samples to prove that the lead levels in Flint's water were dangerously high across the city. Her fight has expanded to other cities and created a push for the EPA to institute policy changes to ensure water safety because "there's no reason for children to ever be poisoned by their water" (Walters, quoted in Brueck 2018). Women continue to crusade for the environment and for the government to protect citizens against the impact of environmental safety failures. Leanne Walters's fight for healthy drinking water exemplifies why scholars and politicians need to appreciate and better understand the gender gap in opinion on environmental issues.

My results provide a good deal of evidence to support the pro-social values hypothesis. The gender gap in environmental attitudes is largely accounted for by gender differences in values. Women's greater endorsement of pro-social values provides insight into their greater support for government spending to protect the environment and for government regulations to protect the environment. This suggests that women likely do rely on their concern for the well-being of other people when evaluating environmental policies. Pro-social values also lead men to support greater spending and regulations; but because women are more likely to hold pro-social values, a gender gap exists on environmental policy attitudes.

Given the focus of the soft media on "going green," the news media's coverage of climate change, and the Obama administration's efforts to pursue environmentally friendly policies, the origins of gender differences in environmental attitudes are of considerable importance. In addition, the Trump administration's policies toward the Environmental Protection Agency, the Dakota Access Pipeline, and conservation through the National Parks and Wildlife Refuge could cause environmental policies to become salient in the 2020 presidential election. This chapter illuminates why these differences exist, which ought to inform how political candidates and policy makers frame environmental issues to garner public support.

Chapter 5 focuses on gender differences in support of various equal rights policies. I again test the pro-social values hypothesis as an explanation for gender differences on support for rights and beneficial policies aimed at three historically disadvantaged groups: gay men and lesbians, African Americans, and women.

# 5

# Gender Gap on Equal Rights

I never doubted that equal rights was the right direction. Most reforms, most problems are complicated. But to me there is nothing complicated about ordinary equality. (Alice Paul, quoted in Rand 2017)

I demonstrated in 1957 for Civil Rights. It's still the same problems. . . . It just upsets me to see us go backwards. (Roberta Safer, quoted in Stuart 2017)

I made the decision to be a part of the Women's March because I stand for equality and I stand for those who cannot stand on their own. Minorities, women, the LGBTQ+ community, undocumented immigrants, and so many more are being attacked by those in power. (Saifa, quoted in Rodriguez 2019)

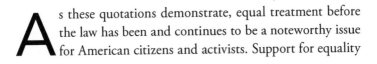s these quotations demonstrate, equal treatment before the law has been and continues to be a noteworthy issue for American citizens and activists. Support for equality

has been a central aspect of the women's movement, dating back to suffrage, as illustrated by the quotation from Alice Paul, a famous suffragette and author of the Equal Rights Amendment. With respect to equal rights for women, women have been seeking equality since the founding of the country. Abigail Adams asked John Adams to "remember the ladies" during the Constitutional Convention in 1776 because of a desire for women to have property rights and better educational opportunities (Ford 2010). In 1848 the Seneca Falls Convention produced the Declaration of Sentiments, which argued for greater gender equality, including a desire for women to have greater access to wealth, property rights, the ability to keep one's wages, changes to divorce laws, and the right to vote (Ford 2010). Unequal treatment, however, continued after women won the right to vote. Women could not serve on a jury until 1973 or get a credit card in their name until 1974. Women could be legally fired from their job if pregnant until 1987 and for taking time off for giving birth until the Family Medical Leave Act of 1993. Finally, equal treatment before the law remains elusive for women, who still do not earn equal pay.

Support for equality of other groups is also of importance to women, as exhibited by the quotations from female participants in the 2017 and 2018 Women's Marches. The first woman notes her past support and activism for civil rights, while the second woman notes her support for minority rights and the rights of members of the LGBTQ community. Women's opinions about equal treatment for these three groups have historically differed from men's opinions. As other scholars have argued, perhaps having the personal experience of unequal treatment promotes greater support for the equal treatment of other historically marginalized groups (Conover 1988).

This chapter investigates how differences in pro-social values illuminate the reasons for gender gaps in support of equal rights for historically disadvantaged groups such as women, African Americans, and the LGBTQ community. As in the previous chapters, I begin with a discussion of the current literature on the gender gap in these areas of public opinion. Next, I provide evidence that value differences between men and women help explain these gender gaps. I find evidence that pro-social values partially mediate the gender gaps on gay rights and equal roles for women. Moreover, pro-social values appear to explain the gender gap on racial attitudes and support for affirmative action for African Americans. These results strongly support the values hypothesis.

## Gender Differences on Equal Rights Attitudes in the Literature

Previous research has shown that there are gender differences in support for equal rights, particularly on race-related attitudes and gay rights, but less so on women's rights. For example, there is not a consistent and sizeable gender gap on support for the Equal Rights Amendment (Mansbridge 1985). In several policy areas, however, there are sizeable and consistent gaps, with women having more liberal positions than men (Norrander 2008; Shapiro and Mahajon 1986). For example, women are more likely to have liberal positions on the rights and role of government with respect to disadvantaged groups such as black people and the LGBTQ community (Hutchings et al. 2004; Norrander 2008; Shapiro and Mahajon 1986).

### Gender Differences in Support for Women's Rights

Public opinion regarding the women's movement has changed considerably since pollsters and researchers first began to measure the public attitudes. Overall opinion has become more positive toward the movement and toward the movement's goals over time. Since the early 1970s, there has been an increase in support among the public for strengthening women's status and in positive evaluations of the women's movement (Huddy, Neely, and Lafay 2000). With respect to women's status, analysis of the General Social Survey data indicates increased support for equal gender roles in the family (Oppenheim and Lu 1988). Recent analysis suggests that support for gender equality is no longer increasing but rather has become stagnant (Cotter, Hermsen, and Vanneman 2011).

Public opinion researchers have also sought to gauge the public's perceptions of the meaning of the women's movement. In general, the women's movement and women's liberation movement generate thoughts having to do with gender equality. A substantial portion of the public thinks of equal pay and equal rights when surveyors ask what comes to mind when thinking about the movement and women's liberation (Huddy, Neely, and Lafay 2000). There is evidence that the public tends to evaluate feminism and feminists less positively than the women's movement (Buschman and Lenart 1996; Cook and Wilcox 1992; Huddy, Neely, and Lafay 2000). This may mean that feminists call to mind more negative thoughts relative to the women's movement and the women's liberation movement. Feminism evokes negative thoughts, such as beliefs about feminists being man-haters and lesbians, for a higher percentage of the public than does the women's movement and women's liberation (Huddy, Neely, and Lafay 2000). It is important to note, however, that these observed differences may be an artifact of differences in the question wording.

Research on support for equal gender roles has found consistent gender differences. According to analysis of pooled cross-sections from the General Social Survey 1972–1996, women have more egalitarian gender attitudes than men, and changes over time are because of cohort succession rather than individual attitude change (Brewster and Padavic 2000). Using General Social Survey data from 1974 to 2006, an analysis reveals that women have more liberal views than men of women's familial responsibilities (Carter, Corra, and Carter 2009). Moreover, black females are the most liberal on gender role attitudes (Bolzendahl and Myers 2004) while over time the gap between black and white females appears to be slowly converging (Carter, Corra, and Carter 2009). Previous work did find women to be more supportive of equal familial roles than men, at least among college students (Helmreich, Spence, and Gibson 1982).

Other research also finds a gender gap on attitudes toward gender equality, including equal rights and feminism. Analysis of the 1996 ANES finds that women are 8 percentage points more likely than men to support equal rights for women (C. Clark and J. Clark 2009). This gap may have reduced over time, with a gap of 4 percentage points on equal rights for women in the 2004 ANES (C. Clark and J. Clark 2009). Women are more likely than men to identify as a feminist (McCabe 2005; Schnittker, Freese, and Powell 2003). Gender differences in feminist identification range from 9 to 40 percentage points (Huddy, Neely, and Lafay 2000).

Other scholars, however, have emphasized the lack of a sizeable, consistent, and statistically significant gender gap on questions of gender equality and women's rights. For example, Virginia Sapiro (2003) argues there is a lack of gender differences in support of women's issues that are unequivocally concerned with women's rights. Another prominent example is the lack of a sizeable gender gap in support of the Equal Rights Amendment. The Equal Rights Amendment, which attempted to advance women's collective interests, produced negligible gender differences (Mansbridge 1985).

There has been discussion at times about the lasting effects of the women's movement. Much has been made of a supposed drop in feminist identity, particularly among younger people (Peltola, Milkie, and Presser 2004). Some people have pointed to specific reasons for a decrease in feminist identification. Lisa Hogeland (1994) claims that young women have a "fear of politics," which prevents them from identifying as feminists. According to Hogeland, young women not only fear becoming politicized but also fear antifeminist sentiments. Similarly, Penny Weiss (1998) claims that young women, along with other women who support gender equality, are choosing not to identify as feminists because feminism is viewed as being radical far beyond the call for equality. This differential finding that more individuals support the aims of feminism than identify as feminists emerged early on (Welch 1975). Perhaps, antifeminists have been successful in characterizing feminism as radical, illegitimate, and worthy of dismissal, leading many women to avoid labeling themselves as feminists even though they believe in gender equality (Weiss 1998).

On the other hand, empirical evidence shows that perhaps there has not been a decrease in feminist identity. Levels of feminist identification among women appear to have remained stable over time with about a quarter to a third of women identifying as feminists (Huddy et al. 2000). In addition, there is a lack of empirical support for the idea that younger women are less likely to identify as feminists. Age was not a predictor of whether one identified as a feminist (McCabe 2005). In fact, young women appear to identify as feminists at the same rate as older women (Huddy, Neely, and Lafay 2000).

Finally, there are a few documented gender differences pertaining to policies such as affirmative action targeted to benefit women. Women are more likely to support affirmative action policies when the question specifically refers to women as the beneficiaries (Conway, Steuernagel, and Ahern 1997). Similar gender differences exist on related policy items that do not specifically reference affirmative action. Gender differences emerge on questions asking about support for government spending to improve women's social and economic status (Sears and Huddy 1990). These gender differences appear to exist across many subgroups, with women of all age groups and education levels being more likely to support affirmative action specifically directed at women (Conway, Steuernagel, Ahern 1997). For example, when the affirmative action policy is directed at helping women attain better jobs and education, the gender differences range from 15 to 31 percentage points, depending on the age group. For policies directed at improving the hiring and promotion of women, the gender differences range from 20 to 26 percentage points, depending on the age group (Conway, Steuernagel, and Ahern 1997).

Although the research to date is not entirely consistent, evidence suggests that women are more supportive of gender equality in comparison to men. Women are more likely than men to support equal gender roles in the home (Brewster and Padavic 2000; Carter, Corra, and Carter 2009). Gender differences exist on feminist identification and in support of the women's movement (C. Clark and J. Clark 2009; Huddy, Neely, and Lafay 2000; McCabe 2005). Women are also more supportive of policies to advance women's economic status (Conway, Steuernagel, and Ahern 1997; Sears and Huddy 1990). Therefore, it is of interest to understand why women compared to men are, at least at times, more supportive of equal rights for women.

## Gender Gap on Racial Attitudes

Similar to the research on equal rights for women, there are inconsistent findings with regard to gender differences in racial attitudes and racial policy positions. Some research has found that women are more liberal than men in their racial attitudes and policy positions on race-related programs (Johnson and Marini 1998; Kuran and McCaffery 2008; Pratto et al. 1997). For example, a study found that men were much more tolerant of discrimination against African American motorists compared to women (Kuran and McCaffery 2008). White women report more favorability than white men toward having a close friend of another race, having next-door neighbors of another race, having friends of one's children be of another race, having the school of one's children be integrated, having colleagues of another race, and having a boss of another race (Johnson and Marini 1998). These gender differences range in size from about 10 to 20 percentage points (Johnson and Marini 1998). Women are more supportive of spending on programs to help black people, with a difference of 4 to 5 percentage points (C. Clark and J. Clark 1996; Kaufmann and Petrocik 1999). Moreover, women were less tolerant of discrimination against other groups, including Arab Americans, overweight individuals, immigrants, and the disabled (Kuran and McCaffery 2008) and have more positive opinions of immigrants (Lay 2012).

Others have found that gender differences on race-related policy questions are not statistically significant or not substantive in size, particularly when demographic control variables are included in the analysis (Hughes and Tuch 2003; Kaufmann and Petrocik 1999). For example, Michael Hughes and Steven Tuch (2003) find in their analysis that white women and white men equally hold racial stereotypes of African Americans. With respect to the gender differences on social distances (Johnson and Marini 1998), only the gap on living in a racially diverse neighborhood remains significant with the inclusion of control variables (Hughes and Tuch 2003). Women are more likely to support spending to improve the standard living of black people, to favor government ensuring fair employment of black people, to favor government action to help black people, and to favor government action promoting school integration; interestingly, these gender differences appear to arise because of a general desire to help other people (Hughes and Tuch 2003). Similarly, women are more liberal in their racial attitudes, which included perceptions of black people as trustworthy, intelligent, and hardworking, but these differences became insignificant when egalitarianism and a willingness to help others were included (Howell and Day 2000).

Finally, there is evidence that women have more liberal views on affirmative action policies targeted at helping African Americans (J. Clark and C. Clark 1993; C. Clark and J. Clark 1996; Cook and Wilcox 1995; Howell and Day 2000; Hughes and Tuch 2003; Kaufmann and Petrocik 1999; Schuman et al. 1997). For support of affirmative action in terms of jobs, the gender difference varies from 4 to 6 percentage points, while support for education quotas results in a 7- to 9-point gender difference (J. Clark and C. Clark 1993; C. Clark and J. Clark 1996; Cook and Wilcox 1995). Again, these gender differences are not all robust to the inclusion of control variables (Cook and Wilcox 1995; Hughes and Tuch 2003). For example, Susan Howell and Christine Day (2000) find women to be more liberal on a racial attitudes index, which includes items on preferential hiring and promotion, but this difference becomes insignificant when controlling for egalitarianism and willingness to help others. In addition, Hughes and Tuch (2003) find that women are significantly more liberal on only one affirmative action–related item when control variables are included in the model. Women are less likely to report being against affirmative action in college admission; there are not, however, any gender differences on affirmative action in employment, special scholarships, government role in employment equality, or giving black people special favors (Hughes and Tuch 2003). Last, James R. Kluegel and Eliot R. Smith (1982) find no effect of gender in their study of white beliefs in the area of preferential treatment.

The extant literature does not provide evidence of a strong and robust gender gap on racial attitudes and racial policy positions. In some of the research, women are more supportive of affirmative action policies, government policies to promote school integration, and spending to help black people (Howell and Day 2000; Hughes and Tuch 2003). On social distance measures, women do appear to be somewhat more favorable toward closeness to other races (Johnson and Marini 1998; Hughes and Tuch 2003). Consistent with the pro-social values hypothesis, there is evidence that when gender differences do arise, egalitarianism or the desire to help others eliminates the gender gap (Howell and Day 2000; Hughes and Tuch 2003). These results, along with the continued issues of racism and discrimination in the United States, demonstrate a need to further investigate the gender gap on race-related issues and the efficacy of the pro-social values explanation of gender differences.

## Gender Gap on Gay Rights Attitudes

Support for gay rights has been a prominent issue since the 2004 presidential election when it arguably became part of the culture wars and national morality debate (Lewis 2005). Existing research establishes that a gender gap exists but does not fully explain the gap. Women are more supportive of consensual sexual relations between same-sex partners being legal; gay adoption rights; the right for gays to serve in the military; and employment protections (Brewer 2003; Herek 2002a; Stoutenborough, Haider-Markel, and Allen 2006; Wilcox and Wolpert 2000). Men have more negative and hostile attitudes than women toward the LGBTQ community (Herek 1988; LaMar and Kite 1998). Women are more likely to believe homosexuality is caused by genetics, believe homosexuality is morally acceptable, support equal rights, and support same-sex marriage, controlling for various demographic and religious variables (Haider-Markel and Joslyn 2008; Olson, Cadge, and Harrison 2006).

The gender gap in support of equal rights for gay men and lesbians appears to be robust to various control variables. Religiosity, gender role attitudes, contact, and traditionalism correlate with attitudes toward lesbians and gay men for heterosexual men and women, but do not explain the gender gap in these attitudes (Herek 1988). Similarly, the gender gap in attitudes toward civil unions persists, controlling for demographic characteristics, religion, religiosity, and ideology (Haider-Markel and Joslyn 2008) as well as moral values (Olson, Cadge, and Harrison 2006). Women's greater internal motivation to respond without prejudice partially explains their less negative attitudes toward gay men (Ratcliff et al. 2006). Finally, consistent with the pro-social values hypothesis, egalitarianism has been shown to predict more favorability toward LGBTQ rights (Brewer 2003; Craig et al. 2005; Jones et al. 2018), but has not been investigated as a mediator of the gender gap on gay rights attitudes.

Of the three policy areas investigated in this chapter, the gender gap on equal rights for gay men and lesbians is the most consistent and robust. Compared to men, women have more positive feelings toward gay men and lesbians as well as more positive views of homosexuality (Brewer 2003; Haider-Markel and Joslyn 2008; Olson, Cadge, and Harrison 2006). Women are also more supportive of civil unions, employment protections, adoption rights, and the right to openly serve in the military (Brewer 2003; Haider-Markel and Joslyn 2008; Olson, Cadge, and Harrison 2006). Although strides have been made in recent years on marriage equality and military service, the issue of equal rights for the LGBTQ community continues to be worthy of study. For example, there are still not national legal protections against employment discrimination, and the issue of adoption rights is currently moving its way through the courts. Thus, it is important to understand public opinion, including gender differences, in this area.

## Recent Polling on Equal Rights Attitudes

Gender differences in polling data are similar to the results in the academic literature. In a 2005 Gallup poll, 61 percent of men versus 45 percent of women stated a belief that women have equal job opportunities to men. In that same poll, 65 percent of men compared to 53 percent of women supported affirmative action programs for women (Jones 2005). In a 2015 Gallup poll, 62 percent of men compared to 72 percent of women favored affirmative action for women. These gender differences were similar across racial groups with a 3-point gap among African Americans, a 14-point gap among Hispanics, and a 9-point gap among whites (Riffkin 2015).

A 2003 Pew Research Center poll finds greater support among white women for affirmative action policies in college admissions compared to white men; 60 percent of women versus 49 percent of men supported this (Pew Research Center 2003a). In a 2015 Gallup poll, 60 percent of women versus 55 percent of men favored affirmative action programs for racial minorities. Gender differences vary in size but exist across racial groups with a 5-point gap among African Americans, a 12-point gap among Hispanics, and a 3-point gap among whites (Riffkin 2015).

Men and women differ on a number of gay rights issues, according to public opinion polls. A gender gap of 5 points emerged on the issue of gay marriage in a 2003 Pew Research Center poll (Pew Research Center 2003b). Women are more supportive of homosexual relations being legal and morally acceptable; they are also more in favor of marriage equality. The largest of these gaps was for the marriage equality question, with 42 percent of men supporting versus 56 percent of women (Saad 2012). Gender differences exist among whites and black people on support for marriage equality, according to a 2013 Pew Research Center report. Among whites, 44 percent of men and 53 percent of women favored legal marriage equality, and among black people, 37 percent of men versus 42 percent of women favored marriage equality (Pew Research Center 2013a). Even after the Supreme Court's marriage equality decision, gender differences persist. In a 2016 PRRI survey, 57 percent of women compared to 50 percent of men support marriage equality (Cooper et al. 2016).

In summary, prior research indicates gender differences exist on support for equal rights and attitudes toward the disadvantaged. The evidence for gender equality and racial equality is less strong, but for gay rights, the evidence is more consistent and stronger. Women are less likely to hold racially resentful attitudes and are more likely than men to support policies such as affirmative action to provide equality for African Americans. Women are also more likely to support marriage equality and legal protections for gay men and lesbians as well as more likely to have positive attitudes toward the LGBTQ community. This evidence indicates a need to understand better why these gender differences exist. Perhaps, gender differences in pro-social values, as discussed in the following hypothesis section, account for these gender gaps in policy positions and attitudes. Overall, the findings provide support for this hypothesis.

## Hypothesis

I hypothesize that gender differences in levels of pro-social values are causing the differences in support for equal rights for historically disadvantaged groups. When women think about the extension of equal rights, the values explanation would predict that women think about how extending equal rights would improve others' well-being. For example, affirmative action would improve African Americans' lives by preventing job discrimination. Gay rights would allow members of the LGBTQ community to live full, secure, and happy lives that are not threatened by job discrimination or discharge from the armed forces; they would also be able to have families through adoption. Conceptually, women may think about how unequal treatment of these groups leads to psychological and material suffering.

## Women Support Greater Equal Rights for Historically Disadvantaged Groups

To test the values explanation for the gender gap, there must be a gap. As is the case throughout the book, I use the American National Election Study (ANES) cumulative data 1980–2012. I do not use the 2011 World Values Survey data in this chapter.

First, the women's role question asks respondents to place themselves on a continuum with 1 indicating the belief that women's place is in the home and 7 indicating the belief that men and women should have an equal role. I treat this variable as if it is continuous using ordinary least squares regression; the results do not substantially differ when using ordered logistic regression. The gender gap on this item is statistically significant, as shown in the Equal role 1 column of Table 5.1. Women are more likely than men to support equal roles for men and women. The predicted probability for women, holding all other variables in the model at their mean, is 5.64 (SE 0.02) and for men is 5.48 (SE 0.02). In addition to gender, many of the other variables are also significant predictors of support for women having an equal role. Older individuals, low-income individuals, whites, frequent church attendees, Protestants, Southerners, and those surveyed during a Republican presidential administration are less likely to believe that men and women should have an equal role. In contrast, college education predicts greater support for women having an equal role. The Catholic identification variable is not significant.

Looking at gender differences across demographic subgroups, we see that the gender gap is highly significant among whites and marginally significant among black people. White women are more likely to support equal roles compared to white men, and the same is true for black women compared to black men. The gender gap is significant in all three age cohorts as well as among those with and without a college degree. The gap is not significant among those with an income below the median. Among individuals with an

TABLE 5.1. GENDER DIFFERENCES IN WOMEN'S RIGHTS AND RACIAL ATTITUDES

| | Equal role 1 | Equal role 2 | Affirmative 1 | Affirmative 2 | Resentment 1 | Resentment 2 |
|---|---|---|---|---|---|---|
| Female | 0.16*** | 0.10*** | 0.07* | -0.01 | -0.09*** | -0.02 |
| | (0.03) | (0.03) | (0.04) | (0.04) | (0.01) | (0.01) |
| Age | -0.01*** | -0.01*** | -0.00 | 0.00 | 0.00*** | -0.00 |
| | (0.00) | (0.00) | (0.00) | (0.00) | (0.00) | (0.00) |
| Education 1 = college | 0.57*** | 0.46*** | 0.29*** | 0.18*** | -0.49*** | -0.42*** |
| | (0.03) | (0.03) | (0.05) | (0.05) | (0.02) | (0.01) |
| Income 1 = low | -0.22*** | -0.24*** | 0.64*** | 0.63*** | -0.09*** | -0.04*** |
| | (0.03) | (0.04) | (0.04) | (0.05) | (0.02) | (0.01) |
| Race 1 = white | -0.22*** | 0.01 | -1.67*** | -1.44*** | 0.59*** | 0.35*** |
| | (0.03) | (0.04) | (0.04) | (0.04) | (0.02) | (0.01) |
| Church attendance | -0.17*** | -0.15*** | -0.00 | 0.02 | 0.00 | -0.02*** |
| | (0.01) | (0.01) | (0.01) | (0.01) | (0.00) | (0.00) |

| | | | | | | |
|---|---|---|---|---|---|---|
| Catholic | 0.05 | 0.12** | -0.33*** | -0.27*** | 0.19*** | 0.15*** |
| | (0.05) | (0.05) | (0.06) | (0.06) | (0.02) | (0.02) |
| Protestant | -0.20*** | -0.14*** | -0.07 | -0.09 | 0.05** | 0.03* |
| | (0.04) | (0.05) | (0.05) | (0.06) | (0.02) | (0.02) |
| Region 1 = South | -0.05* | 0.01 | 0.06 | 0.11** | 0.17*** | 0.13*** |
| | (0.03) | (0.03) | (0.04) | (0.04) | (0.01) | (0.01) |
| Republican president | -0.25*** | -0.17*** | 0.20*** | 0.15*** | -0.17*** | -0.13*** |
| | (0.03) | (0.03) | (0.04) | (0.04) | (0.01) | (0.01) |
| Egalitarianism | | 0.40*** | | 0.77*** | | -0.52*** |
| | | (0.02) | | (0.03) | | (0.01) |
| $R^2$ | .09 | .12 | .13 | .17 | .12 | .29 |
| $N$ | 17,096 | 12,680 | 18,711 | 17,497 | 18,689 | 18,683 |

Note: Data are from the 1980–2012 ANES. Positive coefficients indicate greater support for equal gender roles, greater support for affirmative action policies, and higher levels of racial resentment. To retain respondents, the analysis also includes an income variable (not shown): 1 if people refused to answer and 0 otherwise.

* $p < .10$; ** $p < .05$; *** $p < .01$

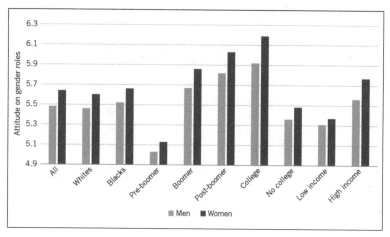

Figure 5.1. Gender differences in equal gender roles
across demographic subgroups

Note: Data are from cumulative 1980–2012 ANES. The scale for gender
roles is from 1 = women's place in home to 7 = equal roles.

income above the median, women are more likely to support equal
gender roles compared to men. Figure 5.1 displays the gender gaps
within each of these demographic groups. It is also interesting to
note the sizeable differences between groups. In particular, the
differences between those with and without a bachelor's degree
are quite drastic; those with a college degree, regardless of gender,
are much more likely to believe in equal gender roles compared
to those with less than a college degree. In addition, those with
an above-median income are more likely, regardless of gender, to
support equal roles in comparison to those with a below-median
income. There are also interesting, though not surprising, differences across birth cohorts, with those born earlier much less likely
to favor equal roles compared to those born later.

Two dependent variables measure policy preferences and attitudes toward black people. The first of these measures attitudes
toward affirmative action. Respondents indicate whether they believe the government should stay out of ensuring fair treatment for
black people when it comes to jobs (0) or the government should

ensure fair treatment (1). Because of the binary nature of this variable, I use logistic regression for the analysis. There is a marginally significant gender gap on support for affirmative action, with women slightly more likely to answer that the government should ensure fair treatment for black people. This is shown in the Affirmative 1 column of Table 5.1. The predicted probability of women giving the pro–affirmative action response is 0.18 (SE 0.00), and for men it is 0.17 (SE 0.00). Age, church attendance, Protestant identification, and being from the South are not significant predictors of affirmative action attitudes. More education, lower income, and a Republican presidency are all associated with greater support. Whites compared to nonwhites and Catholics are less likely to support government involvement to ensure fair treatment of black people. The gender gap is significant among whites, with white women more supportive than white men of affirmative action. Black women and black men are equally supportive of affirmative action. The gender gap is not significant in any of the age cohorts, education levels, or income levels.

The next dependent variable is the well-established racial resentment scale (Feldman and Huddy 2005; Henry and Sears 2002; Kinder and Sears 1981). This is an additive scale of four questions measuring negative and resentful racial attitudes, including special government treatment of black people. The four items create a reliable scale ranging from 1 to 5, with a Cronbach's alpha of 0.75 and inter-item covariance of 0.70. Each item asks respondents to give a degree of agreement or disagreement with the following statements: slavery and discrimination have made it hard for black people to succeed; black people should be given special treatment to succeed; black people need to try harder to succeed; and black people have gotten less than they deserve. These questions are coded and combined so that higher values on the Racial Resentment scale indicate more negative and resentful racial attitudes.

The gender gap on racial resentment is significant, with women being less likely than men to have negative and resentful attitudes toward black people. The predicted probability for women is 2.65 (SE 0.01) and for men is 2.56 (SE 0.01). These predicted probabilities are calculated including the usual control variables held at their means. As shown in the Resentment 1 column of Table 5.1, older individuals, whites, Catholics, Protestants, and Southerners are more likely to hold racially resentful attitudes. Individuals with a low income, those with a college degree, and those surveyed during a Republican presidential administration are less likely to be racially resentful. Church attendance was not a significant predictor.

Turning to the gender gap across subgroups of men and women, Figure 5.2 displays the gender gaps within each of these subgroups. Similar to the affirmative action results, the gender gap is significant among whites but not among black people. White women are less likely than white men to hold racially resentful attitudes. The gender gap is significant in all of the age cohorts. The gender gap is also significant among the college educated and those without a college degree. The gender gap is only marginally significant among those with a below-median income and significant among those with an income above the median.

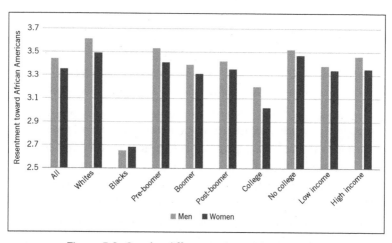

Figure 5.2. Gender differences in racial resentment across demographic subgroups

Note: Data are from cumulative 1980–2012 ANES. Higher values on racial resentment indicate more negative attitudes toward African Americans.

Across different demographic groups, women consistently have lower racial resentment scale scores. Some of the between-group differences are striking. For example, black people have very low racial resentment scores. Also, those with a college education have much lower scores than most of the other subgroups besides African Americans.

The final four questions measure attitudes toward gay rights. The first question asks whether respondents favor (1) or oppose (0) laws to protect homosexuals from job discrimination. The second question asks whether the respondent favors homosexuals being allowed to serve in the military. This question has two parts that ask how they feel about the issue and then their feeling strength. The final response options include (1) feel strongly should not be allowed, (2) feel not strongly should not be allowed, (3) feel not strongly should be allowed, and (4) feel strongly should be allowed. The third question asks if gay couples should be legally permitted to adopt children, with 0 indicating no and 1 indicating yes. The 2016 ANES question on marriage equality is also included in the analysis. Respondents choose between three responses: (1) there should be no legal recognition, (2) gay and lesbian couples should be allowed to form civil unions but not legally marry, and (3) gay and lesbian couples should be allowed to legally marry. I use logistic regression to analyze the two dichotomous dependent variables, job discrimination and adoption. For the other questions, open military service and marriage, I use ordered logistic regression.

For the first item about laws protecting against discrimination, there is a significant and sizeable gender gap. The predicted probability for men is 0.62 (SE 0.01) and for women is 0.74 (SE 0.01). As shown in the Laws 1 column of Table 5.2, college-educated individuals are also more likely to support laws making discrimination illegal. Age and Catholic identification are not significant predictors. During a Republican presidency, low-income individuals, whites, frequent church attendees, Protestants, and Southerners are less likely to support such laws. There is a significant gender gap on this item when limiting the analysis to whites only. There is no gender gap among black people. There

## TABLE 5.2. GENDER DIFFERENCES ON GAY RIGHTS POLICIES

| | Laws 1 | Laws 2 | DADT 1 | DADT 2 | Adopt 1 | Adopt 2 | Marriage 1 | Marriage 2 |
|---|---|---|---|---|---|---|---|---|
| Female | 0.53*** | 0.47*** | 0.85*** | 0.81*** | 0.58*** | 0.53** | 0.25*** | 0.13* |
| | (0.04) | (0.04) | (0.05) | (0.05) | (0.04) | (0.04) | (0.06) | (0.07) |
| Age | −0.00 | 0.00 | −0.01*** | −0.00*** | −0.02*** | −0.02*** | −0.02*** | −0.02*** |
| | (0.00) | (0.00) | (0.00) | (0.00) | (0.00) | (0.00) | (0.00) | (0.00) |
| Education 1 = college | 0.54*** | 0.49*** | 0.58*** | 0.54*** | 0.71*** | 0.68*** | 0.48*** | 0.44*** |
| | (0.05) | (0.05) | (0.06) | (0.06) | (0.05) | (0.05) | (0.07) | (0.08) |
| Income 1 = low | −0.12*** | −0.20*** | −0.16*** | −0.22*** | −0.08* | −0.11** | −0.02*** | −0.02*** |
| | (0.05) | (0.05) | (0.05) | (0.06) | (0.04) | (0.05) | (0.00) | (0.00) |
| Race 1 = white | −0.38*** | −0.04 | −0.24*** | −0.01 | −0.08* | 0.14** | 0.21*** | 0.46*** |
| | (0.05) | (0.05) | (0.05) | (0.06) | (0.04) | (0.05) | (0.07) | (0.08) |
| Church attendance | −0.18*** | −0.16*** | −0.21*** | −0.20*** | −0.34*** | −0.34** | −0.10*** | −0.07*** |
| | (0.01) | (0.01) | (0.02) | (0.02) | (0.01) | (0.01) | (0.02) | (0.02) |

| | | | | | | | | |
|---|---|---|---|---|---|---|---|---|
| Catholic | 0.08 | 0.15** | -0.00 | 0.03 | 0.11* | 0.14** | 0.11 | 0.08 |
| | (0.07) | (0.07) | (0.08) | (0.08) | (0.06) | (0.06) | (0.09) | (0.10) |
| Protestant | -0.45*** | -0.45*** | -0.46*** | -0.46*** | -0.38*** | -0.40*** | 0.05 | -0.03 |
| | (0.06) | (0.06) | (0.07) | (0.07) | (0.05) | (0.05) | (0.19) | (0.21) |
| Region 1 = South | -0.16*** | -0.10** | -0.25*** | -0.23*** | -0.27*** | -0.21*** | -0.67*** | -0.69*** |
| | (0.04) | (0.04) | (0.05) | (0.05) | (0.04) | (0.04) | (0.08) | (0.09) |
| Republican president | -0.21*** | -0.34*** | -0.39*** | -0.51*** | -0.64*** | -0.78*** | | |
| | (0.04) | (0.04) | (0.05) | (0.03) | (0.04) | (0.04) | | |
| Egalitarianism | | 0.76*** | | 0.57*** | | 0.55*** | | 0.67*** |
| | | (0.03) | | (0.03) | | (0.03) | | (0.04) |
| $R^2$ | .05 | .10 | .08 | .10 | .12 | .15 | .05 | .08 |
| $N$ | 12,385 | 11,987 | 11,158 | 10,546 | 12,373 | 21,584 | 4,021 | 3,444 |

Note: Laws, DADT, and adopt data are from the 1980–2012 ANES. Marriage data are from the 2016 ANES. Positive coefficients indicate support for gay rights and legal protections.

$* p < .10; ** p < .05; *** p < .01$

is a gender gap in all age cohorts, for those with and without a bachelor's degree, and in both income groups.

The results are similar for the second gay rights item, with women significantly more likely to support gay men and lesbians being able to openly serve in the military. The predicted probability for men is 0.69 (SE 0.01) and for women is 0.84 (SE 0.00). The results of the analysis are included in the DADT (don't ask, don't tell) 1 column of Table 5.2. Along with women, those with a college education are also more likely to support open military service. Catholic identification is not significant, while all the other variables predict a lower likelihood of support. The gender gap exists for both whites and black people. White women and black women are more supportive of gay men and lesbians being able to openly serve in the military compared to white men and black men, respectively. Women of all birth cohorts are more likely than men of the same cohort to support gay rights to openly serve in the military. The gender gap is also significant in both levels of education and both levels of income.

For the third gay rights item, there is also a significant gender gap. Women are significantly more likely to support the rights of gay men and lesbians to adopt children. The predicted probability for women is 0.58 (SE 0.01) and for men is 0.43 (SE 0.01). The full analysis from which these predicted probabilities are calculated are included in the Adopt 1 column of Table 5.2. In addition to women, college education and Catholic identification is associated with higher levels of support, while the rest of the variables predict a lower likelihood of legal gay adoption. Similar to the DADT results, the gender gap is significant among whites and blacks. White women are more likely to support the right to adopt than white men, and black women are more likely than black men. Pre–baby boomer women, baby boomer women, and post–baby boomer women are all more likely to support adoption rights than men of the same birth cohort. The gender gap is significant among those without a bachelor's degree and those with a bachelor degree. The gender gap is significant in both income groups as well.

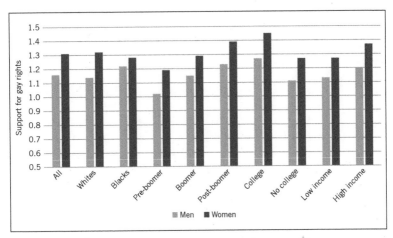

Figure 5.3. Gender differences in gay rights attitudes across demographic subgroups

Note: Data are from cumulative 1980–2012 ANES. Higher values indicate greater support for gay rights.

For ease of depiction of the gender gap in demographic subgroups, I created an additive scale of the three gay rights items in the cumulative ANES data, by which missing values are replaced with the scale mean. The scale has a moderate reliability with a Cronbach's alpha of 0.59 and an inter-item covariance of 0.18. Figure 5.3 displays the gender gap within each demographic subgroup. Women are consistently more likely to support extending these rights to gay men and lesbians. There is variability in support between groups as well. For example, the earliest-born cohort is generally less supportive of gay rights compared to later-born cohorts. Women in all three cohorts, including the pre–baby boomer cohort, in which support is lowest overall, are more supportive of gay rights than men of the same cohort.

The gender gap is also statistically significant for the 2016 marriage question. Women are more likely than men to support legal marriage. The predicted probability of choosing the legal marriage option is 0.56 (SE 0.01) for men compared to 0.62 (SE 0.01) for women. Older individuals, lower-income individuals, Southerners, and frequent church attendees are less likely to

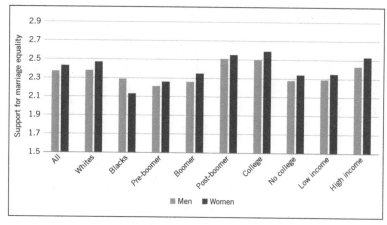

Figure 5.4. Gender differences on marriage equality across demographic subgroups

Note: Data are from 2016 ANES. Higher values indicate greater support for legal marriage for gay men and lesbians.

support marriage equality. Those with more education and those identifying as white are more likely to support marriage equality. Catholic and mainline Protestant identifications are not significant predictors. Figure 5.4 displays the results for the gender gap within demographic subgroups for the 2016 ANES marriage equality item. The gender gap is significant among whites but not blacks, likely because of the small sample of African Americans in the 2016 ANES. The gender gap is significant among those with a college degree but not among the less educated. The gender gap on marriage equality is only significant among the baby boomer generation and not among older or younger cohorts. Gender differences are significant among those with higher incomes but not among those with lower incomes.

## Pro-social Values Provide Insight into Gender Differences on Equal Rights

To test the explanatory power of pro-social values, I add egalitarianism to the analysis discussed above. I find strong support for the pro-social values hypothesis that women's greater endorsement of pro-social values explains the gender gap in support for equal rights policies. First, turning to the women's role question, including egalitarianism in the analysis substantially reduces the gender gap. When egalitarianism is accounted for, there is a much smaller effect of gender on attitudes about women's roles. According to mediational analyses, egalitarianism mediates almost a third of the gender effect with a percent mediated of 32.30 percent. In addition, the size of the female coefficient is reduced when egalitarianism is included in the model. Other conditions necessary for mediation also exist but are not shown. The full analysis is included in the Equal role 2 column of Table 5.1. The results in the table show that the same control variables continue to be significant. Older people, lower-income individuals, those who attend church frequently, Protestants, and times of a Republican presidency are less likely to believe women should have an equal role to men. The race and region variables are not significant in this model. Having a college education continues to predict support for women having an equal role. Being Catholic actually predicts support for women's equal roles. Finally, egalitarianism is a significant and positive predictor. Individuals endorsing egalitarian values are more likely to believe that women should have an equal role to men.

Moreover, the reduction of the gender effect is not merely the result of an underlying gender difference in partisanship related to the gap in women's role beliefs and egalitarianism. Not shown in the table, analysis including party identification did not change the egalitarianism results. Partisanship is significant, with Republicans less likely to support women having an equal role, but egalitarianism continues to be a significant predictor as well. This provides strong support for the values hypothesis. Pro-social values partially explain why gender differences on gender equality exist.

Referring to the race questions, including egalitarianism in the model reduces the size of the gender gap. Egalitarianism considerably reduces the effect of gender for both race-dependent variables. First, for the affirmative action question, mediational analyses indicate that egalitarianism mediates 106.31 percent of the effect of gender on attitudes toward affirmative action. Although they are not shown, the other conditions are also met for mediation. It is likely that the percentage is so high because the gender effect was only marginally significant. The results are in the Affirmative 2 column of Table 5.1. Similar to the prior results, age, Protestant identifiers, and church attendance continue to not be significant predictors. Educated individuals, low-income individuals, Southerners, and Republican presidency are associated with greater support for affirmative action. Whites and Catholics are less likely to support government actions that ensure black people receive fair treatment for jobs. Egalitarianism is also a significant and positive predictor, with those endorsing egalitarian values more likely to support affirmative action. Again, I ensure that the reduction in the effect of gender when egalitarianism is included in the analysis is not just the result of gender differences in partisanship. In analysis not shown, egalitarianism is still significant when party identification is included. Republicans are less likely than Independents and Democrats to support government involvement to ensure jobs for black people. This provides solid support for the values hypothesis.

For the racial resentment variable, including egalitarianism significantly reduces the gender effect. According to the mediation results, egalitarianism reduces the effect of gender by 69.24 percent. Figure 5.5 depicts the gender gap without egalitarianism on the left-hand side and the gender gap with egalitarianism on the right-hand side. The left graph of Figure 5.5 shows a substantial gap, even including the control variables at their mean, and the right graph shows a much smaller gap when pro-social values are included. As is shown in the Resentment 2 column of Table 5.1, the female variable is no longer significant at the $p < 0.01$ level, but has been reduced to significance at the $p < 0.05$ level. In support of the pro-social values hypothesis, egalitarianism is a significant predictor, with individuals holding egalitarian values significantly less likely to express racially resentful attitudes.

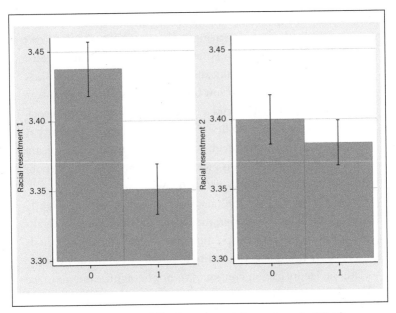

Figure 5.5. Gender differences in racial resentment attitudes

Note: Data are from cumulative 1980–2012 ANES. On the x-axis, 1 = female; 0 = male. Higher values on the y-axis indicate higher values of racial resentment. The left graph shows the marginal effects calculated from the Resentment 1 column of Table 5.1; the right graph shows the marginal effects calculated from the Resentment 2 column. Marginal effects are calculated with demographic variables set at their mean.

The rest of the results are similar to the prior analysis. Whites, Catholics, Protestants, older people, and Southerners are more likely to hold negative racial attitudes. Low-income individuals, frequent church attenders, educated individuals, and a Republican presidential administration are associated with a lower probability of endorsing the racial resentment items. Finally, the effect of egalitarianism is distinct from partisanship. Republicans are more likely than Independents and Democrats to have racially resentful attitudes, but including partisanship does not remove the effect of egalitarianism.

For the first gay rights variable of support for laws protecting against discrimination, including egalitarianism substantially reduces the gender gap. The total effect mediated is 16.82 percent.

Those endorsing egalitarian values are significantly more likely to support laws protecting against discrimination. Age and race are not significant predictors, while the rest of the variables are significant. The college-educated and Catholics are more likely to support such laws, while low income, whites, church attendees, Protestants, Southerners, and a Republican presidency are associated with a lower probability of support for laws to protect gay people. In analysis not shown, egalitarianism remains significant when party identification is included in the analysis, and Republicans are less likely to support such laws.

For the gays in the military variable, egalitarianism slightly reduces the effect of gender, mediating only 8.5 percent. Egalitarianism is a significant predictor, with egalitarian individuals more likely to support the ability to openly serve in the military. Catholic identification continues to not be significant, and race is no longer significant. Along with women, the college-educated are more likely to support open service, while all other variables predict a lower likelihood of support. Finally, including party identification does not change the results; Republicans are less supportive of open service.

The results for the adoption item are similar; including egalitarianism reduces the gender effect. According to the mediation analyses, the gender effect on adoption attitudes is mediated by 12.17 percent when egalitarianism is included. As shown in the Adopt 2 column in Table 5.2, egalitarianism is a significant predictor of support for gay adoption. Older individuals, low-income individuals, frequent church attendees, Protestants, and Southerners, as well as a Republican administration, predict a lower likelihood of support for gay people being allowed to adopt. College-educated, whites, and Catholics have a greater likelihood of support. In analysis not shown, party identification is significant predictor, with Republicans being less supportive. Including party identification does not change the egalitarianism results.

The marriage equality results from the 2016 ANES also support the pro-social values hypothesis. The effect of gender reduces in significance when egalitarianism is included, and according to the mediational analyses, egalitarianism mediates 52.28 percent of the effect of gender on marriage equality attitudes. Egalitarianism is associated with a greater likelihood of supporting legal marriage, and it continues to be significant when party identification is included. These results strongly suggest that women are more likely than men to support the legal marriage of gay men and lesbians because of their tendency to care about other people.

## Testing the Other Explanations

There is also some support for other gender gap theories (see Table A5.1 in the Appendix for a full analysis). As stated earlier, the mediation results of the various explanations are not entirely comparable, given the differences in the number of observations for the different models. Feeling warmly toward feminists predicts greater support for equal gender roles and mediates 25.35 percent of the gender gap. Income and employment status do not mediate the gender gap on women's roles. Having an income below the national median is associated with less support for equal gender roles. Including employment status actually increases the gender gap rather than reducing it. Having children and being a mother are also not mediators, with having children associated with less support for equal roles; motherhood is not a predictor.

The following results are in Table A5.1. The other gender gap theories also provide insight into why women are more supportive of affirmative action compared to men. Feeling warmly toward feminists predicts support for affirmative action and mediates more than 100 percent of the gender gap. A below-median income is associated with greater support for affirmative action and mediates 48.14 percent of the gap. Employment status, parenthood, and motherhood are not mediators of the gender gap. Having children and being employed are associated with lower levels of support for affirmative action.

The other explanations are also somewhat supported with respect to racial resentment attitudes. Feeling warmly toward feminists predicts lower levels of racial resentment and mediates 60.96 percent of the gender gap. Individuals with an income below the national median have less resentful attitudes, and this mediates 9.10 percent of the gender gap. Employment status, parental status, and maternal status are not mediators of the gender gap. Being employed and having children are associated with higher levels of racial resentment, while motherhood is not a predictor. Table A5.2 in the Appendix shows these results.

The results of the other gender gap explanations for LGBTQ rights receive limited support. Feeling warmly toward feminists predicts more support for laws protecting gays and lesbians; this mediates 16.88 percent of the gender gap. Income, being employed, being a parent, and being a mother do not mediate the gender gap. Low income, being employed, and having children are associated with less support for protective laws. Motherhood is not a significant predictor. As displayed in Table A5.3 in the Appendix, feelings of warmth toward feminists are associated with more support for gay and lesbian service in the military; this mediates 13.16 percent of the gender gap. Income, employment, parenthood, and motherhood are not mediators. Below-median income and parenthood predict lower support, while employment predicts more support, and motherhood is not significant.

Warm feelings toward feminists predicts support for gay adoption and mediates 22.11 percent of the gap. The other explanations are not mediators. Being employed and motherhood are not predictors of gay adoption attitudes. Having a below-median income and having children predict lower levels of support for gay adoption rights. As shown in Table A5.4 in the Appendix, feeling warmly toward feminists predicts greater support for marriage equality and mediates 50.02 percent of the gender gap. Income and employment status do not mediate the gender gap; low-income individuals are less supportive of marriage equality, while employment status is unrelated to marriage equality attitudes. Having children and being a mother are not significant predictors; nor are they mediators.

The feminist explanation receives the strongest and most consistent support among the other explanations. Economic circumstances and motherhood do not appear to be explanations for gender differences in attitudes toward historically marginalized groups. The analysis most strongly supports the pro-social values explanation and the feminist explanation. Both provide insight into why women differ from men in their racial attitudes and policy positions regarding women's rights and LGBTQ rights.

## Summary and Conclusion

This chapter provides strong evidence in support of the pro-social values hypothesis. The gender gaps in support for equal rights are mostly explained by gender differences in values. Women's greater endorsement of pro-social values informs their attitudes on gender roles, affirmative action, racial resentment, and gay rights. Women appear to think about the well-being of others when considering the extension of legal protections and rights to historically disadvantaged groups. Men also rely on pro-social values when considering the rights of women, African Americans, and the LGBTQ community. Because women have higher levels of egalitarianism, however, a gender gap in these attitudes exists.

As the quotations and examples at the opening of this chapter elucidate, issues of equality have regularly been a focus of women's activism. Moreover, as the previous research shows, women have often expressed more-progressive attitudes about equal treatment of women, African Americans, and gay men and lesbians. Equal rights continue to be part of ongoing political debates and discourse. For example, the first bill that President Obama signed into law was the Lily Ledbetter Fair Pay Act, which aimed to ensure that women can sue for pay discrimination. Concerning race, much attention has been given to the Black Lives Matter movement, which is an activist group fighting against police brutality toward African Americans and the unjust mass incarceration of African Americans. Regarding gay rights, no federal law protects LGBTQ members from employment discrimination or being turned away as adoptive parents. Therefore, the gender differences on equal rights issues continue to be relevant today and likely of political importance.

Chapter 6 focuses on the gender gap on social welfare programs and spending, including government spending to help the poor, to provide for public schools, and to fund Social Security. Once again, I investigate the pro-social values hypothesis as an explanation for the gap in respect to social welfare issues, which is a well-established and politically consequential gap, according to the extant literature.

# 6

# Gender Gap on Social Welfare Issues

I have a rough time wanting to spend billions and billions and trillions of dollars to help people who won't help
themselves—won't lift a finger—and expect the federal
government to do everything. (Orrin Hatch, quoted in
Sinclair 2017)

Forcing disabled people and seniors into institutions just to
pay for tax cuts, which is what this bill does, is not equality.
It's not liberty. (Dawn Russell, quoted in Diament 2017)

This budget is going to completely decimate SNAP. It's a
program that really provides stability for families. Eighty-
three percent of people who use SNAP, their household
includes an elderly person, a disabled person, or a child.
(Traci Weatherford-Brown, quoted in Delano 2017)

Given the Trump administration's 2018 and 2019 budget
proposals and the public's reaction to his proposed cuts
to various social welfare programs, understanding public

support of social welfare issues and the origins of the gender gap on them is of considerable interest. The Trump budget proposed cutting school lunch funding; Women, Infants, and Children nutrition funding; grants for teacher training; grants for after-school programs; and Housing and Urban Development grants and funding. As Senator Orrin Hatch's quotation illustrates, the Republican support for cuts to various social safety net programs targets those assumed to be unjustifiably dependent on government. Hatch's statement was made while discussing funding health insurance coverage for needy children, which he supported; but, as the quotation illustrates, he did not support other types of government funding for social welfare programs. The other two quotations underscore how budget cuts could have a detrimental impact on the lives of the disabled, the elderly, and children. Thus, people's pro-social value orientations should help us understand their opinions on social welfare programs and social safety net spending, as well as clarify why there is a gender gap on these issues.

Other social welfare issues and spending have been quite salient in recent years, with respect to the Affordable Care Act, public school funding, and childcare tax credits. As mentioned at the outset of Chapter 1, in 2017 people across the country fought to prevent the Affordable Care Act from being repealed (Sganga 2017). In 2018, teacher protests spread across the nation, particularly in more conservative states, as teachers demanded more funding for public schools and raises for themselves. The protests also focused on aging facilities, out-of-date materials, four-day work weeks, and reduced per student capita spending below 2008 figures (Rohlinger 2018). In his 2015 State of the Union Address, President Barack Obama (2015) proposed a childcare tax credit: "My plan will make quality childcare more available and more affordable for every middle-class and low-income family with young children in America." Indicating a general desire for more government subsidies for childcare, women on the left and the right discussed the implications, benefits, and shortcomings of his proposed plan (Friedman 2015; Miller 2015).

Men and women in general differ in their attitudes about social welfare issues. Social welfare issues—including government spending on public schools, childcare, the poor, welfare, and Social Security, as well as the provision of government services, the government guaranteeing jobs, and government provision of healthcare—have been studied quite a bit in the women and politics literature, but it is still not entirely clear why gender differences exist. In this chapter, I seek to demonstrate that women's greater support for social welfare spending is because of their greater concern for others' well-being compared to men. The values explanation would expect that women think about the elderly, disabled, and children, along with those who are struggling for other reasons, such as an economic recession or outsourcing, when they endorse higher levels of government spending for the social safety net.

Social welfare issues are of particular interest now, given the debates over the Affordable Care Act and the recent Republican repeal and replace bill, the American Health Care Act, along with continued concerns about the solvency of Social Security and Medicare. These issues were glaringly absent from the general election presidential debates in 2016, but have otherwise been a constant feature of political campaigns. This area is also of particular interest to pollsters and scholars because it has influenced voting behavior in past elections (Chaney, Alvarez, and Nagler 1998; Kaufmann and Petrocik 1999; Manza and Brooks 1998) and, thus, was likely important in the 2018 congressional midterm elections and could be significant in the 2020 presidential election. Last, the organizers of the historic Women's March on January 21, 2017, included in its list of Unity Principles the belief that the country and industry need to provide affordable childcare and healthcare in addition to other workplace protections.

As in previous chapters, I discuss the relevant literature on public support and the gender gap on social welfare issues. Next, the pro-social values hypothesis is tested as an explanation for gender differences in this area. The findings that women's tendency to care more about other's well-being compared to men partially explains the gaps in support of various social welfare spending and program.

## Gender Differences on Social Welfare
## Issues in the Literature

Several researchers have found gender differences on social welfare issues. These issues can include support for various types of government spending, such as Social Security, the homeless, welfare, food stamps, childcare, and schools (J. Clark and C. Clark 1993; C. Clark and J. Clark 1996; Cook and Wilcox 1995). Others have included support for the government to provide health insurance (J. Clark and C. Clark 1993; C. Clark and J. Clark 1996; Howell and Day 2000), for the government to provide jobs, for more government services in general (J. Clark and C. Clark 1993; C. Clark and J. Clark 1996; Howell and Day 2000; Kaufmann and Petrocik 1999), and, of course, for government spending on the poor (J. Clark and C. Clark 1993; C. Clark and J. Clark 1996; Cook and Wilcox 1995; Howell and Day 2000; Kaufmann and Petrocik 1999).

Women are more liberal on these issues in that they are more likely to support greater government spending on social welfare programs (Eagly et al. 2004; Howell and Day 2000; Kaufmann 2004; Kaufmann and Petrocik 1999; Schlesinger and Heldman 2001; Shapiro and Mahajan 1986; Shirazi and Biel 2005). Overall, women are more likely than men to support policies that provide for the disadvantaged, including policies on housing, childcare, educational opportunities, and financial support such as welfare (Schlesinger and Heldman 2001; Shapiro and Mahajan 1986). A more recent analysis has similar results, finding small but consistent gaps, with women more likely than men to prefer that the government provide more services; guarantee jobs; provide health insurance; and spend more on public schools, childcare, Social Security, welfare programs, aid to poor people, and food stamps (Fox and Oxley 2015).

Gender differences on the issue of social welfare spending vary in size depending on the particular aspect of social welfare. For example, the gap ranges from 4 to 5 percentage points for issues such as government-funded health insurance and government-guaranteed jobs (J. Clark and C. Clark 1993; C. Clark and J. Clark 1996). The differences are much larger, up to 14 or 15 percentage points, in support of increased Social Security spending (J. Clark and C. Clark 1993; C. Clark and J. Clark 1996; Cook and Wilcox 1995). For the issues of spending for the poor, welfare, food stamps, and the homeless, the mean differences tend to be between 4 and 7 points (Kaufmann and Petrocik 1999). These differences persist even when controlling for partisanship (Cook and Wilcox 1995), as well as educational attainment, marital status, income, children, age, cohort, occupational status, and race (Howell and Day 2000; Eagly et al. 2004).

The robustness of these gaps to control variables also depends on which social welfare issue is being investigated. Women are more supportive of reducing the gap in income, aid to the poor, and Social Security, but not welfare, controlling for many other factors such as education, race, income, and religion (Alesina and La Ferrara 2005). Women more supportive of Social Security spending than men, controlling for age, race, social class, education, party identification, and preferences about more or less government (Quadagno and Pederson 2012). Women are more likely to support public school spending, childcare spending, and more government services, controlling for race, region, age, income, religious identification, marital status, education, parental status, and party identification (Lizotte 2017b). These gender differences transcend regional differences, with white women being more supportive of spending on education, food stamps, government health insurance, and government services than white men (Ondercin 2013). Men are less likely to support redistribution, controlling for education, race, age, employment status, income, marital status, worrying about bills, union membership, and beliefs about causes of poverty (Fong 2001).

The gender gap on social welfare issues appears to be politically consequential. Social welfare opinions contribute to the gender gap in party identification and voting (Kaufmann and Petrocik 1999). Interestingly, social welfare attitudes contribute to partisanship for men and women, but more so for men, with men being more conservative on these issues (Kaufmann 2002). Social service spending attitudes mediate the relationship between the changes in the rate of women participating in the labor force and gender differences in presidential vote choice (Manza and Brooks 1998). Attitudes toward government-guaranteed jobs and food stamps are predictive of vote choice for men and women some of the time, controlling for region, education level, age, personal economic retrospections, national economic retrospections, party identification, and ideology (Chaney, Alvarez, and Nagler 1998). These issue gaps account for a large proportion of the voting gap; giving women men's preferences on issues and views on the economy results in substantial reductions in the voting gap in 1984, 1988, and 1992 (Chaney, Alvarez, and Nagler 1998).

## Recent Polling on Social Welfare Attitudes

Recent public opinion polls show similar gender differences on social welfare issues. In a Pew Research Center report (2016b), women were 5 points more likely to approve of the Affordable Care Act compared to men. Women are 34 percentage points more likely than men to believe that poverty is a result of circumstances beyond one's control (Pew Research Center 2016a). This was also the case in a 2013 Pew report that found 40 percent of men versus 52 percent of women believe people are poor because of circumstances beyond their control; among whites, 34 percent of men compared to 48 percent of women responded this way (Drake 2013). In a 2014 Pew survey, women were 9 percentage points more likely to want there to be no benefit reduction for Social Security and 4 percentage points more likely to believe that ensuring all Americans have health care coverage is the responsibility of the federal government. When asked about their midterm election vote choice, 84 percent of women said that healthcare would be important to their vote compared to 70 percent of men (Pew Research Center 2014b). In the same survey, 64 percent of women said that economic inequality would be important to their vote compared to only 49 percent of men (Pew Research Center 2014b).

Other polls indicate the importance and general concern for social welfare programs. A 2007 Pew report finds that, compared to 1994, support for government aid to the needy and guaranteeing food and shelter has increased from 41 percent to 54 percent and 59 percent to 69 percent, respectively (Morin and Neidorf 2007). A majority of Americans expressed support for maintaining entitlement benefits, 69 percent, and spending on the poor, 59 percent, rather than reducing the deficit (Pew Research Center 2013b). In a 2015 Gallup survey, only 16 percent of Americans were satisfied with the federal government's work on poverty (Jones 2015). Likely because of the implementation of the Affordable Care Act, the percentage of Americans satisfied with the government's handling of healthcare went from 29 percent in 2013 to 43 percent in 2015 (Swift and Ander 2015).

In sum, a good deal of evidence shows that there are sizeable and consistent gender differences on social welfare policy preferences. Women are more likely than men to support more government spending and involvement in this area of policy. Recent polls echo the academic research findings. All of this points to a need to understand the origins of these gender differences. In the next section, I state the values hypothesis and conceptualization of the gender gap on social issues. Then the analysis and findings are presented, which offer strong support for the pro-social values hypothesis.

## Hypothesis

I hypothesize that gender differences in levels of pro-social values are causing the differences in support for government spending on social welfare programs and favorability toward more government services. Theoretically, the values explanation would predict that women see social welfare programs and government services as a way to provide citizens with a minimum level of opportunities and to help those who are disadvantaged. Research indicates that social welfare programs do in fact reduce poverty in cross-national data of fifteen industrialized countries from 1960 to

1991 (Kenworthy 1999). The pro-social values explanation asserts that women and men differ on these issues because of women's greater concern for others' well-being and because when women are asked about these programs, they think about their potential to help people. For example, when thinking about welfare and food stamps, women might consider how struggling parents rely on these programs to provide necessities for their children. In general, women may believe that government has the capacity to ensure that all those wanting a job have one, that everyone has access to affordable healthcare, that children go to sufficiently funded public schools, and that working parents can afford reliable and safe childcare.

There are some particularly relevant findings for this hypothesis. Individuals who believe that there are equal opportunities in the United States are less supportive of redistributive policies such as reducing the gap between the rich and the poor (Alesina and Ferrara 2005). Restricting analysis to whites only, egalitarianism predicts support for government spending to aid the undeserving and deserving poor, controlling for income, party identification, ideology, racial stereotyping, and political sophistication, but not gender, in the 1992 and 1996 ANES (Goren 2005). Using the 1996 ANES, Susan Howell and Christine Day (2000) found that including measures of egalitarianism and willingness to help others leads to a sizeable reduction in gender differences on a scale of social welfare issues. Women in the 2008 European Social Survey were more likely to support the welfare state, and egalitarianism was positively associated with support for the welfare state, but did not fully mediate the gender gap (Calzada et al. 2014). Egalitarian attitudes, along with moral attitudes, racial attitudes, education, and income, predict social welfare attitudes for men and women (Kaufmann 2002).

Egalitarianism is predictive of support for government intervention on several policy areas, including medical care, substance abuse, homelessness, and education (Schlesinger and Heldman 2001). Egalitarianism also predicts support for welfare spending, Social Security spending, and government-provided healthcare plans (Winter 2008). My analysis extends these findings to more years of data and looks at these attitudes individually rather than using a scale.

## Women Support Greater Spending on Social Welfare and More Government Services

To test gender differences in pro-social values as an explanation for the gender gap, I rely heavily on 1980–2012 ANES cumulative data. There are significant and sizeable gender gaps on the ten questions included to measure support for various social welfare issues. Not all of the questions are included across all of the years; therefore, the number of respondents for each analysis varies quite a bit. I also include analysis of one item from the 2011 World Values Survey of the United States. There is a sizeable and significant gender gap on this item.

First, I turn to the several spending items regularly included in the ANES. This spending question asks respondents if government spending should be (1) decreased, (2) kept the same, or (3) increased. This question uses the following question stem: "If you had a say in making up the federal budget this year, for which programs would you like to see spending increased and for which would you like to see spending decreased."

Table 6.1 shows the analysis for the childcare spending, public school spending, and Social Security spending. For each of these questions, a column depicts the gender gap, with the inclusion of a list of typical control variables, and a second column depicts the addition of egalitarianism. For childcare spending, the gender gap is significant in both analyses, with women more likely than men to support increased spending on childcare. According to mediational analyses, egalitarianism mediates 28.63 percent of the effect of gender on childcare spending attitudes. Egalitarianism also predicts spending attitudes without gender in the model; this is necessary for mediation to occur, but these results are not shown.

In analysis not shown, including party identification does not change the effect of egalitarianism, and gender remains

TABLE 6.1. GENDER DIFFERENCES IN ATTITUDES ON SPENDING ON CHILDCARE, PUBLIC SCHOOLS, AND SOCIAL SECURITY

| | Childcare 1 | Childcare 2 | Public schools 1 | Public schools 2 | Social Security 1 | Social Security 2 |
|---|---|---|---|---|---|---|
| Female | 0.33*** | 0.25*** | 0.40*** | 0.34*** | 0.44*** | 0.39*** |
| | (0.03) | (0.03) | (0.03) | (0.03) | (0.03) | (0.03) |
| Age | −0.01*** | −0.01*** | −0.02*** | −0.02*** | −0.00 | 0.00 |
| | (0.00) | (0.00) | (0.00) | (0.00) | (0.00) | (0.00) |
| Education 1 = college | −0.12*** | −0.23*** | −0.09*** | −0.20*** | −0.73 | −0.81*** |
| | (0.03) | (0.04) | (0.03) | (0.04) | (0.03) | (0.03) |
| Income 1 = below median | 0.42*** | 0.38*** | 0.19*** | 0.12*** | 0.31*** | 0.29*** |
| | (0.03) | (0.04) | (0.03) | (0.04) | (0.03) | (0.03) |
| Race 1 = white | −0.76*** | −0.43*** | −0.82*** | −0.50*** | −0.72*** | −0.57*** |
| | (0.03) | (0.04) | (0.04) | (0.04) | (0.03) | (0.04) |
| Church attendance | −0.07*** | −0.05*** | −0.06*** | −0.04*** | −0.06*** | −0.05*** |
| | (0.01) | (0.01) | (0.01) | (0.01) | (0.01) | (0.01) |

| | | | | | | |
|---|---|---|---|---|---|---|
| Catholic | 0.18*** | 0.31** | 0.01 | 0.13** | 0.20*** | 0.24*** |
| | (0.04) | (0.05) | (0.05) | (0.05) | (0.01) | (0.04) |
| Protestant | 0.15*** | 0.23** | 0.05 | 0.15*** | 0.25*** | 0.29*** |
| | (0.04) | (0.05) | (0.04) | (0.05) | (0.04) | (0.04) |
| Region 1 = South | −0.04 | 0.03 | 0.13*** | 0.20*** | 0.07*** | 0.10*** |
| | (0.03) | (0.03) | (0.03) | (0.04) | (0.03) | (0.03) |
| Republican president | 0.44*** | 0.36*** | 0.04 | −0.07** | 0.29*** | 0.23*** |
| | (0.03) | (0.03) | (0.03) | (0.03) | (0.03) | (0.03) |
| Egalitarianism | | 0.78*** | | 0.78*** | | 0.41*** |
| | | (0.02) | | (0.02) | | (0.02) |
| $R^2$ | .05 | .09 | .05 | .09 | .06 | .07 |
| $N$ | 20,085 | 17,577 | 22,142 | 19,608 | 24,133 | 21,597 |

Note: Data are from the 1980–2012 ANES. Positive coefficients indicate greater support for social welfare spending. To retain respondents, the analysis also includes an income variable (not shown): 1 if people refused to answer and 0 otherwise.

* $p < .10$; ** $p < .05$; *** $p < .01$

significant. As noted in previous chapters, this indicates that the effect of egalitarianism is not simply the result of the omission of party identification, and the gender gap is not an artifact of gender differences in partisanship. The gender gap in support for increased childcare spending is not significant among blacks, but it is significant among whites. The gender gap is significant in each birth cohort, in both education levels, and for both income levels.

Similar results are found for the public school spending question and the Social Security spending question. Women are more likely than men to support increasing spending for public schools and Social Security. The gender gap on public school spending is significant among whites but not among blacks, while the gender gap on Social Security spending is significant among whites and blacks. The gender gap on public school spending and on Social Security spending is significant in each birth cohort, for both education levels, and for both income levels. Including egalitarianism in the public school spending analysis reduces the effect of gender by 21.97 percent. When party identification is included in the model, egalitarianism and gender remain significant.

Egalitarianism only mediates 10.90 percent of the gender effect on Social Security spending. Party identification inclusion does not influence the significance of egalitarianism or gender. These results provide support for the hypothesis that women are more likely than men to support the government's social welfare spending partially because of their greater concern for others' well-being. As in the prior analysis, the other relationships necessary for mediation also occur but are not shown. Perhaps with a different measure of pro-social values, such as humanitarianism, there would be a better reduction the effect of gender. Table 6.2 includes additional spending questions from the ANES, including spending to aid the poor, spending on welfare, spending on food stamps (Supplemental Nutrition Assistance Program or SNAP), and spending to help the homeless. The results in Table 6.2 are very similar to those on spending for childcare, public schools, and Social Security. Again for each item, the first column shows the gender gap with controls in the model, and the second column includes egalitarianism. The gender gap is significant for aid to the poor spending, with women more supportive than men of increased spending. Egalitarianism mediates 31.75 percent of the effect of gender. This supports the hypothesis that women's greater support for government spending to aid the poor is partially because of their greater propensity to endorse pro-social values. The results are similar for the welfare spending analysis; the gender gap is significant in both models, and egalitarianism mediates 33.30 percent of the gender effect on welfare spending preferences.

The SNAP and homeless spending analysis is quite similar, with women more likely than men to support increased spending on food stamps and to help the homeless. Egalitarianism reduces 25.65 percent of the gender effect on food stamps spending and 14.94 percent of the effect of gender on homeless spending attitudes.

For all four of the dependent variables in Table 6.2, gender and egalitarianism are significant when party identification is included in the analysis. In terms of racial differences, there is a significant gender gap on each of these spending items among whites, with white women more likely to support increased spending to aid the poor and on welfare, food stamps, and the homeless in comparison to white men. These results provide support for the pro-social values hypothesis. A substantial part of the reason for women's greater support for government social welfare spending is because of their concern for others' well-being.

There is not a gender gap among blacks on these spending questions except for a marginally significant gap on the homeless item, where black women are more supportive than black men of increased spending. The gender gap on all four of these spending items is significant for all birth cohorts, for all education levels, and for all income levels, except that the gap on welfare spending is not significant among pre–baby boomers.

Table 6.3 includes analysis for more general attitudes toward social welfare compared to the specific spending questions

TABLE 6.2. GENDER DIFFERENCES IN ATTITUDES ON AID TO THE
POOR, WELFARE SPENDING, FOOD STAMPS SPENDING,
AND SPENDING TO HELP THE HOMELESS

| | Poor 1 | Poor 2 | Welfare 1 | Welfare 2 | SNAP 1 | SNAP 2 | Homeless 1 | Homeless 2 |
|---|---|---|---|---|---|---|---|---|
| Female | 0.35*** | 0.27*** | 0.28*** | 0.20*** | 0.25*** | 0.22*** | 0.57*** | 0.47*** |
| | (0.03) | (0.04) | (0.03) | (0.06) | (0.03) | (0.04) | (0.05) | (0.06) |
| Age | −0.00*** | −0.00** | −0.00 | 0.00** | 0.00 | 0.00*** | −0.01*** | −0.01*** |
| | (0.00) | (0.00) | (0.00) | (0.00) | (0.00) | (0.00) | (0.00) | (0.00) |
| Education 1 = college | −0.35*** | −0.52*** | 0.11*** | 0.01 | 0.10*** | 0.02 | −0.16*** | −0.31*** |
| | (0.04) | (0.04) | (0.04) | (0.04) | (0.04) | (0.04) | (0.06) | (0.07) |
| Income 1 = low | 0.59*** | 0.55*** | 0.73*** | 0.70*** | 0.76*** | 0.71*** | 0.45*** | 0.38*** |
| | (0.04) | (0.04) | (0.04) | (0.04) | (0.04) | (0.04) | (0.06) | (0.07) |
| Race 1 = white | −0.98*** | −0.66*** | −0.80*** | −0.53*** | −0.92*** | −0.65*** | −0.97*** | −0.56*** |
| | (0.04) | (0.04) | (0.03) | (0.04) | (0.04) | (0.04) | (0.07) | (0.08) |
| Church attendance | −0.04*** | −0.01 | −0.06*** | −0.03*** | −0.07*** | −0.06** | −0.04** | −0.01 |
| | (0.01) | (0.01) | (0.01) | (0.01) | (0.01) | (0.01) | (0.02) | (0.02) |

| | | | | | | | |
|---|---|---|---|---|---|---|---|
| Catholic | 0.11** | 0.21*** | -0.18*** | -0.12*** | -0.19*** | -0.08 | 0.08 | 0.25** |
| | (0.05) | (0.05) | (0.04) | (0.04) | (0.06) | (0.06) | (0.09) | (0.10) |
| Protestant | 0.14*** | 0.20*** | -0.11** | -0.09** | -0.20*** | -0.11* | -0.13 | 0.06 |
| | (0.04) | (0.05) | (0.04) | (0.04) | (0.05) | (0.06) | (0.08) | (0.09) |
| Region 1 = South | -0.03 | 0.03 | -0.05 | 0.01 | -0.24*** | -0.17*** | -0.00 | 0.09 |
| | (0.04) | (0.04) | (0.03) | (0.03) | (0.05) | (0.04) | (0.05) | (0.06) |
| Republican president | 0.73*** | 0.63*** | 0.56*** | 0.46*** | 0.54*** | 0.50*** | 0.52*** | 0.41*** |
| | (0.04) | (0.04) | (0.03) | (0.03) | (0.03) | (0.04) | (0.06) | (0.03) |
| Egalitarianism | 0.95*** | 0.73*** | | 0.73*** | | 0.64*** | | 0.89*** |
| | (0.02) | (0.02) | | (0.02) | | (0.02) | | (0.04) |
| $R^2$ | .07 | .14 | .05 | .09 | .05 | .08 | .05 | .11 |
| $N$ | 14,714 | 13,371 | 16,332 | 14,988 | 14,779 | 13,001 | 7,774 | 6,206 |

Note: Data are from the 1980–2012 ANES. Positive coefficients indicate greater support for social welfare spending. To retain respondents, the analysis also includes an income variable (not shown): 1 if people refused to answer and 0 otherwise.

$* p < .10; ** p < .05;$ and $*** p < .01$

TABLE 6.3. GENDER DIFFERENCES IN ATTITUDES ON GUARANTEED JOBS, HEALTHCARE, GOVERNMENT SERVICES, AND INCOME EQUALITY

| | Jobs 1 | Jobs 2 | Health 1 | Health 2 | Services 1 | Services 2 | Income 1 | Income 2 |
|---|---|---|---|---|---|---|---|---|
| Female | 0.33*** | 0.23*** | 0.23*** | 0.14*** | 0.38*** | 0.29*** | 0.34*** | 0.27** |
| | (0.02) | (0.02) | (0.03) | (0.03) | (0.02) | (0.02) | (0.11) | (0.11) |
| Age | -0.01*** | -0.00*** | -0.00 | 0.00 | -0.01*** | -0.00*** | 0.01* | 0.01* |
| | (0.00) | (0.00) | (0.00) | (0.00) | (0.00) | (0.00) | (0.00) | (0.00) |
| Education 1 = college | -0.12*** | -0.22*** | -0.05 | -0.13*** | -0.18*** | -0.27*** | 0.40*** | 0.33*** |
| | (0.03) | (0.03) | (0.04) | (0.03) | (0.02) | (0.02) | (0.12) | (0.12) |
| Income 1 = low | 0.51*** | 0.43*** | 0.50*** | 0.46*** | 0.41*** | 0.36*** | 0.20*** | 0.20*** |
| | (0.03) | (0.03) | (0.04) | (0.04) | (0.02) | (0.02) | (0.03) | (0.03) |
| Race 1 = white | -0.98*** | -0.61*** | -0.65*** | -0.28*** | -0.80*** | -0.47*** | -0.15 | -0.06 |
| | (0.03) | (0.03) | (0.04) | (0.04) | (0.02) | (0.03) | (0.12) | (0.12) |
| Church attendance | -0.04*** | -0.01 | -0.14*** | -0.11*** | -0.08*** | -0.05*** | -0.12*** | -0.13*** |
| | (0.01) | (0.04) | (0.01) | (0.01) | (0.01) | (0.01) | (0.02) | (0.02) |
| Catholic | -0.05 | 0.01 | -0.03 | 0.06 | -0.08** | 0.13*** | — | — |
| | (0.04) | (0.04) | (0.05) | (0.05) | (0.03) | (0.03) | | |

|  | (1) | (2) | (3) | (4) | (5) | (6) | (7) | (8) |
|---|---|---|---|---|---|---|---|---|
| Protestant | −0.14*** | −0.08** | −0.19*** | −0.13*** | −0.05* | −0.01 | — | — |
|  | (0.03) | (0.03) | (0.04) | (0.04) | (0.03) | (0.03) |  |  |
| Region 1 = South | −0.04*** | 0.02 | −0.08** | −0.02 | −0.08** | −0.01 | — | — |
|  | (0.02) | (0.03) | (0.03) | (0.03) | (0.02) | (0.02) |  |  |
| Republican president | 0.08*** | −0.02 | 0.41*** | 0.29*** | 0.34*** | 0.28*** | — | — |
|  | (0.02) | (0.02) | (0.03) | (0.03) | (0.02) | (0.02) |  |  |
| Egalitarianism |  | 0.72*** |  | 0.73*** |  | 0.64*** | — | — |
|  |  | (0.02) |  | (0.02) |  | (0.01) |  |  |
| Universalism |  |  |  |  |  |  |  | 0.29*** |
|  |  |  |  |  |  |  |  | (0.05) |
| Benevolence |  |  |  |  |  |  |  | 0.10* |
|  |  |  |  |  |  |  |  | (0.05) |
| $R^2$ | .11 | .20 | .07 | .16 | .11 | .21 | .04 | .07 |
| N | 23,038 | 18,638 | 15,841 | 14,621 | 21,868 | 18,847 | 2,141 | 2,114 |

Note: Data are from the 1980–2012 ANES. Positive coefficients indicate greater support for social welfare policies.
* $p < .10$; ** $p < .05$; *** $p < .01$

modeled in the first two tables. This table includes support for government-guaranteed jobs and a minimum standard of living, a government-provided health insurance plan, and more government-provided services, with data taken from the ANES, along with a measure of support for income equality in the World Values Survey.

For the first model, respondents place themselves on a continuum from 1, government should let each person get ahead on his own, to 7, government should see to jobs and a good standard of living. Women are more likely than men to support a greater role for government in guaranteeing jobs and a good standard of living. Egalitarianism explains 29.84 percent of the gender effect. The gender gap is statistically significant among whites and among blacks. White women are more likely to support government-guaranteed jobs than white men, and black women are more likely than black men to support the government guaranteeing jobs. Women are consistently more likely to support the government guaranteeing jobs and a standard of living across birth cohorts, education levels, and income levels.

The health insurance question has respondents place themselves on a continuum ranging from 1, a preference for private insurance plan, to 7, a preference for government insurance plan. Women are more supportive compared to men of a greater role for government on the issue of health insurance, and egalitarianism mediates 43.47 percent of the effect of gender on health insurance attitudes. The gender gap is only significant among whites, with white women more supportive of government-provided health insurance than white men; black women and black men are equally likely to support government health insurance. The gender gap is significant for all birth cohorts, education levels, and income levels.

The government services question is similar as are the results. Respondents place themselves on a continuum from 1, government should provide many fewer services and reduce spending a lot, to 7, government should provide many more services and increase spending a lot. Women are significantly more supportive of more government services and spending, with egalitarianism reducing 22.62 percent of the gender effect. The gender gap on government provision of services is significant among whites and blacks. Regardless of race, women are more likely than men of the same race to favor more government services. Women are also more likely to favor more government services regardless of birth cohort, education level, and income level.

I also created a scale of the social welfare items in the ANES. Social Welfare Scale is an additive scale of all social welfare items (spending on poor, childcare, public schools, welfare, homeless, food stamps, and Social Security, as well as guaranteed jobs, government health insurance, and government services) with missing data replaced with the item mean; the scale has a Cronbach's alpha of 0.78 and inter-item covariance of 0.35. Figure 6.1 depicts the gender gaps within various demographic subgroups. Women are consistently more supportive of the social welfare state compared

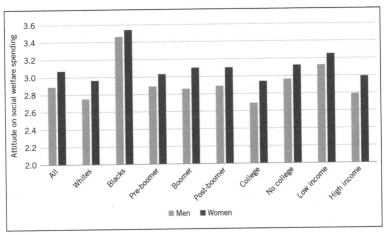

Figure 6.1. Gender differences in social welfare
spending across demographic subgroups

Note: Data are from cumulative 1980–2012 ANES. Higher values indicate greater support for increased spending. Analysis controls for demographic variables are set at their mean.

to men of the same demographic group. The figure also makes evident that large differences exist between groups. For example, blacks are much more likely to support social welfare spending than whites, and low-income individuals are also more likely compared to those with an income above the median.

Finally, in the World Values Survey, respondents place themselves on a continuum from 1, we need larger income differences as incentives for individual effort, to 10, incomes should be made more equal. Women are more supportive of income equality compared to men. As discussed in Chapter 2, universalism and benevolence are Schwartz value types included in the survey; universalism measures concern for the well-being of others, while benevolence measures concern for the well-being of those close to oneself. Including benevolence explains 7.13 percent and including universalism explains 17.69 percent of the effect of gender on income equality attitudes. The results in Table 6.3 provide support for the pro-social values hypothesis. Women's greater endorsement of pro-social values explains a substantial amount of the gender differences in social welfare attitudes.

## Testing Feminism, Income, Employment, and Parenthood

The mediation analysis investigating other gender gap explanations, which is in Table A6.1 in the Appendix, provides support for the feminist and motherhood explanations. Feeling warmly toward feminists predicts support for more government spending on childcare and mediates 32.82 percent of the effect of gender on childcare spending attitudes. The mediation results for the values explanation and the feminist feeling thermometer explanation may not be appropriate to compare because of the much lower number of observations for the feminist model. Income mediates 11.09 percent of the gender effect, while employment does not predict attitudes and mediates 0 percent of the gender gap. Having children and motherhood predict greater support for childcare spending, with being a parent mediating 2.89 percent and motherhood mediating 18.99 percent of the gender effect.

For public school spending, the mediational analyses also provide support for the feminist explanation but not for the other explanations. Feeling warmly toward feminists mediates 26.55 percent of the gender gap on public school spending. Income mediates 3.83 percent, and having children mediates 1.58 percent. Employment and being a mother both mediate 0 percent. The analysis is in Table A6.1.

For Social Security spending, the other gender gap explanations, particularly feminism and motherhood, receive support from the mediational analyses. Feeling warmly toward feminists mediates 12.51 percent of the effect of gender on Social Security spending attitudes. Income mediates 5.91 percent of the gender gap. Employment status again mediates 0 percent. Having children mediates only 1.62 percent, but motherhood mediates 13.16 percent of the gender effect. These results are in Table A6.2 in the Appendix.

For government spending to aid the poor, the feminist, low-income, and motherhood explanations receive support; the full results are in Table A6.2. Warm feelings toward feminists mediate 32.89 percent of the effect of gender on government spending to aid the poor. Income mediates 12.59 percent of the gender effect. Motherhood mediates 12.07 percent of the effect of gender. Being employed mediates only 2.21 percent, and having children only mediates 1.01 percent of the gender gap. And for the welfare spending dependent variable, the mediational analyses also support the feminist, economic, and social role explanations. Feelings toward feminists mediates 40.64 percent of the gender effect. Income mediates 19.62 percent, and being employed mediates 13.52 percent. Having children only mediates 0.81 percent, but being a mother mediates 16.10 percent of the gender effect. See Table A6.3 in the Appendix for the full analysis.

The feminist explanation mediates 11.20 percent of the gender gap on support for SNAP spending and 4.20 percent of the gender gap on homeless spending. Income mediates 28.85 percent of the effect of gender on support for food stamp spending and 8.53 percent on spending to help the homeless. Being employed mediates 24.22 percent of the gender on SNAP spending and 2.78 percent on homeless spending attitudes. Parenthood mediates 2.96 percent and motherhood mediates 36.61 percent of the effect of gender on support for SNAP spending. Parenthood only mediates 1.34 percent and motherhood mediates 0 percent of the gender effect on homeless spending. Tables A6.3 and A6.4 in the Appendix have the full results for the other explanations.

The results for other explanations on the government-guaranteed jobs are in Table A6.4. The feminist feeling thermometer ratings mediates 27.78 percent of the gender gap. The income and employment variables mediate 13.60 percent and 7.36 percent, respectively. Having children mediates 1.24 percent, and being a mother mediates 18.33 percent of the gender gap. For the government-provided healthcare, the analysis including the other explanations is displayed in Table A6.5 in the Appendix. Feelings toward feminists mediates 47.7 percent. Income mediates 18.39 percent, and being employed mediates 4.80 percent of the effect of gender. Having children mediates 0 percent, and being a mother mediates 29.03 percent of the gender gap. Finally, for the government services dependent variable, the results for the other explanations are in Table A6.5. Feelings toward feminists mediates 27.64 percent of the gender effect. Income mediates 9.50 percent and employment status mediates 3.71 percent of the effect of gender on support for government services. Parenthood mediates 0 percent, and motherhood mediates 19.79 percent of the gender gap.

Again, the feminist explanation receives more consistent and stronger support than the other explanations. Compared to the other issue areas, however, economic circumstances and parental status receive more support as explanations for the gender gap in social welfare attitudes. The analysis provides the most support for the pro-social values and feminism explanations.

## Summary and Conclusion

In this chapter the results provide a good deal of evidence to support the pro-social values hypothesis. The gender gap in social welfare attitudes is partially accounted for by gender differences in values. Women's greater endorsement of pro-social values influences their positions on social welfare spending and government services. Their endorsement also provides insight into their greater support for government spending on childcare, public schools, Social Security, the poor, welfare, food stamps, and the homeless. In addition, gender differences in pro-social values partially explains why women are more likely to support government-guaranteed jobs, government-provided health insurance, the government providing more services, and greater income equality. This suggests that women likely do think about others, relying on their concern for the well-being of other people, when evaluating social welfare spending and programs. Pro-social values also lead men to support greater spending and more services, but because women are more likely to hold pro-social values, a gender gap emerges on these policy attitudes.

As discussed at the beginning of the chapter, social welfare spending and policies have been extremely salient in the past few years. The Affordable Care Act was the first and one of the major legislative achievements of President Obama's two terms in office. Paul Ryan (R-WI) rose to prominence for his proposals to reduce entitlement program spending (i.e., spending on Social Security and Medicare). The Trump administration has proposed various cuts in spending to these programs at the federal level, while at the state level, low public school funding levels have triggered multistate protests. Knowing the influence that social welfare policy positions have had on vote choice in the past, it is of particular interest to understand opinions and the gender gap on these issues (Chaney, Alvarez, and Nagler 1998; Kaufmann and Petrocik 1999; Manza and Brooks 1998).

In Chapter 7, I provide evidence of the political consequences of the gender differences in public opinion discussed throughout the book, propose some avenues for future work, and offer some conclusions. Finally, I discuss the implications of this research for studying public opinion.

# Political Consequences of Gender Differences and Conclusions

> I must sojourn once to the ballot-box before I die. I
> hear the ballot-box is a beautiful glass globe, so you
> can see all the votes as they go in. Now, the first time
> I vote I'll see if the woman's vote looks any different
> from the rest—if it makes any stir or commotion. If it
> don't inside, it need not outside.
>
> —SOJOURNER TRUTH, "Sojourner Truth on the Press"

> Last year, it was really about the day. . . . [T]his year,
> it's about following that through to our individual
> states, to our individual communities and pushing that
> one-time event into a long-lasting movement that's
> going to carry us through, really, the next four years.
>
> —SAVANNAH PEARLMAN, quoted in Domenica Bongiovanni,
> "Hoosier Women's March Participants Talk 2018 Wishes"

The electoral consequences of public opinion are of considerable interest. The vote and ability to participate fully in American democracy is something that was hard earned for women. In 1840, Elizabeth Cady Stanton and Lucretia Mott, along with other American women fighting for the abolition of slavery, attended the World Anti-slavery Convention in London. Women were not permitted to participate in the convention, only to observe. Their awareness that their lack of a political voice or their paucity of political influence would prevent them from effecting change eventually gave rise to the women's rights and suffrage movement in the United States (Ford 2017). Sojourner

Truth was one of the speakers at the resulting Seneca Falls Convention, which Stanton and Mott organized.

In more recent times, women have never been a solid voting block; their vote has never looked vastly different from that of men. But on average, women are more likely to vote for Democratic candidates (Center for American Women and Politics 2017). As the Women's March participant quoted in the epigraph highlights, the current engagement of women in politics, including the Women's Marches of 2017 and 2018, could have major electoral consequences.

This chapter includes a summary of findings, a discussion of implications, and an outline of possibilities for future research. The discussion of implications focuses a great deal on the political consequences of gender differences in issue positions, specifically how these opinion differences contribute to party identification and vote choice. I also discuss the implications of the findings from the previous chapters for studying public opinion and values endorsement. Finally, I note avenues for future research to better understand American public opinion and gender gaps.

This book adds to the existing research on public opinion, gender differences, and the importance of political values. As discussed in Chapter 1, prior work establishes that the gender gap in public opinion contributes to the gender gap in voting (Chaney, Alvarez, and Nagler 1998; C. Clark and J. Clark 2008; Kaufmann and Petrocik 1999). Furthermore, research also demonstrates that public opinion influences policy makers (Page and Shapiro 1983; Powlick 1991; Zaller 1992). Thus, the gender gaps studied throughout this book have potentially important political consequences for partisanship and elections. This research contributes to a better understanding of how appeals to different values can garner more support from women on public policies related to these topics, as well as appeal to women during campaigns. I hope that these results advance political scientists' understanding of the gender gap and the importance of values when examining the public's attitudes toward these issues.

## Gender Gap in Voting and Partisanship:
## An Overview of the Literature

Research tends to point to the 1980 presidential election as the emergence of the gender gap in vote choice, with women consistently more likely than men to vote for the Democratic presidential nominee since that election (Huddy, Cassese, and Lizotte 2008b). In 2016, women were also more likely than men to vote for Hillary Clinton for president (Burden, Crawford, and DeCrescenzo 2016). These gender differences exist across many different demographic groups (C. Clark and J. Clark 2009; Huddy, Cassese, and Lizotte 2008a). For example, the gender gap in the 1980 presidential election, with women being more likely to vote for Carter compared to men, appeared across most of the income categories, among all levels of education, among all racial and ethnic groups, among parents and non-parents, in all age categories, and in all regions (C. Clark and J. Clark 2009). The gender gap is similarly robust across demographic groups for presidential vote choice in the 1996, 2000, and 2004 elections (C. Clark and J. Clark 2009).

Gender differences in candidate preferences has also emerged within parties during presidential primaries. In the 2000 Democratic presidential primaries, men were more likely to vote for former senator Bill Bradley than were women, who were more likely to vote for Vice President Al Gore. In the 2000 Republican presidential primary, men were more likely to vote for Senator John McCain than were women, who were more likely to vote for former governor George W. Bush (Norrander 2003). Women voting in the 2016 Republican presidential primary were much less likely than men to vote for Donald Trump, while in the Democratic primary, women were more likely to vote for former secretary of state Hillary Clinton, and men were more likely to vote for Senator Bernie Sanders (Presidential Gender Watch 2017).

The gender gap in party identification emerged in 1968 but did not appear in 1970; in 1972 it came back and has existed ever since (Kenski 1988). Although the focus has often been on why the gap exists, several researchers found evidence that the gap is the result of men's movement away from the Democratic Party (Kaufmann and Petrocik 1999; Kaufmann, Petrocik, and Shaw 2008; Norrander 1999; Wirls 1986). The gender gap is the result of white men in the North and South leaving the Democratic Party over time (Kaufmann, Petrocik, and Shaw 2008), but white Southern men moved at a faster rate than those in the North (Norrander 1999). The gender gap in the 2004 presidential election was quite small in comparison to other years, largely because white Southern women did not contribute the gap as usual; instead white Southern women voted more in line with white Southern men (Kaufmann 2006). Challenging these earlier findings that it was men's movement away from the Democratic Party, recent analysis of the gender gap in partisanship using Gallup poll data finds evidence of movement by men and women in response to the political parties' symbolic images, including the gender composition of congressional delegations; the presence of more women in the Democratic Party delegation compared to the Republican Party delegation signifies that the Democratic Party better represents the gendered social identity of women and that the Democratic Party is more likely to pursue policies that benefit women in the electorate (Ondercin 2017).

In addition to understanding the cause of its emergence, researchers have focused on what factors, such as issue positions and demographic characteristics, precipitate the gap. Differences in issue positions and differences in salience of issues both contributed to the gender gaps in voting in 1992 and 1996 (Kaufmann and Petrocik 1999). In terms of issue salience for party identification, social welfare attitudes matter more for men than for women (Kaufmann, Petrocik, and Shaw 2008). In the 1980 and 1984 presidential and congressional elections, women were more likely to rely on perceptions of the national economy than men when voting, while men were more likely to rely on perceptions of their own personal financial situation (Welch and Hibbing

1992). Recent research demonstrates that beliefs about income equality, racial equality, and gender equality also predict party identification, with all forms of equality leading to a lower likelihood of identifying as Republican (Blinder and Rolfe 2017). In addition, the personality trait of compassion is associated with a greater likelihood of Democratic identification among men and women (McDermott 2016).

Various issue areas appear to bring about gender differences in vote choice. Social welfare opinions contribute most to the gender gap in voting (Kaufmann and Petrocik 1999). Cultural values, including reproductive rights, gender equality, and gay rights, were predictive of party identification for women and men from 1988 to 2000, but more determinant for women. Social welfare attitudes, racial attitudes, and defense attitudes were predictive of party identification for men and women from 1988 to 2000 (Kaufmann 2002). Attitudes about gender roles and racial resentment predicted party identification in the 1985 ANES pilot study data (Conover 1988). The gender gap varies in size depending on the presidential candidate's stances on race, and the gap is reduced when a Republican candidate takes a more compassionate stance (Hutchings et al. 2004). Support for the Equal Rights Amendment did not contribute to the gender gap in the 1980 presidential election (Mansbridge 1985). Preferences about the military and social welfare attitudes contributed to the gender gap on approval for President Ronald Reagan (Gilens 1988).

Some research has focused on the changing contribution of particular issues to the vote gap over time. Social welfare attitudes increased in importance for women's partisanship but not men's partisanship from 1988 to 2000. Perhaps because of the ending of the Cold War and general peaceful times, defense attitudes became less important to women and men's partisanship from 1988 to 2000 (Kaufmann 2002). The gender gap in partisanship from 1979 to 2000 grew, apparently in response to a deteriorating economy and an increase in economically vulnerable women (Box-Steffensmeier, De Boef, and Lin 2004). Increasing rates of women's participation in the labor force appears to have contributed to the gender gap in presidential elections from 1952 to 1992 (Manza and Brooks 1998).

There is disagreement in the literature as to whether economically vulnerable and/or economically autonomous women contribute to the gap in voting. Economically vulnerable women are low-income women who may be reliant on social welfare programs. Economically autonomous women are those who are economically independent, such as professional women participating in the labor force or those who are psychologically independent, such as unmarried women (Box-Steffensmeier, De Boef, and Lin 2004; Carroll 1988; Huddy, Cassese, and Lizotte 2008b). In 1980 and 1982 data ANES data investigating presidential vote and approval, supporting evidence shows that economically vulnerable and economically autonomous women are causing the gaps, but the analysis does not control for party identification (Carroll 1988). With respect to the gender gap in partisanship from 1979 to 2000, there is support for the economically vulnerable women explanation, but not for the economically autonomous explanation (Box-Steffensmeier, De Boef, and Lin 2004). Others have presented evidence that labor force participation among women contributes to the gender gap in presidential elections from 1952 to 1992 (Manza and Brooks 1998). Neither the inclusion of economic vulnerability measures nor economic autonomy measures appears to mediate the gap in voting or party identification (Huddy, Cassese, and Lizotte 2008b).

## Evidence from Polling

Gender differences on which issues were important to vote choice existed in 2012. Women were more likely to state that several issues were very important in comparison to men, with the gap sizes varying quite a bit, such as a 14-point gap on education, a 13-point gap on birth control, an 11-point gap on healthcare, a 10-point gap on abortion, 9-point gaps on the environment and

Medicare, a 6-point gap on gun control, a 5-point gap on gay marriage, a 4-point gap on jobs, 3-point gaps on the economy, terrorism, and Afghanistan, and a 1-point gap on foreign policy (Pew Research Center 2012b). There was no gender gap on the importance of immigration, and men were more likely than women to say that the following were very important to their vote choice: taxes by 2 points, Iran by 3 points, the budget deficit by 5 points, and energy by 8 points (Pew Research Center 2012b).

Exit polls in 2012 revealed a 10-point gap, with 55 percent of women versus 45 percent of men voting for Obama (CNN Politics 2012). Gender gaps existed among all racial and ethnic groups. There was a 7-point gap among whites, with 35 percent of white men and 42 percent of white women voting for Obama. The majority of white men, 62 percent, and the majority of white women, 56 percent, voted for Romney. Among blacks, 87 percent of men and 96 percent of women voted for Obama. Among Latinos, 65 percent of men and 76 percent of women voted for Obama.

In 2016, gender gaps on issues of importance to vote choice also emerged among registered voters. Some of these gender differences were quite small, such as 85 percent of men versus 83 percent of women stating that the economy was a very important issue to their vote. Small gaps with men more likely to state an issue is very important included a 2-point gap on foreign policy and a 2-point gap on Supreme Court appointments. Small gaps, with women more likely to state that an issue is very important, included 6-point gaps on healthcare and education, a 5-point gap on gun policy, a 4-point gap on terrorism, a 3-point gap on Social Security, and a 2-point gap on immigration. Other gaps were larger, such as the treatment of racial and ethnic minorities, which produced a 14-point gap, with women more likely to rate the issue as very important. Women were more likely to state that the environment by a 10-point difference, abortion by a 14-point difference, and treatment of the LGBTQ community by a 17-point difference were very important to their vote. Men were 10 points more likely to state that trade policy would be very important to their vote (Chaturvedi 2016).

Exit polls reveal a gender gap among voters, with women 13 points more likely than men to vote for Clinton (CNN Politics 2016), with 54 percent of women and 41 percent of men voting for Clinton. Gender differences existed across racial groups, although the gaps varied in size. The gap was 12 points among whites, with 43 percent of white women versus 31 percent of white men voting for Clinton. The majority of white men, at 62 percent, and the majority of white women, at 52 percent, voted for Trump. The gap was also 12 points among blacks, with 82 percent of black men and 94 percent of black women voting for Clinton. The gap was smallest among Latinos, with 63 percent of Latinos and 69 percent of Latinas voting for Clinton. All of this points to a need to understand the origins of these gender differences. The following section outlines the pro-social values hypothesis as it applies to the gender gap in party identification and vote choice.

## Hypothesis

I hypothesize that the gender gaps in public opinion investigated throughout this book contribute to the gender gaps in party identification and vote choice. Because men and women differ on force issues, environmental protection policy, equal rights, and social welfare issues, there is a consistent and sizeable gender gap in vote choice, with women being more likely to identify as Democrats and vote for Democratic candidates compared to men. Furthermore, I hypothesize that gender differences in pro-social values also partially explain gender difference in party identification and vote choice. I suspect that women are more likely to identify as Democrats and vote for Democratic presidential candidates because of a greater concern for the well-being of other people.

## Gender Differences in Party Identification and Vote Choice

To explore the political consequences of the gender gaps discussed throughout the book, I investigated whether these opinions and attitudes predicted vote choice and how their inclusion influenced the gender gap in party identification and voting. As is the case throughout the book, I use the 1980–2012 American National Election Study (ANES) cumulative data. The analysis in this chapter does not include the 2011 World Values Survey data.

I chose to use the standard party identification question, which asks respondents, "Generally speaking, do you usually think of yourself as a Republican, a Democrat, an Independent, or what?" I coded party identification so 1 = Strong Republican, 2 = Weak Republican, 3 = Independent, leans Republican, 4 = Independent, 5 = Independent, leans Democrat, 6 = Weak Democrat, and 7 = Strong Democrat. I chose to use the presidential vote choice question and code the response options so 1 is equal to voting for the Democratic presidential nominee and 0 otherwise, which is an established method of analysis (Huddy, Cassese, and Lizotte 2008b). I include in the analysis all of the control variables used throughout the book including age, education, income, race, church attendance, religious identification, region, Republican presidential administration, and party identification.

For the vote choice models, I also include two variables measuring respondent perceptions of the economy and a variable measuring respondent perceptions of his or her family's personal financial situation. The first of these is often referred to as economic retrospection, which asks respondents how much better or worse the economy has been in the past year. The second of these is known as economic prospection, which asks respondents how much better or worse the economy will be in the next year. The third question asks respondents how much better or worse their family's personal financial situation has gotten over the last year. Past research indicates that these are important predictors of presidential vote choice (Markus 1988; Nadeau and Lewis-Beck 2001) and that women are more likely to rely on national economic perceptions, while men are more likely to rely on personal financial perceptions (Chaney, Alvarez, and Nagler 1998; Welch and Hibbing 1992). Finally, I use the scale of the social welfare items in Chapter 6. The social welfare scale is an additive scale of all social welfare items (spending on poor, childcare, public schools, welfare, homeless, food stamps, and Social Security as well as government-guaranteed jobs, government-provided health insurance, and government services), with missing data replaced with the item mean; the scale has a Cronbach's alpha of 0.78 and inter-item covariance of 0.35.

## Party Identification Results

Table 7.1 provides a summary of the results for the party identification analyses. I include in this table how the inclusion of each issue or attitude influences the gender gap in party identification. In addition, I include what the predicted values of men's and women's party identification are when each issue or attitude is included in the model. The gender gap in the baseline model, which includes the control variables listed in the prior paragraph, is sizeable and significant with a $p$-value of 0.000. Women's party identification is significantly different from men's party identification in this baseline model; on the 7-point scale, men's party identification is 4.20 (SE 0.02) compared to women's at 4.50 (SE 0.02).

Each subsequent row of the table summarizes the results when different issues and/or attitudes are included along with the baseline variables. The models are as follows: defense spending and use of military force, environmental spending and environmental regulations, equal role, affirmative action and racial resentment, laws to protect gay men and lesbians against discrimination, LGBTQ open military service and adoption, and social welfare issues. All of these issues are significant predictors, with each having only a slight influence on the size and significance of the

TABLE 7.1. GENDER DIFFERENCES IN PARTY
IDENTIFICATION

| | Men | Women | Gender gap ($p$) | $N$ |
|---|---|---|---|---|
| Baseline model | 4.20 (0.02) | 4.50 (0.02) | 0.000 | 28,866 |
| International force: defense spending and use of military force | 4.08 (0.05) | 4.45 (0.05) | 0.000 | 3,504 |
| Environment: spending and regulations | 4.08 (0.06) | 4.42 (0.06) | 0.000 | 2,116 |
| Women's rights: equal roles for women | 4.15 (0.02) | 4.44 (0.02) | 0.000 | 16,984 |
| Racial attitudes: affirmative action and racial resentment | 4.19 (0.02) | 4.48 (0.02) | 0.000 | 15,994 |
| Gay rights: discrimination laws, military service, and adoption | 4.32 (0.03) | 4.50 (0.03) | 0.000 | 8,904 |
| Social welfare scale | 4.26 (0.02) | 4.44 (0.02) | 0.000 | 28,201 |
| Pro-social values: egalitarianism | 4.22 (0.02) | 4.43 (0.02) | 0.000 | 23,328 |

Note: Data are from the cumulative 1980–2012 ANES. The scale for the dependent variable is from 1 = Strong Republican to 7 = Strong Democrat; OLS regression is used. The marginal values are calculated including the following variables in the model: age, education, income, no income response, race, church attendance, Catholic identification, Protestant identification, region, and Republican presidential administration.

gender gap in party identification. For the most part, the gender gap is highly significant and about the same size when each of the issues is included as a predictor.

The mediation results also show that these issues do not mediate much of the gender gap in party identification. The percent mediated for defense spending is 16.09 percent, while it is only 3.22 percent for the use of force. The percent mediated for spending to protect the environment is 6.06 percent, and the percent mediated for regulations to protect the environment is 23.81 percent. For the equal rights measures, women's equal role mediates only 0.36 percent of the effect of gender, while affirmative action and racial resentment mediate 6.28 percent and 12.98 percent, respectively. Support for laws to prevent discrimination against gay men and lesbians mediates 15.41 percent, support for open military service mediates 36.08 percent, and support for adoption mediates 19.45 percent. Given that the indicator of statistical significance, the $p$-value, does not change, some of these percent-mediated results may be surprising. As shown in Table 7.1, the gender gap is 0.30-point difference, with men at a 4.20 and women at a 4.50 on the 7-point scale. When all three of the gay rights measures are included, the gender gap is 0.18 compared to the baseline of 0.30 difference. The percent mediated by the social welfare attitudes scale is 42.11 percent. When the social welfare scale is included, the gap reduced to a 0.18-point difference, with men at 4.26 and women at 4.44. So even though the $p$-value does not change, the gender gap is smaller, and the percent mediated reflects that. Egalitarianism mediates 32.44 percent of the effect of gender, with a 0.21-point difference compared to the baseline 0.30 difference. Not shown in the table, feelings toward feminists mediates 37.79 percent of the gender effect on party identification. Given the smaller number of observations in the feminist feeling thermometer analysis, it is not appropriate to compare the mediation results to the egalitarianism results. Income mediates 8.99 percent and motherhood mediates 13.64 percent of the gender differences in party identification. Employment status and having children each mediate 0 percent of the effect of gender.

Additional results are displayed in Table 7.2. Running separate models for men and women, reveals much similarity in the way these issues and attitudes influence men and women's party identification. The only difference that exists is that the use of military force predicts women's party identification but not men's. Otherwise, the rest of the issues and attitudes significantly predicts both men's and women's party identification. I also ran separate models for whites and blacks. Among whites, all of the issues and attitudes significantly predicted party identification

TABLE 7.2. THE INFLUENCE OF ISSUES AND ATTITUDES ON PARTY IDENTIFICATION

| Model | All | Gender gap ($p$) | Men | Women | Whites | Gender gap ($p$) | Blacks | Gender gap ($p$) |
|---|---|---|---|---|---|---|---|---|
| Baseline | | 0.000 | | | | 0.000 | | 0.000 |
| Defense spending | + | 0.000 | + | + | + | 0.000 | + | 0.000 |
| Use of military | n.s. | | n.s. | − | n.s. | | n.s. | |
| Environmental spending | + | 0.000 | + | + | + | 0.000 | + | 0.000 |
| Environmental regulations | + | | + | + | + | | − | — |
| Equal roles | + | 0.000 | + | + | + | 0.000 | + | 0.008 |
| Affirmative action | + | 0.000 | + | + | + | 0.000 | n.s. | 0.000 |
| Resentment | − | | − | − | − | | − | |
| Laws | + | 0.000 | + | + | + | 0.001 | + | 0.101 |
| Don't ask, don't tell | + | | + | + | + | | + | |
| Adoption | + | | + | + | + | | n.s. | |
| Social welfare scale | + | 0.000 | + | + | + | 0.000 | + | 0.000 |
| Egalitarianism | + | 0.000 | + | + | + | 0.000 | + | 0.000 |

Note: Data are from the cumulative 1980–2012 ANES. The scale for the dependent variable is from 1 = Strong Republican to 7 = Strong Democrat; OLS regression is used. Analysis includes the following variables: age, education, income, no income response, race, church attendance, Catholic identification, Protestant identification, region, and Republican presidential administration. + = positive significance, − = negative significance, n.s. = not significant; an em dash means there were not sufficient data to model.

except for the use of military force. The gender gap in party identification among whites is highly significant, regardless of what
issues or attitudes are included in the models. For black respondents, the use of military force, environmental regulations, affirmative action, and adoption by gay men and lesbians are not
significant predictors of party identification. The rest of the issues and attitudes are significant predictors of party identification
among blacks. The gender gap among black respondents is highly
significant except when the gay rights questions are included in
the model.

To summarize, the results are significant, but none of these
issues alone appear to reduce the gender gap in party identification by much. These issues and attitudes predict partisanship,
but the gender gap remains highly significant with the inclusion
of these different policy positions and attitudes. Environmental
regulations, gay rights, social welfare issues, and egalitarianism
all mediate the gender gap quite a bit, but again the effect of
gender continues to be very significant. These results highlight
the notable political consequences of these issues and pro-social
values. Gender differences in public opinion significantly and
substantially contribute to the gender gap in party identification.

Next I discuss the presidential vote choice results, which provide even stronger support for the hypothesis that these issues
reduce the gender gap in vote choice.

### Presidential Vote Choice Results

Table 7.3 summarizes the presidential vote choice results when
including the different measures of issues and attitudes from each
chapter. This table includes whether an issue was a significant
predictor of vote choice and whether it was a positive or negative
predictor. I also include the significance of the gender gap. I summarize if the issue and/or attitude predicts men's vote choice, if
it predicts women's vote choice, and if it is a positive or negative
predictor. Finally, I summarize the influence of each issue and/or

TABLE 7.3. GENDER DIFFERENCES IN VOTE CHOICE

| | Men | Women | Gender gap ($p$) | $N$ |
|---|---|---|---|---|
| Baseline model | 0.52 (0.01) | 0.58 (0.01) | 0.000 | 11,684 |
| International force: defense spending and use of military force | 0.43 (0.02) | 0.52 (0.02) | 0.004 | 2,419 |
| Environment: spending and regulations | 0.47 (0.03) | 0.58 (0.03) | 0.009 | 1,428 |
| Women's rights: equal roles for women | 0.43 (0.01) | 0.49 (0.01) | 0.005 | 6,568 |
| Racial attitudes: affirmative action and racial resentment | 0.59 (0.01) | 0.64 (0.01) | 0.006 | 7,821 |
| Gay rights: discrimination laws, military service, and adoption | 0.58 (0.02) | 0.58 (0.02) | 0.782 | 5,653 |
| Social welfare scale | 0.54 (0.01) | 0.57 (0.01) | 0.045 | 11,682 |
| Pro-social values: egalitarianism | 0.53 (0.01) | 0.58 (0.01) | 0.005 | 11,656 |

Note: Data are from the cumulative 1980–2012 ANES. Coding for the dependent variable is 1 = voted for Democratic Party presidential nominee and 0 = otherwise; logistic regression is used. The marginal values are calculated including the following variables in the model: age, education, income, no income response, race, church attendance, Catholic identification, Protestant identification, region, Republican presidential administration, party identification, national economy retrospection, national economy prospection, and personal financial situation retrospection.

attitude on the vote choice of whites and blacks as well as the significance of the gender gap for each model. The gender gap in the baseline model, which includes the control variables listed previously, is sizeable and significant with a $p$-value of 0.000. Women are significantly more likely to vote for the Democratic presidential candidate, with a probability of 0.58 (SE 0.01) versus men's predicted probability of 0.52 (SE 0.01). In analysis not shown of the baseline model, the gender gap in voting is significant among pre–baby boomers and baby boomers but not among post–baby

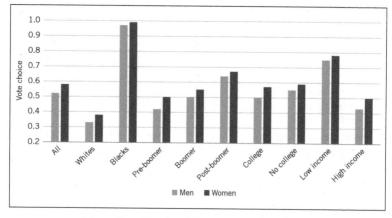

Figure 7.1. Gender differences in vote choice
across demographic subgroups

Note: Data are from cumulative 1980–2012 ANES. 1 = Democratic
presidential candidate; 0 = otherwise. Analysis controls for demographic
variables are set at their mean.

boomers. The gender gap is significant for both education levels, but only for those with above-median income, not those with below-median income. Racial differences are discussed at length in a few paragraphs; the gender gap in vote choice is significant among whites and blacks.

The gender gaps within each group are displayed in Figure 7.1. As is quite noticeable, the differences between subgroups of women are often larger than the gender gaps within a particular group. For example, blacks are much more likely to vote for a Democratic presidential candidate than whites. Another example is that individuals with lower incomes are much more likely to vote for Democratic presidential candidates compared to individuals with higher incomes. In other words, not all women have the same likelihood of voting for the Democratic Party's presidential nominee. Other group memberships exert a strong influence on vote choice as well. Across almost every subgroup, women are consistently more likely to vote for the Democratic presidential nominee.

Next I focus on the significance of each issue. The use of military force is not a significant predictor of vote choice. It is likely, however, that in individual years, when the use of military force is salient and not abstract, but specific to a particular conflict, it would be a significant predictor of presidential vote choice. Supporting an increase in defense spending makes one less likely to vote for the Democratic presidential nominee. Supporting greater spending and increased regulations to protect the environment leads to a greater likelihood of voting for the Democratic presidential candidate. Believing in equal gender roles leads to a greater likelihood of voting for the Democratic candidate. Supporting affirmative action predicts voting for the Democratic candidate, while holding racially resentful attitudes makes one less likely to vote for the Democrat. Supporting laws to protect gay men and lesbians against discrimination, supporting openly serving in the military, and supporting the right to adopt predict a greater likelihood to vote for the Democratic nominee. Supporting greater social welfare spending, more government services, government-guaranteed jobs, and government-provided health insurance predicts voting for the Democrat. Finally, the more one endorses egalitarianism, the more one is likely to vote for the Democratic presidential candidate.

Now we turn to the gender gap for each model. For several models, the $p$-value for the gender gap remains highly significant, but mediational analyses reveal that including these issues partially reduces the effect of gender on vote choice. Defense spending mediates 22.36 percent of the gender effect. The use of military force variable, however, does not mediate the gender gap in voting. Spending to protect the environment mediates 14.81 percent, and regulations to protect the environment mediates 20.93 percent of the gender effect. Women's rights issues only mediate 3.6 percent of the gender effect. Affirmative action only mediates 2.53 percent of the gender effect. Racial resentment mediates 18.21 percent of the gender effect. The gay rights issues together eliminate the gender gap ($p = 0.782$), with the discrimination laws mediating 25.47 percent, military service mediating 69.03 percent, and adoption mediating 28.99 percent. The social welfare attitudes scale also substantially reduces the gender gap ($p = 0.045$) and mediates 60.95 percent of the effect of gender on vote choice. The effect of gender on vote choice also reduces when egalitarianism is included in the model ($p = 0.005$) and is mediated by 34.56 percent. Finally, with respect to the other gender gap explanations, only feminism receives support. Warmth toward feminists mediates 41.52 percent of the gender gap in vote choice. Income, employment status, parenthood, and motherhood each mediate 0 percent of the effect of gender on vote choice.

Turning to the separate analyses for men and women with a focus on any differences, men and women mainly rely on the same issues when determining their vote choice. For the most part, women do not appear to largely differ from men in terms of what issues influence their vote choice. Both men and women rely on their attitudes toward environmental regulation, gender equality, racial resentment, gay rights, social welfare programs, and egalitarianism. Only women rely on defense spending and environmental spending attitudes, while only men rely on affirmative action attitudes. The use of military force does not predict the vote choice of men or women. These results are shown in Table 7.4.

Finally, I examine the separate models for whites and blacks. In the baseline model, there is a significant and sizeable gender gap among only whites ($p = 0.001$) and among only blacks ($p = 0.006$). The predicted probabilities reflect the vast racial differences in vote choice. Among whites, the probability of women voting for the Democratic presidential candidate is 0.38 (SE 0.01) and for men is 0.33 (SE 0.01). Among blacks, the probability for women is 0.99 (SE 0.00) and for men is 0.97 (SE 0.01). Use of military force and affirmative action are not significant predictors of vote choice among whites or blacks. Only racial resentment, social welfare attitudes, and egalitarianism predict vote choice

TABLE 7.4. THE INFLUENCE OF ISSUES AND ATTITUDES ON VOTE CHOICE

| Model | All | Gender gap (p) | Men | Women | Gender gap (p) | Whites | Blacks | Gender gap (p) |
|---|---|---|---|---|---|---|---|---|
| Baseline | | 0.000 | | | 0.001 | − | + | 0.006 |
| Defense spending | − | 0.004 | n.s. | − | 0.003 | n.s. | + | 0.017 |
| Use of military | n.s. | | n.s. | n.s. | 0.98 | n.s. | n.s. | 0.017 |
| Environmental spending | + | 0.009 | + | + | | + | + | |
| Environmental regulations | + | | + | + | | + | − | — |
| Equal roles | + | 0.005 | + | + | 0.026 | + | n.s. | 0.019 |
| Affirmative action | + | 0.006 | + | n.s. | 0.026 | n.s. | n.s. | 0.036 |
| Resentment | − | | − | − | | − | — | — |
| Laws | + | 0.782 | + | + | 0.574 | + | n.s. | 0.222 |
| Don't ask, don't tell | + | | + | + | | + | n.s. | |
| Adoption | + | | + | + | | + | n.s. | |
| Social welfare scale | + | 0.045 | + | + | 0.106 | + | + | 0.004 |
| Egalitarianism | + | 0.005 | + | + | 0.036 | + | + | 0.143 |

Note: Data are from the cumulative 1980–2012 ANES. Coding for the dependent variable is 1 = voted for Democratic Party presidential nominee and 0 = otherwise; logistic regression is used. Analysis includes the following variables: age, education, income, no income response, race, church attendance, Catholic identification, Protestant identification, region, Republican presidential administration, party identification, national economy retrospection, national economy prospection, and personal financial situation retrospection. + = positive significance, − = negative significance, n.s. = not significant; an em dash means there were not sufficient data to model.

among blacks; all three also predict vote choice among whites, as do defense spending, environment spending, environment regulations, women's rights, and gay rights. These results are also shown in Table 7.4.

In sum, gender differences in public opinion have important political consequences. Voters in presidential elections rely on these issues and attitudes on which gender gaps arise. The strongest results are for defense spending, environmental regulations, gay rights, and social welfare issues. All four of these issues substantially reduce the gender gap in presidential vote choice with high levels—over 20 percent—of percent mediation. This means that women are more likely to vote for Democratic presidential candidates because of their positions on these public policy issues. The Democratic Party should take note of these findings to continue to benefit from the gender gap in vote choice and emphasize these issues. For example, during the 2020 presidential election, the Democratic Party could emphasize recent increases in defense spending, problems with healthcare, the need for regulations to deal with climate change, and continued discrimination against the LGBTQ community to garner women's votes. On the other hand, the Republican Party may want to consider these findings when thinking about how to court women's votes. Perhaps deemphasizing these issues or proposing more moderate policy solutions could increase the Republican Party's share of women's vote.

A couple of the issues do not appear very important for presidential vote choice, including use of military force, affirmative action, and women's rights. I would suspect that in particular presidential elections when these issues are salient, they do contribute to the gender gap in vote choice. For example, women's rights may have contributed to the gender gap during the War on Women in 2012, during which Democrats argued that state legislation restricting reproductive rights and the push to eliminate the birth control mandate of the Affordable Care Act were part of a conservative legislative agenda to reduce women's rights. This may have been an instance when the issue of gender equality would have contributed the gender gap in vote choice. There is some evidence that these issues influenced women's vote choice more than men's (Deckman and McTague 2015). With respect to military force, women fearing a terrorist attack were more likely to vote for John Kerry, the Democratic Party candidate, than President George W. Bush in the 2004 presidential election (Carroll 2008).

## Summary of Findings from the Previous Chapters

Overall, the findings throughout the book suggest that there are robust gender differences in many important areas of public opinion and that differences in the endorsement of pro-social values between men and women illuminate their existence. For mediation to exist, there must be a gender gap in the mediator. As discussed in Chapter 2, there are sizeable and significant gender differences in egalitarianism, benevolence, and universalism. Women are more likely to be egalitarian, care about the well-being of those close to them, and have concern for the well-being of all. The gender differences in egalitarianism transcend several demographic subgroups, including birth cohort, education level, and income level. Moreover, among whites, women are more likely to endorse egalitarianism as well.

Chapter 3 discusses the prior research establishing the gender gap in support for the use of force. I argue that these gender differences arise because of women's greater propensity toward concern for others. In the data analysis, I find significant gaps on defense spending, the use of military force to solve international crises, and whether war is ever necessary. Women are less likely than men to support increased government spending on defense, to support the use of military force, or to believe that war is ever necessary. I find moderate support for the pro-social values hypothesis. Egalitarianism partially explains gender differences on defense spending, and universalism partially explains gender differences on whether war is ever necessary. Chapter 3 also provides some detracting evidence. Specifically, egalitarianism does not appear to explain much of the gender gap on the use of military force. On the whole, the evidence suggests that pro-social values are an important part of why this gender gap on the use of force exists.

Chapter 4 summarizes the existing research investigating the gender gap on environmental policy preferences and argues that it is a result of women's greater concern for the well-being of others. I find strong support for the values hypothesis. There is a sizeable gender gap on government spending and regulations to protect the environment. The inclusion of egalitarianism fully mediates the gap on spending and substantially mediates the gap on regulations. At the center of these gender differences appears to be women's greater concern for others' well-being.

The focus of Chapter 5 is gender differences in support of equal rights for three historically disadvantaged groups: women, African Americans, and the LGBTQ community. My analysis reveals significant gender differences in support of equal gender roles, affirmative action for blacks, racial resentment toward blacks, laws to protect gay people from discrimination, the rights of gay people to openly serve in the military, and the rights of gay people to adopt children. Generally, the results provide evidence in support of the pro-social values hypothesis. Gender differences in egalitarianism partially or fully mediate each of these opinion and attitudinal gaps. The results are strongest for affirmative action and racial resentment, where the inclusion of egalitarianism appears to fully explain the gender gap. Pro-social values also appear to be part of the reason for women's greater support of equal gender roles and gay rights.

Chapter 6 investigates the gender gap on social welfare issues. This gap is very well established in the literature, with women consistently more supportive of government spending to aid the poor, provide more services, guarantee a minimum standard of living, provide health insurance, fund public schools, and so on. Again, the values explanation contends that this gap can be better understood as resulting from women's caring and concern for others. I find significant and sizeable gender gaps on all of the social welfare policies asked about in the data. My analysis provides a great deal of support for the pro-social values hypothesis. Egalitarianism and universalism explain a substantial percentage of the effect of gender across the various social welfare issues that I examine. Women's concern for others appears to drive their support for increased spending for aid to the poor, welfare, public schools, Social Security, the homeless, food stamps, and childcare. Women's desire to help and care for others also appears to explain their greater support for government-guaranteed jobs and a minimum standard of living, government health insurance, government provision of more services, and government reduction of income inequality.

Throughout this book, I discuss how the gender gap often exists within various demographic subgroups, such as race, birth cohort, education level, and income level. It is not always the case that women within each of these subgroups differ from men, but it is true more often than not. It is important to note, however, that often the gender gap is quite small in comparison to differences between these demographic groups. For example, the differences between whites and blacks on several issues and in their endorsement of egalitarianism are very large. I contend that the gender gap remains to be of considerable interest. Women not only make up half of the population but also turn out to vote at higher rates than men (Center for American Women and Politics 2012).

Finally, the analysis firmly establishes that the observed gender differences in public opinion and vote choice are not merely the result of differences in income, educational attainment, or any other demographic factor. Gender gaps in public opinion are significant even with the inclusion of these other factors.

## Implications of Findings

My findings have several implications for understanding gender gaps in public opinion, the gender gap in vote choice, public opinion more generally, and the importance of values. Gender differences in public opinion across seemingly unrelated policy and attitude areas can be better understood via gender differences in concern for others. Gender gaps in public opinion are not merely the result of differences in self-interest or political knowledge. For example, it is not the case that low-income women are behind the gaps in social welfare spending because they benefit from funding social welfare programs. Women are not more supportive of equal rights for women simply out of self-interest either. It is also not the case that uneducated or politically unaware women are causing these gender gaps because they are unknowledgeable about political issues. Rather, women, often regardless of race, birth cohort, education level, and income level, are more likely to oppose military interventions, to oppose defense spending, to support gun control, to support environmental protections, to believe climate change is happening, to support equal rights for women, to support LGBTQ rights, and to prefer more government spending on social welfare programs because of their propensity to think about and have concern for the well-being of other people.

The results for the previously tested explanations indicate a great deal of support for the feminist explanation and more limited support for the other three explanations. Although the measure of feminist identity is imperfect, feelings toward feminists mediates a substantial percentage of the gender gap across most of the policy positions investigated throughout the book as well as party identification and vote choice. The feminist explanation deserves further investigation, particularly with a measure of actual feminist identity rather than the feeling thermometer measure. The economically marginalized explanation receives less support with low income mediating a moderate percentage of the gender effect on environmental spending, affirmative action, childcare spending, spending to aid the poor, and welfare spending attitudes. The economic autonomy explanation receives the least amount of support; employment only moderately mediates welfare spending attitudes. Finally, the social role theory and motherhood explanation receives a moderate level of support; motherhood substantially mediates attitudes toward defense spending, childcare spending, Social Security spending, spending to aid the poor, welfare spending, and party identification. In addition, the tests of the social role theory and motherhood explanation demonstrate that parenthood and motherhood have differential effects on policy positions. Mainly, parenthood rarely mediated the gender gap on any policy areas, and motherhood mediated certain gaps.

As noted in Chapter 3, sample sizes differ quite a bit depending on which variables are included in the models. Thus, the number of observations for the feminist analysis is much smaller than the values analysis. Because of this difference in sample size, the feminist identity mediation results might be so strong compared to the other explanations simply because of the smaller number of observations and not because it is a better mediator. Directly comparing the mediation results should be done with caution. The values explanation and feminist identity explanation perform the best throughout the results; it is not entirely fair, however, to directly compare the mediation results for the values to the feminist feeling thermometer because of the differences in sample sizes.

Moreover, gender differences in party identification and presidential vote choice are tied to these differences in public opinion, meaning that these gender gaps are politically consequential. Support for environmental regulations, LGBTQ rights, and social welfare spending is predictive of party identification and substantially mediates the gender gap in party identification. In other words, part of the reason why women are more likely to identify as Democrats compared to men is because of their positions on environmental, gay rights, and social welfare policies. With respect to vote choice, women, who are against the use of force, are more likely to vote Democrat, as are those who want more environmental protections, equal rights, and social welfare programs. This does not mean that all women identify as Democrats or vote for the Democratic presidential candidate. It also does not mean that women holding these opinions will always favor the Democratic presidential candidate. It likely depends on the individuating characteristics of the candidates and on the salience of particular issues during an election.

My results also indicate the need to incorporate values into investigations of public opinion more broadly. Earlier research in social psychology on values often focused on providing an exhaustive list of values that people hold and establishing which core values are universal. More-recent research has investigated the predictive power and consequences of values, but political scientists, in particular public opinion scholars in the American context, have regularly failed to incorporate values into their research. Values not only govern our individual behavior and relationships but also influence our perspective on government policy and group attitudes. My results suggest that egalitarianism in particular is at the center of how Americans think about public policies, and it influences party identification and presidential vote choice.

## Future Research

My results raise many questions and possibilities for future research. First, there are issue areas that I do not investigate or do not have the best measures of to examine. For example, I do not analyze gender differences on morality issues, such as legality of drugs and abortion. There is evidence that women may be more conservative than men on morality issues, largely because of their higher levels of religiosity (Eagly et al. 2004; Elder and Greene 2019; Lizotte 2015). It is possible that gender differences on morality issues can also be better understood by theorizing and investigating how values play a part in these attitudes. I am unable to investigate the gender gap on police brutality, though the pro-social values explanation would predict that it would also substantially mediate these gender gaps. The cumulative data do not include measures of support for specific military interventions. The pro-social values theory would expect that values would partially mediate gender differences in specific instances of international use of force.

Second, more work is needed to understand the intersection of race and gender with respect to public opinion. For example, gender gaps were not always significant among African Americans in the analysis. This may be a result of smaller sample sizes, or it could be because black men and black women simply have the same levels of support for various public policies. In addition, the pro-social values explanation may not explain any gender differences in public opinion that do exist among African Americans, seeing how men had higher average egalitarianism scores than women. It is also possible that pro-social values would still shed light on any differences but that other measures of pro-social values would be better.

This brings me to a third area for future research: better and more diverse measures of pro-social values, as well as better measures of the other explanations. In particular, it would be vastly superior to have a more direct measure of concern for others, such as humanitarianism. Including measures of the Schwartz value types in more public opinion data sets would also be valuable. It would be beneficial to extend the analysis done here on benevolence and universalism to other issues not included in the 2011 World Values Survey. Perhaps this would lead to even stronger mediation results. It would also be great to have a measure such as individualism to get at concern for oneself and support for self-reliance rather than help from government or other people. Having a measure of individualism would also allow for testing whether men's opinions are driven more by individualism and whether women's opinions are compelled more by concern for others. Having a more direct measure of feminist identity would be better than using the feeling thermometer rating of feminists. Other measures of the economic explanations may also lend more support to these theories of the gender gap. For example, knowing the specifics of receipt of government aid or services would be better than simply using income, or using a different measure of economic independence would be better than knowing whether a woman is employed outside of the home.

Future work should also investigate the origins of values differences. As mentioned in Chapter 2, cross-sectional data is not suited to answer if values differences arise because of gender socialization. As social roles change, with fathers becoming more hands-on caregivers to children, and possibly socialization practices changing, with girls and boys being encouraged to pursue activities such as athletics and careers once considered suitable for only one gender or the other, values differences might reduce considerably in the future. And in turn, many of the gender gaps in policy positions may decrease.

Last, as new public policy issues arise, such as the Syrian refugee crisis, the Russian interference into American elections, the 2017 travel ban, voter suppression, the border wall, the treatment of undocumented immigrants, including the separation of children from their parents, and the extension of school choice to include religious schools, or as different issues become salient, such as sexual harassment or transgender rights, continued investigation of the existence of gender gaps on these issues and testing of the prosocial values hypothesis is necessary to understand its usefulness, its strength, and its limitations. On some of these issues, it is likely that there would be significant gender differences and that prosocial values would help to explain these gender differences. For example, the values explanations would predict that women are more likely to oppose the travel ban for individuals coming from some Muslim majority countries and that pro-social values would account for these differences. This would be because women would be more likely to think about the adverse effects of such a ban for some people and have concern for those potentially negatively affected, and would thus be more likely to oppose the travel ban.

## Conclusion

The gender gap in vote choice has been of considerable interest since its emergence, and because of the differences in vote choice, the gender gap in public opinion has garnered attention from scholars, the media, and the public. The election of President Donald Trump seems to have caused a resurgence in activism among women voters. In turn, this renaissance in political engagement among women generates a renewed interest in the gender gaps in vote choice, party identification, and public opinion. The negative reactions to women's increased activism, as noted at the outset of Chapter 1, do not appear to have diminished women's resolve. Congress members complaining about women increasingly voicing their concerns, as Representative Dave Brat from Virginia did, has not caused women to recede. Referring to women as "vagina screechers" and calling for doing away with women's suffrage, as school board member Dathan Paterno did, has not discouraged women activists. Instead, women's engagement keeps "stirring," as Sojourner Truth encouraged. The results discussed throughout this book indicate that women, regardless of birth cohort, race, education level, and income, differ on a vast number of issue areas. This suggests that it is not just the women attending marches and calling their Congress members who want more government services for those in need, more government protections for historically marginalized groups, more government regulations to protect the environment, and less governmental use of force. Rather, a significant proportion of women favor liberal policies and do so largely because of their endorsement of pro-social values.

Furthermore, the quotations from women marchers at the outset of Chapter 2 about caring about others and believing in equality illustrate some of the reasons for the revival of women's political involvement. The analysis throughout the book also points to how caring about other people and wanting equal treatment for all is at the heart of women's opinions on several political issues, as well as a major cause of gender differences on these issues. Regarding the use of force and women-led peace movements, First Lady Jacqueline Kennedy noted women's pervasive concern for the welfare of other people, as quoted in Chapter 3. Women's activism with respect to force issues mirrors the attitudes of a large portion of American women. As the results in Chapter 3 demonstrate, women are much more likely to have liberal positions on the use of international force, gun control, and the death penalty partially because of their pro-social values. As discussed in Chapter 4, this concern for others is evident in the environmental activism of Lois Gibbs and more recently Leanne Walters, who were both concerned with the impact of environmental hazards on the well-being of their family members and their community members. The results show that women are more supportive of government action to protect the environment because of their greater commitment to the well-being of other people. In Chapter 5, women marchers are quoted, noting their participation is driven by support for gender equality, racial equality, and equal rights for the LGBTQ community. These quotations parallel the findings in this chapter, which illustrate that American women are significantly more supportive of government protections for these historically disadvantaged groups because of a strong belief in equality. Unlike Utah Senator Orrin Hatch, who is quoted in Chapter 6 stating his opposition to many forms of government assistance, women activists have been very vocal in their fight to keep the Affordable Care Act intact, as well as in their desire to maintain funding for welfare and food stamps. Women in the electorate echo these sentiments in that they are much more likely than men to support social welfare spending and programs largely because of their greater endorsement of pro-social values.

At the outset of this chapter, Savannah Pearlman is quoted stating that the Women's March of 2018 was about more than just a single event but rather "pushing that one-time event into a long-lasting movement that's going to carry us through, really, the next four years but especially the midterm elections in 2018" (Bongiovanni 2018). In addition, the importance of voting is underlined by the words and actions of Suffragists such as Sojourner Truth, Elizabeth Cady Stanton, and Lucretia Mott. As shown in the analysis in this chapter, public opinion differences between men and women are connected to gender differences in party identification and vote choice. Women's recent activism has gotten much attention, and this activism corresponds to the attitudes and policy positions of women in the electorate. And women's greater endorsement of pro-social values is one of the chief reasons for these attitudinal and policy differences.

In conclusion, gender differences in public opinion are substantial and of considerable interest to pollsters and political scientists alike. Even though there may be much to divide women of different backgrounds, there are consistent and significant gender gaps on many areas of public opinion. During a time of what appears to be increased political activism among women, gender differences in public opinion are particularly relevant and worthy of study. The analysis in this book demonstrates that differences between men and women in the endorsement of pro-social values are clearly an important reason as to why these gaps in opinion exist. Women's concern and caring for others leads them to be more likely to oppose the use of force, to support environmental protections, to support equal rights for disadvantaged groups, and to support social welfare programs. The analysis also shows that these gaps in opinion are politically consequential. Gender differences on policy preferences and political attitudes predict vote choice and contribute to the gender gap in party identification and voting, leading women to be more likely to vote for the Democratic presidential candidate. Scholars, the media, and politicians should not only take note of women's recent political activism but also understand that such activism reflects a larger phenomenon among women in the electorate regarding a greater concern for others and how this influences women's public opinion and political behavior.

# Appendix

TABLE A3.1. EXPLANATIONS FOR ATTITUDES ON DEFENSE SPENDING
AND USE OF FORCE

| | Defense 1 | Defense 2 | Defense 3 | Force 1 | Force 2 | Force 3 |
|---|---|---|---|---|---|---|
| Female | -0.131 | -0.219 | -0.169 | -0.082 | -0.127 | -0.192 |
| | (0.030)*** | (0.021)*** | (0.030)*** | (0.037)** | (0.024)*** | (0.044)*** |
| White | 0.141 | 0.234 | 0.285 | -0.027 | -0.059 | -0.033 |
| | (0.034)*** | (0.025)*** | (0.028)*** | (0.047) | (0.029)** | (0.042) |
| Church | 0.047 | 0.035 | 0.033 | 0.003 | 0.016 | 0.017 |
| | (0.010)*** | (0.007)*** | (0.008)*** | (0.013) | (0.008)** | (0.012) |
| Age | 0.006 | 0.004 | 0.005 | 0.000 | -0.001 | 0.001 |
| | (0.001)*** | (0.001)*** | (0.001)*** | (0.001) | (0.001) | (0.001) |
| Low income | -0.088 | -0.132 | -0.116 | -0.071 | -0.026 | -0.049 |
| | (0.034)** | (0.025)*** | (0.028)*** | (0.044) | (0.028) | (0.041) |
| College | -0.462 | -0.478 | -0.501 | -0.184 | -0.182 | -0.214 |
| | (0.033)*** | (0.025)*** | (0.028)*** | (0.043)*** | (0.028)*** | (0.040)*** |
| South | 0.292 | 0.337 | 0.332 | 0.129 | 0.086 | 0.101 |
| | (0.032)*** | (0.023)*** | (0.026)*** | (0.040)*** | (0.025)*** | (0.037)*** |

| | (1) | (2) | (3) | (4) | (5) | (6) |
|---|---|---|---|---|---|---|
| Protestant | 0.275 | 0.304 | 0.322 | 0.170 | 0.097 | 0.101 |
| | (0.040)*** | (0.030)*** | (0.034)*** | (0.055)*** | (0.036)*** | (0.052)** |
| Catholic | 0.285 | 0.229 | 0.242 | 0.164 | 0.104 | 0.093 |
| | (0.044)*** | (0.033)*** | (0.038)*** | (0.062)*** | (0.040)*** | (0.057) |
| Republican administration | -0.282 | -0.147 | -0.197 | | -0.123 | -0.156 |
| | (0.032)*** | (0.022)*** | (0.028)*** | | (0.023)*** | (0.035)*** |
| Feminist | -0.008 | | | -0.002 | | |
| | (0.001)*** | | | (0.001)*** | | |
| Employed | | -0.013 | | | 0.021 | |
| | | (0.025) | | | (0.028) | |
| Children | | | 0.156 | | | -0.004 |
| | | | (0.037)*** | | | (0.056) |
| Mother | | | -0.136 | | | 0.053 |
| | | | (0.049)*** | | | (0.073) |
| N | 10,201 | 22,432 | 17,784 | 1,997 | 5,251 | 2,638 |

Note: Data are from the 1980–2012 ANES. Positive coefficients indicate support for increased defense spending and support for using force. To retain respondents, the analysis also includes an income variable (not shown): 1 if people refused to answer and 0 otherwise.

* $p < .10$; ** $p < .05$; *** $p < .01$

## TABLE A3.2. EXPLANATIONS FOR ATTITUDES ON GUN CONTROL AND DEATH PENALTY

| | Gun 1 | Gun 2 | Gun 3 | Death 1 | Death 2 | Death 3 |
|---|---|---|---|---|---|---|
| Female | 0.421 | 0.565 | 0.640 | -0.164 | -0.298 | -0.313 |
| | (0.077)*** | (0.067)*** | (0.082)*** | (0.069)** | (0.062)*** | (0.076)*** |
| White | -0.615 | -0.860 | -0.870 | 0.473 | 0.625 | 0.635 |
| | (0.090)*** | (0.079)*** | (0.079)*** | (0.078)*** | (0.070)*** | (0.070)*** |
| Church | -0.062 | -0.124 | -0.121 | -0.009 | 0.039 | 0.038 |
| | (0.021)*** | (0.018)*** | (0.018)*** | (0.019) | (0.017)** | (0.017)** |
| Age | 0.004 | 0.007 | 0.005 | 0.006 | 0.005 | 0.005 |
| | (0.002)** | (0.002)*** | (0.002)** | (0.002)*** | (0.002)*** | (0.002)** |
| Low income | -0.239 | -0.177 | -0.197 | -0.178 | -0.129 | -0.139 |
| | (0.082)*** | (0.073)** | (0.073)*** | (0.074)** | (0.068)** | (0.068)** |
| College | 0.095 | 0.137 | 0.138 | -0.148 | -0.173 | -0.167 |
| | (0.018)*** | (0.016)*** | (0.015)*** | (0.016)*** | (0.015)*** | (0.015)*** |
| South | -0.321 | -0.321 | -0.322 | 0.019 | 0.027 | 0.030 |
| | (0.103)*** | (0.090)*** | (0.090)*** | (0.093) | (0.084) | (0.084) |

| | (1) | (2) | (3) | (4) | (5) | (6) |
|---|---|---|---|---|---|---|
| Protestant | 0.078 | 0.159 | 0.154 | -0.156 | -0.260 | -0.265 |
| | (0.240) | (0.210) | (0.210) | (0.211) | (0.194) | (0.194) |
| Catholic | 0.225 | 0.306 | 0.301 | -0.191 | -0.199 | -0.207 |
| | (0.111)** | (0.097)*** | (0.097)*** | (0.098)** | (0.089)** | (0.089)** |
| Feminist | 0.028 | | | -0.018 | | |
| | (0.002)*** | | | (0.001)*** | | |
| Employed | 0.065 | | | | 0.181 | |
| | (0.076) | | | | (0.071)** | |
| Children | | -0.058 | -0.058 | | | 0.160 |
| | | (0.107) | (0.107) | | | (0.102) |
| Mother | | -0.209 | -0.209 | | | -0.021 |
| | | (0.140) | (0.140) | | | (0.131) |
| N | 3,386 | 4,019 | 4,018 | 3,339 | 3,964 | 3,963 |

Note: Data are from the 2016 ANES. Positive coefficients indicate support for increased gun control and support for the death penalty. To retain respondents, the analysis also includes an income variable (not shown): 1 if people refused to answer and 0 otherwise.

* $p < .10$; ** $p < .05$; *** $p < .01$

## TABLE A4.1. EXPLANATIONS FOR ATTITUDES ON ENVIRONMENTAL SPENDING AND REGULATIONS

| | Spending 1 | Spending 2 | Spending 3 | Regulations 1 | Regulations 2 | Regulations 3 |
|---|---|---|---|---|---|---|
| Female | 0.061 | 0.068 | 0.062 | 0.373 | 0.379 | 0.262 |
| | (0.038) | (0.027)** | (0.039) | (0.126)*** | (0.059)*** | (0.113)** |
| White | −0.442 | −0.505 | −0.608 | −0.115 | −0.343 | −0.402 |
| | (0.043)*** | (0.031)*** | (0.036)*** | (0.157) | (0.073)*** | (0.115)*** |
| Church | −0.062 | −0.089 | −0.084 | −0.020 | −0.089 | −0.098 |
| | (0.013)*** | (0.009)*** | (0.010)*** | (0.046) | (0.021)*** | (0.032)*** |
| Age | −0.011 | −0.009 | −0.011 | −0.014 | −0.012 | −0.012 |
| | (0.001)*** | (0.001)*** | (0.001)*** | (0.004)*** | (0.002)*** | (0.003)*** |
| Low income | 0.241 | 0.221 | 0.165 | 0.146 | 0.057 | 0.074 |
| | (0.043)*** | (0.031)*** | (0.035)*** | (0.148) | (0.071) | (0.107) |
| College | 0.072 | 0.167 | 0.193 | 0.039 | 0.009 | 0.046 |
| | (0.043)** | (0.032)*** | (0.037)*** | (0.136) | (0.065) | (0.102) |
| South | −0.084 | −0.095 | −0.136 | −0.004 | 0.048 | 0.008 |
| | (0.040)** | (0.028)*** | (0.033)*** | (0.141) | (0.063) | (0.098) |
| Protestant | −0.047 | −0.135 | −0.120 | −0.369 | −0.203 | −0.063 |
| | (0.050) | (0.037)*** | (0.044)*** | (0.193)** | (0.088)** | (0.137) |

| | (1) | (2) | (3) | (4) | (5) | (6) |
|---|---|---|---|---|---|---|
| Catholic | 0.085 | 0.039 | 0.021 | −0.082 | −0.037 | −0.097 |
| | (0.055) | (0.042) | (0.048) | (0.203) | (0.095) | (0.147) |
| Republican administration | 0.880 | 0.632 | 0.728 | | | |
| | (0.040)*** | (0.027)*** | (0.035)*** | | | |
| Feminist | 0.022 | | | 0.018 | | |
| | (0.001)*** | | | (0.003)*** | | |
| Employed | | 0.007 | | | 0.008 | |
| | | (0.031) | | | (0.069) | |
| Children | | | −0.166 | | | 0.044 |
| | | | (0.049)*** | | | (0.150) |
| Mother | | | −0.006 | | | 0.092 |
| | | | (0.063) | | | (0.196) |
| N | 11,994 | 22,874 | 16,905 | 669 | 3,191 | 1,302 |

Note: Data are from the 1980–2012 ANES. Positive coefficients indicate support for spending and regulations to protect the environment. To retain respondents, the analysis also includes an income variable (not shown): 1 if people refused to answer and 0 otherwise.

* $p < .10$; ** $p < .05$; *** $p < .01$

## TABLE A4.2. EXPLANATIONS FOR ATTITUDES ON CLIMATE CHANGE

|  | Climate 1 | Climate 2 | Climate 3 |
|---|---|---|---|
| Female | 0.141 | 0.230 | 0.231 |
|  | (0.068)** | (0.061)*** | (0.074)*** |
| White | −0.062 | −0.213 | −0.218 |
|  | (0.079) | (0.070)*** | (0.070)*** |
| Church | −0.125 | −0.170 | −0.168 |
|  | (0.018)*** | (0.016)*** | (0.017)*** |
| Age | −0.015 | −0.010 | −0.012 |
|  | (0.002)*** | (0.002)*** | (0.002)*** |
| Low income | 0.016 | 0.048 | 0.032 |
|  | (0.072) | (0.066) | (0.066) |
| College | −0.067 | −0.135 | −0.133 |
|  | (0.226) | (0.191) | (0.191) |
| South | 0.085 | 0.113 | 0.115 |
|  | (0.016)*** | (0.014)*** | (0.014)*** |
| Protestant | −0.197 | −0.233 | −0.233 |
|  | (0.091)** | (0.082)*** | (0.082)*** |
| Catholic | 0.170 | 0.145 | 0.139 |
|  | (0.209) | (0.190) | (0.190) |
| Republican administration | −0.095 | −0.039 | −0.044 |
|  | (0.096) | (0.087) | (0.087) |
| Feminist | 0.019 |  |  |
|  | (0.001)*** |  |  |
| Employed |  | 0.066 |  |
|  |  | (0.069) |  |
| Children |  |  | −0.089 |
|  |  |  | (0.099) |
| Mother |  |  | −0.005 |
|  |  |  | (0.128) |
| N | 3,388 | 4,019 | 4,018 |

Note: Data are from the 2016 ANES. Positive coefficients indicate greater belief that human beings are a major cause of climate change.

$^*p < .10;$ $^{**}p < .05;$ $^{***}p < .01$

## TABLE A5.1. EXPLANATIONS FOR ATTITUDES ON EQUAL ROLES AND AFFIRMATIVE ACTION

| | Equal Role 1 | Equal Role 2 | Equal Role 3 | Affirmative 1 | Affirmative 2 | Affirmative 3 |
|---|---|---|---|---|---|---|
| Female | 0.184 | 0.190 | 0.127 | -0.078 | 0.054 | 0.040 |
| | (0.040)*** | (0.027)*** | (0.041)*** | (0.053) | (0.041) | (0.060) |
| White | -0.014 | -0.224 | -0.296 | -1.500 | -1.671 | -1.644 |
| | (0.047) | (0.032)*** | (0.039)*** | (0.054)*** | (0.042)*** | (0.050)*** |
| Church | -0.130 | -0.173 | -0.163 | 0.040 | -0.000 | 0.019 |
| | (0.014)*** | (0.009)*** | (0.011)*** | (0.018)** | (0.014) | (0.016) |
| Age | -0.013 | -0.010 | -0.015 | -0.003 | -0.003 | -0.003 |
| | (0.001)*** | (0.001)*** | (0.001)*** | (0.002)** | (0.001)** | (0.002)** |
| Low income | -0.165 | -0.161 | -0.289 | 0.606 | 0.603 | 0.582 |
| | (0.046)*** | (0.031)*** | (0.037)*** | (0.056)*** | (0.046)*** | (0.052)*** |
| College | 0.371 | 0.547 | 0.570 | 0.179 | 0.307 | 0.267 |
| | (0.046)*** | (0.032)*** | (0.039)*** | (0.061)*** | (0.049)*** | (0.057)*** |
| South | -0.013 | -0.053 | -0.049 | 0.064 | 0.055 | 0.038 |
| | (0.043) | (0.028)** | (0.034) | (0.054) | (0.042) | (0.049) |

(continued)

## TABLE A5.1 (CONTINUED)

| | Equal Role 1 | Equal Role 2 | Equal Role 3 | Affirmative 1 | Affirmative 2 | Affirmative 3 |
|---|---|---|---|---|---|---|
| Protestant | -0.150 | -0.204 | -0.216 | -0.060 | -0.062 | -0.026 |
| | (0.062)** | (0.042)*** | (0.052)*** | (0.067) | (0.055) | (0.063) |
| Catholic | 0.041 | 0.058 | 0.036 | -0.438 | -0.322 | -0.336 |
| | (0.068) | (0.046) | (0.057) | (0.076)*** | (0.062)*** | (0.071)*** |
| Republican administration | -0.216 | -0.243 | -0.361 | -0.046 | 0.208 | 0.125 |
| | (0.059)*** | (0.028)*** | (0.047)*** | (0.054) | (0.042)*** | (0.049)** |
| Feminist | 0.016 | | | 0.019 | | |
| | (0.001)*** | | | (0.001)*** | | |
| Employed | | 0.254 | | | -0.148 | |
| | | (0.031)*** | | | (0.046)*** | |
| Children | | | -0.277 | | | -0.169 |
| | | | (0.051)*** | | | (0.078)** |
| Mother | | | 0.095 | | | 0.084 |
| | | | (0.066) | | | (0.100) |
| N | 6,128 | 17,089 | 12,026 | 10,961 | 17,702 | 12,217 |

Note: Data are from the 1980–2012 ANES. Positive coefficients indicate greater support for equal roles and affirmative action policies. The analysis includes an income variable (not shown): 1 if people refused to answer and 0 otherwise.

* $p < .10$; ** $p < .05$; *** $p < .01$

## TABLE A5.2. EXPLANATIONS FOR RACIAL RESENTMENT AND ATTITUDES ON LAWS TO PROTECT LGBTQ

| | Resentment 1 | Resentment 2 | Resentment 3 | Laws 1 | Laws 2 | Laws 3 |
|---|---|---|---|---|---|---|
| Female | −0.035 | −0.082 | −0.085 | 0.481 | 0.538 | 0.503 |
| | (0.016)** | (0.014)*** | (0.020)*** | (0.047)*** | (0.041)*** | (0.062)*** |
| White | 0.491 | 0.586 | 0.612 | −0.234 | −0.381 | −0.350 |
| | (0.018)*** | (0.015)*** | (0.017)*** | (0.053)*** | (0.046)*** | (0.054)*** |
| Church | −0.012 | 0.004 | 0.000 | −0.153 | −0.175 | −0.187 |
| | (0.005)** | (0.005) | (0.005) | (0.016)*** | (0.014)*** | (0.017)*** |
| Age | 0.002 | 0.002 | 0.002 | −0.003 | −0.000 | −0.006 |
| | (0.000)*** | (0.000)*** | (0.001)*** | (0.001)** | (0.001) | (0.002)*** |
| Low income | −0.076 | −0.076 | −0.061 | −0.177 | −0.093 | −0.149 |
| | (0.018)*** | (0.016)*** | (0.018)*** | (0.052)*** | (0.047)** | (0.055)*** |
| College | −0.456 | −0.494 | −0.470 | 0.539 | 0.530 | 0.572 |
| | (0.018)*** | (0.016)*** | (0.018)*** | (0.055)*** | (0.049)*** | (0.060)*** |
| South | 0.172 | 0.171 | 0.163 | −0.134 | −0.163 | −0.205 |
| | (0.017)*** | (0.014)*** | (0.017)*** | (0.048)*** | (0.042)*** | (0.051)*** |

*(continued)*

## TABLE A5.2 (CONTINUED)

| | Resentment 1 | Resentment 2 | Resentment 3 | Laws 1 | Laws 2 | Laws 3 |
|---|---|---|---|---|---|---|
| Protestant | 0.043 | 0.047 | 0.051 | −0.463 | −0.455 | −0.319 |
| | (0.021)** | (0.019)** | (0.021)** | (0.066)*** | (0.058)*** | (0.070)*** |
| Catholic | 0.223 | 0.193 | 0.197 | 0.036 | 0.070 | 0.135 |
| | (0.023)*** | (0.021)*** | (0.023)*** | (0.076) | (0.067) | (0.080)** |
| Republican administration | −0.104 | −0.177 | −0.211 | −0.372 | −0.212 | −0.335 |
| | (0.017)*** | (0.014)*** | (0.016)*** | (0.049)*** | (0.041)*** | (0.054)*** |
| Feminist | −0.010 | | | 0.020 | | |
| | (0.000)*** | | | (0.001)*** | | |
| Employed | | 0.044 | | | 0.106 | |
| | | (0.016)*** | | | (0.047)** | |
| Children | | | 0.118 | | | |
| | | | (0.025)*** | | | |
| Mother | | | −0.010 | | | −0.197 |
| | | | (0.033) | | | (0.077)** |
| | | | | | | 0.001 |
| | | | | | | (0.102) |
| N | 13,084 | 18,678 | 14,239 | 10,032 | 12,379 | 8,684 |

Note: Data are from the 1980–2012 ANES. Positive coefficients indicate higher levels of racial resentment and support for legal protections for gay people. The analysis includes an income variable (not shown): 1 if people refused to answer and 0 otherwise.

* $p < .10$; ** $p < .05$; *** $p < .01$

TABLE A5.3. EXPLANATIONS FOR ATTITUDES ON OPEN MILITARY SERVICE
AND ABILITY TO ADOPT

| | DADT 1 | DADT 2 | DADT 3 | Adopt 1 | Adopt 2 | Adopt 3 |
|---|---|---|---|---|---|---|
| Female | 0.756 | 0.828 | 0.770 | 0.469 | 0.585 | 0.601 |
| | (0.044)*** | (0.038)*** | (0.058)*** | (0.044)*** | (0.041)*** | (0.057)*** |
| White | −0.213 | −0.396 | −0.368 | 0.055 | −0.083 | −0.008 |
| | (0.049)*** | (0.042)*** | (0.051)*** | (0.047) | (0.043)** | (0.049) |
| Church | −0.187 | −0.198 | −0.209 | −0.331 | −0.345 | −0.369 |
| | (0.015)*** | (0.013)*** | (0.016)*** | (0.015)*** | (0.014)*** | (0.015)*** |
| Age | −0.006 | −0.003 | −0.004 | −0.018 | −0.015 | −0.020 |
| | (0.001)*** | (0.001)** | (0.002)*** | (0.001)*** | (0.001)*** | (0.002)*** |
| Low income | −0.111 | −0.027 | −0.086 | −0.091 | −0.074 | −0.092 |
| | (0.049)** | (0.043) | (0.053) | (0.048)** | (0.046) | (0.051)** |
| College | 0.450 | 0.470 | 0.406 | 0.674 | 0.705 | 0.660 |
| | (0.050)*** | (0.044)*** | (0.055)*** | (0.050)*** | (0.047)*** | (0.053)*** |
| South | −0.173 | −0.213 | −0.248 | −0.214 | −0.268 | −0.280 |
| | (0.045)*** | (0.039)*** | (0.048)*** | (0.045)*** | (0.042)*** | (0.047)*** |

(continued)

## TABLE A5.3 (CONTINUED)

|  | DADT 1 | DADT 2 | DADT 3 | Adopt 1 | Adopt 2 | Adopt 3 |
|---|---|---|---|---|---|---|
| Protestant | −0.379 | −0.409 | −0.200 | −0.400 | −0.381 | −0.181 |
|  | (0.059)*** | (0.051)*** | (0.063)*** | (0.055)*** | (0.051)*** | (0.058)*** |
| Catholic | −0.043 | −0.024 | 0.053 | 0.048 | 0.109 | 0.260 |
|  | (0.066) | (0.057) | (0.070) | (0.062) | (0.057)** | (0.065)*** |
| Republican administration | −0.606 | −0.327 | −0.420 | −0.797 | −0.640 | −0.663 |
|  | (0.045)*** | (0.037)*** | (0.049)*** | (0.045)*** | (0.041)*** | (0.048)*** |
| Feminist | 0.021 |  |  | 0.022 |  |  |
|  | (0.001)*** |  |  | (0.001)*** |  |  |
| Employed |  | 0.120 |  |  | 0.024 |  |
|  |  | (0.043)*** |  |  | (0.045) |  |
| Children |  |  | −0.112 |  |  | −0.217 |
|  |  |  | (0.074) |  |  | (0.073)*** |
| Mother |  |  | −0.020 |  |  | −0.035 |
|  |  |  | (0.099) |  |  | (0.096) |
| N | 8,647 | 11,151 | 7,212 | 11,095 | 12,362 | 9,582 |

Note: Data are from the 1980–2012 ANES. Positive coefficients indicate support for gay rights and legal protections. To retain respondents, the analysis includes an income variable (not shown): 1 if people refused to answer and 0 otherwise.

* $p < .10$; ** $p < .05$; *** $p < .01$

## TABLE A5.4. EXPLANATIONS FOR SUPPORT FOR MARRIAGE EQUALITY

|  | Marriage 1 | Marriage 2 | Marriage 3 |
|---|---|---|---|
| Female | 0.209 | 0.394 | 0.399 |
|  | (0.077)*** | (0.068)*** | (0.083)*** |
| White | 0.428 | 0.118 | 0.107 |
|  | (0.089)*** | (0.077) | (0.077) |
| Church | −0.422 | −0.446 | −0.444 |
|  | (0.021)*** | (0.019)*** | (0.019)*** |
| Age | −0.021 | −0.018 | −0.019 |
|  | (0.002)*** | (0.002)*** | (0.002)*** |
| Low income | −0.222 | −0.169 | −0.172 |
|  | (0.081)*** | (0.073)** | (0.073)** |
| College | 0.108 | 0.137 | 0.135 |
|  | (0.018)*** | (0.016)*** | (0.015)*** |
| South | −0.417 | −0.455 | −0.455 |
|  | (0.099)*** | (0.087)*** | (0.088)*** |
| Protestant | 0.207 | 0.318 | 0.314 |
|  | (0.225) | (0.201) | (0.201) |
| Catholic | 0.568 | 0.635 | 0.636 |
|  | (0.104)*** | (0.093)*** | (0.093)*** |
| Feminist | 0.026 |  |  |
|  | (0.002)*** |  |  |
| Employed |  | −0.072 |  |
|  |  | (0.077) |  |
| Children |  |  | −0.175 |
|  |  |  | (0.108) |
| Mother |  |  | 0.026 |
|  |  |  | (0.142) |
| N | 3,369 | 3,995 | 3,994 |

Note: Data are from the 2016 ANES. Positive coefficients indicate support for gay rights and legal protections. To retain respondents, the analysis also includes an income variable (not shown): 1 if people refused to answer and 0 otherwise.

* $p < .10$; ** $p < .05$; *** $p < .01$

### TABLE A6.1. EXPLANATIONS FOR ATTITUDES ON CHILDCARE AND PUBLIC SCHOOL SPENDING

| | Childcare 1 | Childcare 2 | Childcare 3 | School 1 | School 2 | School 3 |
|---|---|---|---|---|---|---|
| Female | 0.235 | 0.333 | 0.225 | 0.330 | 0.408 | 0.364 |
| | (0.036)*** | (0.029)*** | (0.041)*** | (0.040)*** | (0.030)*** | (0.042)*** |
| White | −0.663 | −0.764 | −0.906 | −0.687 | −0.827 | −0.880 |
| | (0.041)*** | (0.033)*** | (0.039)*** | (0.048)*** | (0.037)*** | (0.042)*** |
| Church | −0.040 | −0.072 | −0.064 | −0.044 | −0.061 | −0.063 |
| | (0.012)*** | (0.010)*** | (0.011)*** | (0.013)*** | (0.010)*** | (0.012)*** |
| Age | −0.016 | −0.014 | −0.010 | −0.022 | −0.018 | −0.016 |
| | (0.001)*** | (0.001)*** | (0.001)*** | (0.001)*** | (0.001)*** | (0.001)*** |
| Low income | 0.462 | 0.421 | 0.461 | 0.209 | 0.210 | 0.212 |
| | (0.041)*** | (0.033)*** | (0.039)*** | (0.046)*** | (0.035)*** | (0.040)*** |
| College | −0.137 | −0.122 | −0.079 | −0.169 | −0.102 | −0.033 |
| | (0.040)*** | (0.033)*** | (0.039)** | (0.044)*** | (0.034)*** | (0.040) |
| South | −0.027 | −0.038 | −0.055 | 0.126 | 0.132 | 0.105 |
| | (0.038) | (0.030) | (0.036) | (0.042)*** | (0.032)*** | (0.037)*** |

| | | | | | |
|---|---|---|---|---|---|
| Protestant | 0.182 | 0.148 | 0.030 | 0.172 | 0.040 | -0.045 |
| | (0.047)*** | (0.038)*** | (0.045) | (0.053)*** | (0.041) | (0.048) |
| Catholic | 0.105 | 0.176 | 0.056 | 0.049 | 0.003 | -0.067 |
| | (0.052)** | (0.043)*** | (0.050) | (0.058) | (0.046) | (0.052) |
| Republican administration | 0.600 | 0.436 | 0.913 | 0.151 | 0.034 | 0.257 |
| | (0.037)*** | (0.029)*** | (0.036)*** | (0.041)*** | (0.030) | (0.038)*** |
| Feminist | 0.022 | | | 0.022 | | |
| | (0.001)*** | | | (0.001)*** | | |
| Employed | | 0.016 | | | 0.087 | |
| | | (0.033) | | | (0.035)** | |
| Children | | | 0.069 | | | 0.117 |
| | | | (0.054) | | | (0.055)** |
| Mother | | | 0.193 | | | 0.039 |
| | | | (0.071)*** | | | (0.073) |
| N | 12,878 | 20,074 | 14,132 | 13,013 | 22,130 | 16,109 |

Note: Data are from the 1980–2012 ANES. Positive coefficients indicate greater support for social welfare spending. To retain respondents, the analysis also includes an income variable (not shown): 1 if people refused to answer and 0 otherwise.

* p < .10; ** p < .05; *** p < .01

## TABLE A6.2. EXPLANATIONS FOR ATTITUDES ON SOCIAL SECURITY AND AID TO THE POOR

| | SocSec 1 | SocSec 2 | SocSec 3 | Poor 1 | Poor 2 | Poor 3 |
|---|---|---|---|---|---|---|
| Female | 0.382 | 0.448 | 0.352 | 0.254 | 0.341 | 0.289 |
| | (0.037)*** | (0.027)*** | (0.039)*** | (0.039)*** | (0.034)*** | (0.048)*** |
| White | −0.684 | −0.725 | −0.752 | −0.913 | −0.981 | −1.048 |
| | (0.042)*** | (0.032)*** | (0.037)*** | (0.044)*** | (0.038)*** | (0.044)*** |
| Church | −0.056 | −0.063 | −0.067 | −0.010 | −0.041 | −0.029 |
| | (0.012)*** | (0.009)*** | (0.011)*** | (0.013) | (0.011)*** | (0.013)** |
| Age | 0.001 | 0.001 | 0.003 | −0.006 | −0.006 | −0.003 |
| | (0.001) | (0.001) | (0.001)*** | (0.001)*** | (0.001)*** | (0.001)** |
| Low income | 0.319 | 0.330 | 0.296 | 0.604 | 0.570 | 0.651 |
| | (0.042)*** | (0.032)*** | (0.036)*** | (0.044)*** | (0.039)*** | (0.046)*** |
| College | −0.660 | −0.746 | −0.674 | −0.412 | −0.344 | −0.310 |
| | (0.041)*** | (0.031)*** | (0.036)*** | (0.042)*** | (0.038)*** | (0.044)*** |
| South | 0.064 | 0.074 | 0.073 | −0.043 | −0.026 | −0.087 |
| | (0.039)** | (0.029)*** | (0.033)** | (0.041) | (0.035) | (0.042)** |
| Protestant | 0.296 | 0.250 | 0.215 | 0.143 | 0.144 | 0.065 |
| | (0.049)*** | (0.038)*** | (0.044)*** | (0.050)*** | (0.044)*** | (0.051) |

| | (1) | (2) | (3) | (4) | (5) | (6) |
|---|---|---|---|---|---|---|
| Catholic | 0.207 | 0.194 | 0.184 | 0.054 | 0.114 | −0.000 |
| | (0.054)*** | (0.042)*** | (0.048)*** | (0.055) | (0.048)** | (0.056) |
| Republican administration | 0.193 | 0.285 | 0.471 | 0.747 | 0.728 | 0.952 |
| | (0.038)*** | (0.028)*** | (0.035)*** | (0.041)*** | (0.035)*** | (0.043)*** |
| Feminist | 0.010 | | | 0.021 | | |
| | (0.001)*** | | | (0.001)*** | | |
| Employed | 0.093 | | | | −0.079 | |
| | (0.032)*** | | | | (0.039)** | |
| Children | | | 0.044 | | | 0.000 |
| | | | (0.049) | | | (0.064) |
| Mother | | | 0.148 | | | 0.135 |
| | | | (0.065)** | | | (0.084) |
| N | 12,943 | 24,122 | 18,139 | 11,359 | 14,705 | 10,403 |

Note: Data are from the 1980–2012 ANES. Positive coefficients indicate greater support for social welfare spending. To retain respondents, the analysis also includes an income variable (not shown): 1 if people refused to answer and 0 otherwise.

* $p < .10$; ** $p < .05$; *** $p < .01$

TABLE A6.3. EXPLANATIONS FOR ATTITUDES ON WELFARE AND FOOD STAMPS SPENDING

| | Welfare 1 | Welfare 2 | Welfare 3 | SNAP 1 | SNAP 2 | SNAP 3 |
|---|---|---|---|---|---|---|
| Female | 0.159 | 0.255 | 0.248 | 0.199 | 0.205 | 0.055 |
| | (0.037)*** | (0.031)*** | (0.046)*** | (0.057)*** | (0.033)*** | (0.067) |
| White | −0.657 | −0.787 | −0.833 | −0.694 | −0.918 | −0.845 |
| | (0.041)*** | (0.034)*** | (0.041)*** | (0.072)*** | (0.040)*** | (0.070)*** |
| Church | −0.030 | −0.059 | −0.058 | −0.056 | −0.076 | −0.036 |
| | (0.012)** | (0.010)*** | (0.013)*** | (0.020)*** | (0.011)*** | (0.020)** |
| Age | −0.003 | −0.004 | 0.000 | 0.002 | −0.002 | 0.003 |
| | (0.001)** | (0.001)*** | (0.001) | (0.002) | (0.001)** | (0.002) |
| Low income | 0.703 | 0.656 | 0.721 | 0.694 | 0.686 | 0.821 |
| | (0.041)*** | (0.035)*** | (0.043)*** | (0.067)*** | (0.039)*** | (0.067)*** |
| College | 0.053 | 0.140 | 0.097 | 0.164 | 0.140 | 0.123 |
| | (0.041) | (0.035)*** | (0.044)** | (0.066)** | (0.039)*** | (0.070)** |
| South | −0.068 | −0.048 | −0.076 | −0.313 | −0.236 | −0.349 |
| | (0.038)** | (0.032) | (0.039)** | (0.061)*** | (0.035)*** | (0.061)*** |
| Protestant | −0.031 | −0.101 | −0.079 | −0.110 | −0.198 | −0.283 |
| | (0.048) | (0.040)** | (0.049) | (0.090) | (0.052)*** | (0.092)*** |

| | | | | | | |
|---|---|---|---|---|---|---|
| Catholic | −0.164 | −0.168 | −0.163 | −0.168 | −0.189 | −0.328 |
| | (0.053)*** | (0.045)*** | (0.053)*** | (0.098)** | (0.057)*** | (0.101)*** |
| Republican administration | 0.371 | 0.571 | 0.629 | 0.154 | 0.529 | 0.800 |
| | (0.038)*** | (0.032)*** | (0.040)*** | (0.063)** | (0.034)*** | (0.109)*** |
| Feminist | 0.019 | | | 0.013 | | |
| | (0.001)*** | | | (0.001)*** | | |
| Employed | | −0.338 | | | −0.324 | |
| | | (0.035)*** | | | (0.039)*** | |
| Children | | | −0.020 | | | 0.727 |
| | | | (0.062) | | | (0.045)*** |
| Mother | | | 0.099 | | | 0.118 |
| | | | (0.080) | | | (0.082) |
| N | 11,350 | 16,320 | 10,390 | 4,868 | 14,777 | 5,027 |

Note: Data are from the 1980–2012 ANES. Positive coefficients indicate greater support for social welfare spending. To retain respondents, the analysis also includes an income variable (not shown): 1 if people refused to answer and 0 otherwise.

* $p < .10$; ** $p < .05$; *** $p < .01$

## TABLE A6.4. EXPLANATIONS FOR ATTITUDES ON HOMELESS SPENDING AND GOVERNMENT GUARANTEED JOBS

| | Homeless 1 | Homeless 2 | Homeless 3 | Jobs 1 | Jobs 2 | Jobs 3 |
|---|---|---|---|---|---|---|
| Female | 0.578 | 0.556 | 0.535 | 0.219 | 0.309 | 0.262 |
| | (0.078)*** | (0.051)*** | (0.078)*** | (0.034)*** | (0.024)*** | (0.033)*** |
| White | −1.024 | −0.965 | −0.928 | −0.813 | −0.979 | −1.004 |
| | (0.123)*** | (0.071)*** | (0.087)*** | (0.038)*** | (0.027)*** | (0.031)*** |
| Church | −0.025 | −0.038 | −0.042 | −0.027 | −0.039 | −0.037 |
| | (0.027) | (0.017)** | (0.022)** | (0.011)** | (0.008)*** | (0.009)*** |
| Age | −0.013 | −0.012 | −0.006 | −0.007 | −0.009 | −0.007 |
| | (0.002)*** | (0.002)*** | (0.002)*** | (0.001)*** | (0.001)*** | (0.001)*** |
| Low income | 0.461 | 0.432 | 0.578 | 0.479 | 0.477 | 0.537 |
| | (0.098)*** | (0.063)*** | (0.077)*** | (0.038)*** | (0.027)*** | (0.030)*** |
| College | −0.131 | −0.153 | −0.037 | −0.119 | −0.101 | −0.110 |
| | (0.089) | (0.059)*** | (0.074) | (0.038)*** | (0.027)*** | (0.031)*** |
| South | −0.017 | −0.001 | −0.003 | −0.084 | −0.040 | −0.060 |
| | (0.086) | (0.055) | (0.068) | (0.036)** | (0.025) | (0.028)** |

| | | | | | | |
|---|---|---|---|---|---|---|
| Protestant | −0.104 | −0.124 | −0.143 | −0.101 | −0.134 | −0.106 |
| | (0.125) | (0.079) | (0.099) | (0.045)** | (0.033)*** | (0.037)*** |
| Catholic | 0.083 | 0.080 | 0.089 | −0.081 | −0.051 | −0.051 |
| | (0.142) | (0.089) | (0.112) | (0.049)** | (0.037) | (0.041) |
| Republican administration | | 0.520 | 0.277 | −0.027 | 0.088 | 0.018 |
| | | (0.058)*** | (0.116)** | (0.036) | (0.024)*** | (0.029) |
| Feminist | 0.016 | | | 0.014 | | |
| | (0.002)*** | | | (0.001)*** | | |
| Employed | −0.082 | | | | −0.163 | |
| | (0.063) | | | | (0.027)*** | |
| Children | | | 0.145 | | | −0.014 |
| | | | (0.093) | | | (0.042) |
| Mother | | | 0.068 | | | 0.142 |
| | | | (0.128) | | | (0.055)*** |
| N | 3,520 | 7,773 | 5,198 | 10,545 | 23,025 | 18,201 |

Note: Data are from the 1980–2012 ANES. Positive coefficients indicate greater support for social welfare spending. To retain respondents, the analysis also includes an income variable (not shown): 1 if people refused to answer and 0 otherwise.

* $p < .10$; ** $p < .05$; *** $p < .01$

TABLE A6.5. EXPLANATIONS FOR ATTITUDES ON GOVERNMENT
HEALTH INSURANCE AND SERVICES

| | Health 1 | Health 2 | Health 3 | Services 1 | Services 2 | Services 3 |
|---|---|---|---|---|---|---|
| Female | 0.107 | 0.221 | 0.149 | 0.270 | 0.364 | 0.293 |
| | (0.037)*** | (0.031)*** | (0.046)*** | (0.030)*** | (0.021)*** | (0.030)*** |
| White | −0.521 | −0.649 | −0.748 | −0.678 | −0.802 | −0.836 |
| | (0.042)*** | (0.035)*** | (0.041)*** | (0.034)*** | (0.025)*** | (0.028)*** |
| Church | −0.116 | −0.136 | −0.144 | −0.052 | −0.076 | −0.072 |
| | (0.012)*** | (0.010)*** | (0.012)*** | (0.010)*** | (0.007)*** | (0.008)*** |
| Age | −0.003 | −0.003 | −0.001 | −0.006 | −0.006 | −0.005 |
| | (0.001)*** | (0.001)*** | (0.001) | (0.001)*** | (0.001)*** | (0.001)*** |
| Low income | 0.463 | 0.482 | 0.491 | 0.427 | 0.385 | 0.395 |
| | (0.041)*** | (0.036)*** | (0.042)*** | (0.034)*** | (0.025)*** | (0.028)*** |
| College | −0.039 | −0.042 | 0.004 | −0.206 | −0.168 | −0.177 |
| | (0.041) | (0.035) | (0.042) | (0.033)*** | (0.025)*** | (0.028)*** |
| South | −0.113 | −0.086 | −0.125 | −0.098 | −0.082 | −0.093 |
| | (0.039)*** | (0.033)*** | (0.039)*** | (0.032)*** | (0.023)*** | (0.026)*** |

| | (1) | (2) | (3) | (4) | (5) | (6) |
|---|---|---|---|---|---|---|
| Protestant | -0.155 | -0.190 | -0.169 | 0.037 | -0.051 | -0.027 |
| | (0.049)*** | (0.041)*** | (0.049)*** | (0.039) | (0.030)** | (0.034) |
| Catholic | -0.110 | -0.032 | -0.089 | 0.046 | 0.082 | 0.081 |
| | (0.053)** | (0.046) | (0.054)** | (0.043) | (0.033)** | (0.037)** |
| Republican administration | 0.420 | 0.410 | 0.438 | 0.306 | 0.342 | 0.384 |
| | (0.039)*** | (0.032)*** | (0.039)*** | (0.031)*** | (0.022)*** | (0.026)*** |
| Feminist | 0.017 | | | 0.018 | | |
| | (0.001)*** | | | (0.001)*** | | |
| Employed | | -0.104 | | | -0.103 | |
| | | (0.036)*** | | | (0.025)*** | |
| Children | | | -0.083 | | | -0.098 |
| | | | (0.060) | | | (0.038)** |
| Mother | | | 0.153 | | | 0.176 |
| | | | (0.077)** | | | (0.050)*** |
| N | 10,523 | 15,831 | 11,040 | 10,027 | 21,859 | 17,319 |

Note: Data are from the 1980–2012 ANES. Positive coefficients indicate greater support for social welfare spending. To retain respondents, the analysis also includes an income variable (not shown): 1 if people refused to answer and 0 otherwise.

* $p < .10$; ** $p < .05$; *** $p < .01$

# References

Abell, John D. 1994. "Military Spending and Income Inequality." *Journal of Peace Research* 31 (1): 35–43.

Alesina, Alberto, and Eliana La Ferrara. 2005. "Ethnic Diversity and Economic Performance." *Journal of Economic Literature* 43 (3): 762–800.

Applegate, Brandon K., Francis T. Cullen, and Bonnie S. Fisher. 2002. "Public Views toward Crime and Correctional Policies: Is There a Gender Gap?" *Journal of Criminal Justice* 30 (2): 89–100.

Archer, John. 2004. "Sex Differences in Aggression in Real-World Settings: A Meta-analytic Review." *Review of General Psychology* 8 (4): 291–322.

Bardi, Anat, and Shalom H. Schwartz. 2003. "Values and Behavior: Strength and Structure of Relations." *Personality and Social Psychology Bulletin* 29 (10): 1207–1220.

Baron, Reuben M., and David A. Kenny. 1986. "The Moderator-Mediator Variable Distinction in Social Psychological Research: Conceptual, Strategic, and Statistical Considerations." *Journal of Personality and Social Psychology* 51 (6): 1173–1182.

Beckwith, Karen. 2002. "Women, Gender, and Nonviolence in Political Movements." *PS: Political Science and Politics* 35 (1): 75–81.

Bendyna, Mary E., Tamata Finucane, Lynn Kirby, John P. O'Donnell, and Clyde Wilcox. 1996. "Gender Differences in Public Attitudes toward the Gulf War: A Test of Competing Hypotheses." *Social Science Journal* 33 (1): 1–22.

Bettencourt, B., and Norman Miller. 1996. "Gender Differences in Aggression as a Function of Provocation: A Meta-analysis." *Psychological Bulletin* 119 (3): 422–447.

Beutel, Ann, and Monica Kirkpatrick Johnson. 2004. "Gender and Prosocial Values during Adolescence: A Research Note." *Sociological Quarterly* 45 (2): 379–393.

Beutel, Ann M., and Margaret Mooney Marini. 1995. "Gender and Values." *American Sociological Review* 60:436–448.

Bittner, Amanda, and Elizabeth Goodyear-Grant. 2017. "Sex Isn't Gender: Reforming Concepts and Measurements in the Study of Public Opinion." *Political Behavior* 39 (4): 1019–1041.

Blinder, Scott, and Meredith Rolfe. 2018. "Rethinking Compassion: Toward a Political Account of the Partisan Gender Gap in the United States." *Political Psychology* 39 (4): 889–906.

Blocker, T. Jean, and Douglas Lee Eckberg. 1997. "Gender and Environmentalism: Results from the 1993 General Social Survey." *Social Science Quarterly* 78 (4): 841–858.

Bolzendahl, Catherine I., and Daniel J. Myers. 2004. "Feminist Attitudes and Support for Gender Equality: Opinion Change in Women and Men, 1974–1998." *Social Forces* 83 (2): 759–789.

Bongiovanni, Domenica. 2018. "Hoosier Women's March Participants Talk 2018 Wishes and What's Next for #MeToo." *IndyStar*, January 20. Available at https://www.indystar.com/story/news/local/2018/01/20/hoosier-womens-march-participants-talk-2018-wishes-and-whats-next-metoo/1044753001.

Boots, Denise Paquette, and John L. Cochran. 2011. "The Gender Gap in Support for Capital Punishment: A Test of Attribution Theory." *Women and Criminal Justice* 21 (3): 171–197.

Bord, Richard J., and Robert A. O'Conner. 1997. "The Gender Gap in Environmental Attitudes: The Case of Perceived Vulnerability to Risk." *Social Science Quarterly* 78 (4): 830–840.

Box-Steffensmeier, Janet M., Suzanna De Boef, and Tse-Min Lin. 2004. "The Dynamics of the Partisan Gender Gap." *American Political Science Review* 98 (3): 515–528.

Brandes, Lisa. 1992. "The Gender Gap and Attitudes toward War." Paper presented at the annual meeting of the Midwest Political Science Association, Chicago, April 9.

Brennan, Pauline Gasdow, Alan J. Lizotte, and David McDowall. 1993. "Guns, Southernness, and Gun Control." *Journal of Quantitative Criminology* 9 (3): 289–307.

Brewer, Paul R. 2003. "The Shifting Foundations of Public Opinion about Gay Rights." *Journal of Politics*, 65 (4): 1208–1220.

Brewster, Karin L., and Irene Padavic. 2000. "Change in Gender-Ideology, 1977–1996: The Contributions of Intracohort Change and Population Turnover." *Journal of Marriage and Family* 62 (2): 477–487.

Brock-Utne, Birgit. 1985. *Educating for Peace: A Feminist Perspective.* New York: Pergamon.

Broverman, Inge K., Susan Raymond Vogel, Donald M. Broverman, Frank E. Clarkson, and Paul S. Rosenkrantz. 1972. "Sex-Role Stereotypes: A Current Appraisal." *Journal of Social Issues* 28 (2): 59–78.

Brueck, Hilary. 2018. "A Mother in Flint, Michigan Collected More than 800 Neighborhood Water Samples to Help Uncover the City's Lead Crisis." *Business Insider*, April 23. Available at http://www.businessinsider.com/flint-water-crisis-crusader-leeanne-walters-wins-goldman-prize-2018-4.

Burden, Barry C., Evan Crawford, and Michael G. DeCrescenzo. 2016. "The Unexceptional Gender Gap of 2016." *The Forum* 14 (4): 415–432.

Buschman, Joan K., and Silvo Lenart. 1996. "'I Am Not a Feminist, but . . .': College Women, Feminism, and Negative Experiences." *Political Psychology* 17:59–75.

Calzada, Inés, María Gómez-Garrido, Luis Moreno, and Francisco Javier Moreno-Fuentes. 2014. "It Is Not Only about Equality: A Study on the (Other) Values That Ground Attitudes to the Welfare State." *International Journal of Public Opinion Research* 26 (2): 178–201.

Campbell, Karlyn Kohrs, ed. 1989. *Man Cannot Speak for Her.* Vol. 2, *Key Texts of the Early Feminists.* New York: Praeger.

Carlisle, Juliet, and Eric R.A.N. Smith. 2005. "Postmaterialism vs. Egalitarianism as Predictors of Energy-Related Attitudes." *Environmental Politics* 14 (4): 527–540.

Carroll, Susan J. 1988. "Women's Autonomy and the Gender Gap: 1980 and 1982." In *The Politics of the Gender Gap*, edited by C. M. Mueller, 236–257. Newbury Park, CA: Sage.

———. 2006. "Voting Choices: Meet You at the Gender Gap." In *Gender and Elections: Shaping the Future of American Politics*, edited by Susan J. Carroll and Richard L. Fox, 74–96 . New York: Cambridge University Press.

———. 2008. "Security Moms and Presidential Politics: Women Voters in the 2004 Election." In *Voting the Gender Gap*, edited by Lois Duke Whitaker, 75–90. Champaign: University of Illinois Press.

Carter, Scott J., Mamadi Corra, and Shannon K. Carter. 2009. "The Interaction of Race and Gender: Changing Gender-Role Attitudes, 1974–2006." *Social Science Quarterly* 90 (1): 196–211.

Caughell, Leslie A. 2016. *The Political Battle of the Sexes: Exploring the Sources of Gender Gaps in Policy Preferences*. Lanham, MD: Rowman and Littlefield.

Celinska, Katarzyna. 2007. "Individualism and Collectivism in America: The Case of Gun Ownership and Attitudes toward Gun Control." *Sociological Perspectives* 50 (2): 229–247.

Center for American Women and Politics. 2012. "The Gender Gap: Attitudes on Public Policy Issues." Available at http://www.cawp.rutgers .edu/sites/default/files/resources/gg_issuesattitudes-2012.pdf.

———. 2014. "The Gender Gap: Party Identification and Presidential Performance Ratings." Available at http://www.cawp.rutgers.edu/ sites/default/files/resources/ggprtyid.pdf.

———. 2017. "The Gender Gap: Voting Choices in Presidential Elections." Available at http://www.cawp.rutgers.edu/sites/default/files/ resources/ggpresvote.pdf.

———. 2019. "Gender Differences in Voter Turnout." Available at http:// www.cawp.rutgers.edu/sites/default/files/resources/genderdiff.pdf.

Center for Health, Environment and Justice. n.d. "Our History." Available at http://chej.org/about-us/story (accessed July 19, 2019).

Chaney, Carole Kennedy, R. Michael Alvarez, and Jonathan Nagler. 1998. "Explaining the Gender Gap in U.S. Presidential Elections, 1980–1992." *Political Research Quarterly* 51 (2): 311–339.

Chaturvedi, Richa. 2016. "A Closer Look at the Gender Gap in Presidential Voting." Pew Research Center, July 28. Available at http://www .pewresearch.org/fact-tank/2016/07/28/a-closer-look-at-the-gender -gap-in-presidential-voting.

Ciuk, David J., Robert N. Lupton, and Judd R. Thornton. 2018. "Values Voters: The Conditional Effect of Income on the Relationship between Core Values and Political Attitudes and Behavior." *Political Psychology* 39 (4): 869–888.

Clark, Cal, and Janet Clark. 1996. "The Gender Gap: A Manifestation of Women's Dissatisfaction with the American Polity?" In *Broken Contract? Changing Relationships between Americans and Their Government*, edited by Stephen C. Craig, 167–182. Boulder, CO: Westview Press.

———. 2009. *Women at the Polls: The Gender Gap, Cultural Politics, and Contested Constituencies in the United States*. Newcastle upon Tyne, UK: Cambridge Scholars.

———. 2008. "The Reemergence of the Gender Gap in 2004." In *Voting the Gender Gap*, edited by Louis Duke Whitaker, 50–74. Urbana: University of Illinois Press.

Clark, Janet, and Cal Clark. 1993. "The Gender Gap 1988: Compassion, Pacifism, and Indirect Feminism." In *Women in Politics: Insiders or*

*Outsiders? A Collection of Readings*, edited by Lois L. Duke, 32–45. Englewood Cliffs, NJ: Prentice-Hall.

CNN Politics. 2012. "America's Choice 2012: President." Available at http://www.cnn.com/election/2012/results/race/president.

———. 2016. "Election 2016: Exit Polls." Available at http://www.cnn .com/election/results/exit-polls.

Cochran, John K., and Beth A. Sanders. 2009. "The Gender Gap in Death Penalty Support: An Exploratory Study." *Journal of Criminal Justice* 37 (6): 525–533.

Combs, Michael W., and Susan Welch. 1982. "Blacks, Whites, and Attitudes toward Abortion." *Public Opinion Quarterly* 46 (4): 510–520.

Conover, Pamela Johnston. 1988. "Feminists and the Gender Gap." *Journal of Politics* 50 (4): 985–1010.

Conover, Pamela Johnston, and Virginia Sapiro. 1993. "Gender, Feminist Consciousness, and War." *American Journal of Political Science* 37:1079–1099.

Conway, M. Margaret, Gertrude A. Steuernagel, and David W. Ahern. 1997. *Women and Political Participation—Cultural Change in the Political Arena*. Washington, DC: CQ Press.

Cook, Elizabeth Adell, Ted G. Jelen, and Clyde Wilcox. 1992. *Between Two Absolutes: Public Opinion and the Politics of Abortion*. Boulder, CO: Westview Press.

Cook, Elizabeth Adell, and Clyde Wilcox. 1991. "Feminism and the Gender Gap—a Second Look." *Journal of Politics* 53 (4): 1111–1122.

———. 1992. "A Rose by Any Other Name: Measuring Support for Organized Feminism Using ANES Feeling Thermometers." *Women and Politics* 12 (1): 35–51.

———. 1995. "Women Voters in the 'Year of the Woman.'" In *Democracy's Feast: Elections in America*, edited by Herbert F. Weisberg, 195–219. Chatham, NJ: Chatham House.

Cooper, Betsy, Daniel Cox, Rachel Lienesch, and Robert P. Jones. 2016. "Beyond Same-Sex Marriage: Attitudes on LGBT Nondiscrimination Laws and Religious Exemptions from the 2015 American Values Atlas." Public Religion Research Institute, February 18. Available at https://www.prri.org/research/poll-same-sex-gay-marriage-lgbt -nondiscrimination-religious-liberty.

Costain, Anne N. 2000. "Women's Movements and Nonviolence." *PS: Political Science and Politics* 33 (2): 175–180.

Cott, Nancy F. 1987. *The Grounding of Modern Feminism*. New Haven, CT: Yale University Press.

Cotter, David, Joan M. Hermsen, and Reeve Vanneman. 2011. "The End of the Gender Revolution? Gender Role Attitudes from 1977 to 2008." *American Journal of Sociology* 117 (1): 259–289.

Craig, Stephen C., Michael D. Martinez, James G. Kane, and Jason Gainous. 2005. "Core Values, Value Conflict, and Citizens' Ambivalence about Gay Rights." *Political Research Quarterly* 58 (1): 5–17.

Crawford, Kerry F., Eric D. Lawrence, and James H. Lebovic. 2017. "Aversion, Acceptance, or Apprehension? The Effects of Gender on US Public Opinion concerning US-Inflicted Civilian Casualties." *Journal of Global Security Studies* 2 (2): 150–169.

Davidson, Debra J., and William R. Freudenburg. 1996. "Gender and Environmental Risk Concerns: A Review and Analysis of Available Research." *Environment and Behavior* 28:302–339.

Deckman, Melissa. 2016. *Tea Party Women: Mama Grizzlies, Grassroots Leaders, and the Changing Face of the American Right.* New York: NYU Press.

Deckman, Melissa, and John McTague. 2015. "Did the 'War on Women' Work? Women, Men, and the Birth Control Mandate in the 2012 presidential Election." *American Politics Research* 43 (1): 3–26.

Deitch, Cynthia. 1988. "Sex Differences in Support for Government Spending." In *The Politics of the Gender Gap*, edited by Carol M. Mueller, 192–216. Newbury Park, CA: Sage.

Delano, Jon. 2017. "Trump's Proposed Food Stamp Changes, Including Work Requirement, Elicits Protests." *CBS Pittsburgh*, May 30. Available at http://pittsburgh.cbslocal.com/2017/05/30/trump-food-stamp-changes-pennsylvania.

Diament, Michelle. 2017. "Disability Advocates Arrested Protesting Medicaid Cuts." *Disability Scoop*, September 26. Available at https://www.disabilityscoop.com/2017/09/26/disability-advocates-arrest-cuts/24213.

Diekman, Amanda B., and Monica C. Schneider. 2010. "A Social Role Theory Perspective on Gender Gaps in Political Attitudes." *Psychology of Women Quarterly* 34 (4): 486–497.

Dietz, Mary G. 1985. "Citizenship with a Feminist Face: The Problem with Maternal Thinking." *Political Theory* 13 (1): 19–37.

Dietz, Thomas, Linda Kalof, and Paul C. Stern. 2002. "Gender, Values, and Environmentalism." *Social Science Quarterly* 83 (1): 353–364.

Dotson, Hilary, and J. Scott Carter. 2012. "Changing Views toward the Death Penalty? The Intersecting Impact of Race and Gender on Attitudes, 1974–2006." *Justice System Journal* 33 (1): 1–21.

Drake, Bruce. 2013. "Americans See Growing Gap Between Rich and Poor." Pew Research Center, December 5. Available at http://www.pewresearch.org/fact-tank/2013/12/05/americans-see-growing-gap-between-rich-and-poor.

Eagly, Alice H. 1987. *Sex Differences in Social Behavior: A Social-Role Interpretation.* Hillsdale, NJ: Lawrence Erlbaum.

Eagly, Alice H., and Amanda B. Diekman. 2006. "Examining Gender Gaps in Sociopolitical Attitudes: It's Not Mars and Venus." *Feminism and Psychology* 16 (1): 26–34.

Eagly, Alice H., Amanda B. Diekman, Mary C. Johannesen-Schmidt, and Anne M. Koenig. 2004. "Gender Gaps in Sociopolitical Attitudes: A Social Psychological Analysis." *Journal of Personality and Social Psychology* 87 (6): 796–816.

Eagly, Alice H., and Anne M. Koenig. 2006. "Social Role Theory of Sex Differences and Similarities: Implication for Prosocial Behavior." In *Sex Differences and Similarities in Communication*, edited by Daniel J. Canary and Kathryn Dindia, 161–178. Mahwah, NJ: Lawrence Erlbaum.

Eagly, Alice H., and Valerie J. Steffen. 1984. "Gender Stereotypes Stem from the Distribution of Women and Men into Social Roles." *Journal of Personality and Social Psychology* 46, (4): 735–754.

Eagly, Alice H., and Wendy Wood. 2012. "Social Role Theory." In *Handbook of Theories of Social Psychology*, edited by Arie W. Kruglanski, Paul A. M. Van Lange, and Tory Higgins, 458–476. Thousand Oaks, CA: Sage.

Eichenberg, Richard C. 2003. "Gender Differences in Public Attitudes toward the Use of Force by the United States, 1990–2003." *International Security* 28 (1): 110–141.

Elder, Laurel, and Steven Greene. 2006. "The Children Gap on Social Welfare and the Politicization of American Parents, 1984–2000." *Politics and Gender* 2 (4): 451–472.

———. 2007. "The Myth of 'Security Moms' and 'NASCAR Dads': Parenthood, Political Stereotypes, and the 2004 Election." *Social Science Quarterly* 88 (1): 1–19.

———. 2012. "The Politics of Parenthood: Parenthood Effects on Issue Attitudes and Candidate Evaluations in 2008." *American Politics Research* 40 (3): 419–449.

———. 2019. "Gender and the Politics of Marijuana." *Social Science Quarterly* 100 (1): 109–122.

Elshtain, Jean Bethke. 1985. "Reflections on War and Political Discourse: Realism, Just War, and Feminism in a Nuclear Age." *Political Theory* 13 (1): 39–57.

———. 1986. "The New Feminist Scholarship." *Salmagundi* 70–71:3–26.

"Environment: CBS News Poll." 2019. *Polling Report.* Available at http://www.pollingreport.com/enviro.htm.

Erskine, Hazel. 1972. "The Polls: Gun Control." *Public Opinion Quarterly* 36 (3): 455–469.

Feinstein, Yuval. 2017. "The Rise and Decline of 'Gender Gaps' in Support for Military Action: United States, 1986–2011." *Politics and Gender* 13 (4): 618–655.

Feldman, Stanley. 1988. "Structure and Consistency in Public Opinion: The Role of Core Beliefs and Values." *American Journal of Political Science* 32:416–440.

———. 2003. "Values, Ideology, and the Structure of Political Attitudes." In *Oxford Handbook of Political Psychology*, edited by David O. Sears, Leonie Huddy, and Robert Jervis, 477–510. New York: Oxford University Press.

Feldman, Stanley, and Leonie Huddy. 2005. "Racial Resentment and White Opposition to Race-Conscious Programs: Principles or Prejudice?" *American Journal of Political Science* 49 (1): 168–183.

Feldman, Stanley, and Marco R. Steenbergen. 2001. "The Humanitarian Foundation of Public Support for Social Welfare." *American Journal of Political Science* 45 (3): 658–677.

Fong, Christina. 2001. "Social Preferences, Self-Interest, and the Demand for Redistribution." *Journal of Public Economics* 82 (2): 225–246.

Ford, Lynne E. 2010. *Encyclopedia of Women and American Politics*. New York: Infobase.

———. 2017. *Women and Politics: The Pursuit of Equality*. 4th ed. Boulder, CO: Westview Press.

Fox, Richard L., and Zoe M. Oxley. 2016. "Women's Support for an Active Government." In *Minority Voting in the United States*, edited by Kyle Kreider and Thomas J. Baldino, 148–167. Denver: Praeger.

Friedman, Ann. 2015. "Can We Solve Our Child-Care Problem?" *The Cut*, January 22. Available at http://nymag.com/thecut/2015/01/can-we-solve-our-child-care-problem.html.

Funk, Cary, and Brian Kennedy. 2016. "The Politics of Climate." Pew Research Center, October 4. Available at https://www.pewinternet.org/wp-content/uploads/sites/9/2016/10/PS_2016.10.04_Politics-of-Climate_FINAL.pdf.

Gallup. 2000. "Gun Laws and Women." May 12. Available at http://www.gallup.com/poll/2908/gun-laws-women.aspx.

Gibbs, Lois Marie. 1998. "Learning from Love Canal: A 20th Anniversary Retrospective." *Orion Afield*. Previously available at http://arts.envirolink.org/arts_and_activism/LoisGibbs.html.

Gidengil, Elisabeth. 1995. "Economic Man—Social Woman? The Case of the Gender Gap in Support for the Canada-United States Free Trade Agreement." *Comparative Political Studies* 28 (3): 384–408.

Gilens, Martin. 1988. "Gender and Support for Reagan: A Comprehensive Model of Presidential Approval." *American Journal of Political Science* 32 (1): 19–49.

Goertzel, Ted. 1983. "The Gender Gap: Sex, Family Income and Political Opinions in the Early 1980's." *JPMS: Journal of Political and Military Sociology* 11 (2): 209–222.

Goren, Paul. 2005. "Party Identification and Core Political Values." *American Journal of Political Science* 49 (4): 881–896.

Goren, Paul, Harald Schoen, Jason Reifler, Thomas Scotto, and William Chittick. 2016. "A Unified Theory of Value-Based Reasoning and U.S. Public Opinion." *Political Behavior* 38 (4): 977–997.

Greenlee, Jill S. 2014. *The Political Consequences of Motherhood.* Ann Arbor: University of Michigan Press.

Gupte, Manjusha. 2002. "Gender, Feminist Consciousness, and the Environment: Exploring the 'Natural' Connection." *Women and Politics* 24 (1): 47–62.

Gwartney-Gibbs, Patricia A., and Denise H. Lach. 1991. "Sex Differences in Attitudes toward Nuclear War." *Journal of Peace Research* 28 (2): 161–174.

Haider-Markel, Donald P., and Mark R. Joslyn. 2001. "Gun Policy, Opinion, Tragedy, and Blame Attribution: The Conditional Influence of Issue Frames." *Journal of Politics* 63 (2): 520–543.

———. 2008. "Beliefs about the Origins of Homosexuality and Support for Gay Rights: An Empirical Test of Attribution Theory." *Public Opinion Quarterly* 72 (2): 291–310.

Halim, Shaheen, and Beverly L. Stiles. 2001. "Differential Support for Police Use of Force, the Death Penalty, and Perceived Harshness of the Courts: Effects of Race, Gender, and Region." *Criminal Justice and Behavior* 28 (1): 3–23.

Hare, Christopher, Tzu-Ping Liu, and Robert N. Lupton. 2018. "What Ordered Optimal Classification Reveals about Ideological Structure, Cleavages, and Polarization in the American Mass Public." *Public Choice* 176 (1): 57–78.

Hayes, Bernadette. 2001. "Gender, Scientific Knowledge, and Attitudes toward the Environment." *Political Research Quarterly* 54 (3): 657–671.

Helmreich, Robert L., Janet T. Spence, and Robert H. Gibson. 1982. "Sex-Role Attitudes: 1972–1980." *Personality and Social Psychology Bulletin* 8 (4): 656–663.

Henry, Patrick J., and David O. Sears. 2002. "The Symbolic Racism 2000 Scale." *Political Psychology* 23 (2): 253–283.

Herek, Gregory M. 1988. "Heterosexuals' Attitudes toward Lesbians and Gay Men: Correlates and Gender Differences." *Journal of Sex Research* 25 (4): 451–477.

———. 2002a. "Gender Gaps in Public Opinion about Lesbians and Gay Men." *Public Opinion Quarterly* 66 (1): 40–66.

———. 2002b. "Heterosexuals' Attitudes toward Bisexual Men and Women in the United States." *Journal of Sex Research* 39 (4): 264–274.

Hetherington, Marc J., and Michael Nelson. 2003. "Anatomy of a Rally Effect: George W. Bush and the War on Terrorism." *PS: Political Science and Politics* 36 (1): 37–42.

Hevesi, Dennis. 2011. "Dagmar Wilson, Anti-nuclear Leader, Dies at 94." *New York Times*, January 23. Available at https://www.nytimes.com/2011/01/24/us/24wilson.html.

Hicks, Raymond, and Dustin Tingley. 2011. "Causal Mediation Analysis." *Stata Journal* 11 (4), 605–619.

Hogeland, Lisa Maria. 1994. "Fear of Feminism: Why Young Women Get the Willies." *Ms.*, November–December, pp. 18–21.

Howell, Susan E., and Christine L. Day. 2000. "Complexities of the Gender Gap." *Journal of Politics* 62 (3):858–874.

Huddy, Leonie, Joshua Billig, John Bracciodieta, Lois Hoeffler, Patrick J. Moynihan, and Patricia Pugliani. 1997. "The Effect of Interviewer Gender on the Survey Response." *Political Behavior* 19 (3): 197–220.

Huddy, Leonie, Erin Cassese, and Mary-Kate Lizotte. 2008a. "Gender, Public Opinion, and Political Reasoning." In *Political Women and American Democracy*, edited by Christina Wolbrecht, Karen Beckwith, and Lisa Baldez, 31–49. New York: Cambridge University Press.

———. 2008b. "Sources of Political Unity and Disunity among Women: Placing the Gender Gap in Perspective." In *Voting the Gender Gap*, edited by Lois Duke Whitaker, 141–169. Champaign: University of Illinois Press.

Huddy, Leonie, Stanley Feldman, and Erin Cassese. 2009. "Terrorism, Anxiety, and War." In *Terrorism and Torture: An Interdisciplinary Perspective*, edited by W. Stritzke, S. Lewandowsky, D. Denemark, F. Morgan, and J. Clare, 290–312. Cambridge: Cambridge University Press.

Huddy, Leonie, Stanley Feldman, Charles Taber, and Gallya Lahav. 2005. "Threat, Anxiety, and Support of Antiterrorism Policies." *American Journal of Political Science* 49:593–608.

Huddy, Leonie, Francis K. Neely, and Marilyn R. Lafay. 2000. "Trends: Support for the Women's Movement." *Public Opinion Quarterly* 64 (3): 309–350.

Hughes, Michael, and Steven A. Tuch. 2003. "Gender Differences in Whites' Racial Attitudes: Are Women's Attitudes Really More Favorable?" *Social Psychology Quarterly* 66 (4): 384–401.

Hurwitz, Jon, and Shannon Smithey. 1998. "Gender Differences on Crime and Punishment." *Political Research Quarterly* 51 (1): 89–115.

Hutchings, Vincent L., Nicholas A. Valentino, Tasha S. Philpot, and Ismail K. White. 2004. "The Compassion Strategy: Race and the Gender Gap in Campaign 2000." *Public Opinion Quarterly* 68 (4): 512–541.

Jaggar, Alison M. 1991. *Feminist Politics and Human Nature*. Totowa, NJ: Rowman and Allanheld.

Jelen, Ted G., and Clyde Wilcox. 2005. "Continuity and Change in Attitudes toward Abortion: Poland and the United States." *Politics and Gender* 1 (2): 297–317.

Johnson, Monica Kirkpatrick, and Margaret Mooney Marini. 1998. "Bridging the Racial Divide in the United States: The Effect of Gender." *Social Psychology Quarterly* 61 (3): 247–258.

Jones, Jeffrey M. 2001. "Men, Women Equally Likely to Support Military Retaliation for Terrorist Attacks." Gallup, October 5. Available at http://news.gallup.com/poll/4963/men-women-equally-likely-support-military-retaliation-terrorist-attacks.aspx.

———. 2005. "Gender Differences in Views of Job Opportunity." Gallup, August 2. Available at http://www.gallup.com/poll/17614/gender-differences-views-job-opportunity.aspx.

———. 2015. "U.S. Satisfaction with Federal Poverty Efforts at New Low." Gallup, May 7. Available at http://www.gallup.com/poll/183023/satisfaction-federal-poverty-efforts-new-low.aspx.

Jones, Philip Edward, Paul R. Brewer, Dannagal G. Young, Jennifer L. Lambe, and Lindsay H. Hoffman. 2018. "Explaining Public Opinion toward Transgender People, Rights, and Candidates." *Public Opinion Quarterly* 82 (2): 252–278. Available at https://doi.org/10.1093/poq/nfy009.

Kamo, Yoshinori, and Ellen L. Cohen. 1998. "Division of Household Work between Partners: A Comparison of Black and White Couples." *Journal of Comparative Family Studies* 29 (1): 131–145.

Kaufmann, Karen M. 2002. "Culture Wars, Secular Realignment, and the Gender Gap in Party Identification." *Political Behavior* 24 (3): 283–307.

———. 2004. "The Partisan Paradox Religious Commitment and the Gender Gap in Party Identification." *Public Opinion Quarterly* 68 (4): 491–511.

———. 2006. "The Gender Gap." *PS: Political Science and Politics* 39 (3): 447–453.

Kaufmann, Karen M., and John R. Petrocik. 1999. "The Changing Politics of American Men: Understanding the Sources of the Gender Gap." *American Journal of Political Science* 43:864–887.

Kaufmann, Karen M., John R. Petrocik, and Daron R. Shaw. 2008. *Unconventional Wisdom: Facts and Myths about American Voters*. New York: Oxford University Press.

Kenski, Henry C. 1988. "The Gender Factor in a Changing Electorate." In *The Politics of the Gender Gap: The Social Construction of Political Influence*, edited by Carol M. Mueller, 38–60. Beverly Hills, CA: Sage.

Kenworthy, Lane. 1999. "Do Social-Welfare Policies Reduce Poverty? A Cross-National Assessment." *Social Forces* 77 (3): 1119–1139.

Kessler, Suzanne J., and Wendy McKenna. 1978. *Gender: An Ethnomethological Approach.* New York: John Wiley.

Kimenyi, Mwangi S., and John Mukum Mbaku. 1995. "Female Headship, Feminization of Poverty and Welfare." *Southern Economic Journal* 62 (1): 44–52.

Kinder, Donald R., and David O. Sears. 1981. "Prejudice and Politics: Symbolic Racism versus Racial Threats to the Good Life." *Journal of Personality and Social Psychology* 40 (3): 414.

Kleck, Gary, Marc Gertz, and Jason Bratton. 2009. "Why Do People Support Gun Control?: Alternative Explanations of Support for Handgun Bans." *Journal of Criminal Justice* 37 (5): 496–504.

Klineberg, Stephen L., Matthew McKeever, and Bert Rothenbach. 1998. "Demographic Predictors of Environmental Concern: It Does Make a Difference How It's Measured." *Social Science Quarterly* 79 (4): 734–753.

Kluegel, James R., and Eliot R. Smith. 1982. "Whites' Beliefs about Blacks' Opportunity." *American Sociological Review* 47 (4): 518–532.

Kriesberg, Louis, and Ross Klein. 1980. "Changes in Public Support for U.S. Military Spending." *Journal of Conflict Resolution* 24 (1): 79–111.

Kuran, Timur, and Edward J. McCaffery. 2008. "Sex Differences in the Acceptability of Discrimination." *Political Research Quarterly* 61 (2): 228–238.

Kutateladze, Besiki, and Angela M. Crossman. 2009. "An Exploratory Analysis of Gender Differences in Punitiveness in Two Countries." *International Criminal Justice Review* 19 (3): 322–343.

LaMar, Lisa, and Mary Kite. 1998. "Sex Differences in Attitudes toward Gay Men and Lesbians: A Multidimensional Perspective." *Journal of Sex Research* 35 (2): 189–196.

Lambert, Eric G., Alan Clarke, Kasey A. Tucker-Gail, and Nancy L. Hogan. 2009. "Multivariate Analysis of Reasons for Death Penalty Support between Male and Female College Students: Empirical Support for Gilligan's 'Ethic of Care.'" *Criminal Justice Studies* 22 (3): 239–260.

Lay, J. Celeste. 2012. *A Midwestern Mosaic: Immigration and Political Socialization in Rural America.* Philadelphia: Temple University Press.

Lehmann, Peter S., and Justin T. Pickett. 2017. "Experience versus Expectation: Economic Insecurity, the Great Recession, and Support for the Death Penalty." *Justice Quarterly* 34 (5): 873–902.

Lewis, Gregory B. 2005. "Same-Sex Marriage and the 2004 Presidential Election." *PS: Political Science and Politics* 38 (2): 195–199.

Liberman, P. 2014. "War and Torture as 'Just Deserts.'" *Public Opinion Quarterly* 78 (1): 47–70.

Lizotte, Mary-Kate. 2009. "The Dynamics and Origins of the Gender Gap in Support for Military Interventions." Ph.D. diss., Stony Brook University.

———. 2015. "The Abortion Attitudes Paradox: Model Specification and Gender Differences." *Journal of Women, Politics and Policy* 36 (1): 22–42.

———. 2016a. "Gender, Voting, and Reproductive Rights Attitudes." In *Minority Voting in the United States*, edited by Kyle L. Kreider and Thomas J. Baldino, 127–147. Santa Barbara, CA: Praeger.

———. 2016b. "Investigating Women's Greater Support of the Affordable Care Act." *Social Science Journal* 53 (2): 209–217.

———. 2017a. "Gender Differences in Support for Torture." *Journal of Conflict Resolution* 61 (4): 772–787.

———. 2017b. "The Gender Gap in Public Opinion: Exploring Social Role Theory as an Explanation." In *Gender and Political Psychology*, edited by Angela L. Bos and Monica C. Schneider, 51–70. New York: Routledge.

Lizotte, Mary-Kate, and Andrew H. Sidman. 2009. "Explaining the Gender Gap in Political Knowledge." *Politics and Gender* 5 (2): 127–151.

Lupton, Robert N., Steven M. Smallpage, and Adam M. Enders. 2017. "Values and Political Predispositions in the Age of Polarization: Examining the Relationship between Partisanship and Ideology in the United States, 1988–2012." *British Journal of Political Science*, December 19. Available at https://doi.org/10.1017/S0007123417000370.

Lyons, Sean, Linda Duxbury, and Christopher Higgins. 2005. "Are Gender Differences in Basic Human Values a Generational Phenomenon?" *Sex Roles* 53 (9–10): 763–778.

Mansbridge, Jane J. 1985. "Myth and Reality: The ERA and the Gender Gap in the 1980 Election." *Public Opinion Quarterly* 49 (2): 164–178.

Manza, Jeff, and Clem Brooks. 1998. "The Gender Gap in U.S. Presidential Elections: When? Why? Implications?" *American Journal of Sociology* 103 (5): 1235–1266.

Markus, Gregory B. 1988. "The Impact of Personal and National Economic Conditions on the Presidential Vote: A Pooled Cross-Sectional Analysis." *American Journal of Political Science* 32 (1): 137–154.

Mason, Karen Oppenheim, and Yu-Hsia Lu. 1988. "Attitudes toward Women's Familial Roles: Changes in the United States, 1977–1985." *Gender and Society* 2 (1): 39–57.

Mata, Jessieka, Negin Ghavami, and Michele A. Wittig. 2010. "Understanding Gender Differences in Early Adolescents' Sexual Prejudice." *Journal of Early Adolescence* 30 (1): 50–75.

Mattei, Franco. 2000. "The Gender Gap in Presidential Evaluations: Assessments of Clinton's Performance in 1996." *Polity* 33 (2): 199–228.

McCabe, Janice. 2005. "What's in a Label? The Relationship between Feminist self-Identification and 'Feminist' Attitudes among US Women and Men." *Gender and Society* 19 (4): 480–505.

McClosky, Herbert, and John Zaller. 1984. *The American Ethos: Public Attitudes toward Capitalism and Democracy.* Cambridge, MA: Harvard University Press.

McCright, Aaron. 2010. "The Effects of Gender on Climate Change Knowledge and Concern in the American Public." *Population and Environment* 32:66–87.

McDermott, Monika L. 2016. *Masculinity, Femininity, and American Political Behavior.* New York: Oxford University Press.

Miller, Lisa. 2015. "Obama's Right-Wing Feminist Critics." *Intelligencer,* January 22. Available at http://nymag.com/daily/intelligencer/2015/01/obamas-right-wing-feminist-critics.html.

Mohai, Paul. 1992. "Men, Women, and the Environment." *Society and Natural Resources* 5:1–19.

Morin, Richard, and Shawn Neidorf. 2007. "Surge in Support for Social Safety Net." Pew Research Center, May 2. Available at http://www.pewresearch.org/2007/05/02/surge-in-support-for-social-safety-net.

Mueller, John E. 1973. *War, Presidents, and Public Opinion.* New York: Wiley.

Nadeau, Richard, and Michael S. Lewis-Beck. 2001. "National Economic Voting in US Presidential Elections." *Journal of Politics* 63 (1): 159–181.

Nincic, Miroslav, and Donna J. Nincic. 2002. "Race, Gender, and War." *Journal of Peace Research* 39 (5): 547–568.

Norrander, Barbara. 1999. "The Evolution of the Gender Gap." *Public Opinion Quarterly* 63 (4): 566–576.

———. 2003. "The Intraparty Gender Gap: Differences between Male and Female Voters in the 1980–2000 Presidential Primaries." *PS: Political Science and Politics* 36 (2): 181–186.

———. 2008. "The History of the Gender Gaps." In *Voting the Gender Gap,* edited by Lois Duke Whitaker, 9–32. Champaign: University of Illinois Press.

Obama, Barack. 2015. "Remarks by the President in State of the Union Address." White House, January 20. Available at https://www.whitehouse.gov/the-press-office/2015/01/20/remarks-president-state-union-address-january-20-2015.

Oliphant, J. Baxter. 2016. "Support for Death Penalty Lowest in More than Four Decades." Pew Research Center, September 29. Available at http://www.pewresearch.org/fact-tank/2016/09/29/support-for-death-penalty-lowest-in-more-than-four-decades.

Olson, Laura R., Wendy Cadge, and James T. Harrison. 2006. "Religion and Public Opinion about Same-Sex Marriage." *Social Science Quarterly* 87 (2): 340–360.

Ondercin, Heather. 2013. "What Scarlett O'Hara Thinks: Political Attitudes of Southern Women." *Political Science Quarterly* 128 (2): 233–259.

———. 2017. "Who Is Responsible for the Gender Gap? The Dynamics of Men's and Women's Democratic Macropartisanship, 1950–2012." *Political Research Quarterly* 70 (4): 749–761.

Ondercin, Heather L., and Jeffrey L. Bernstein. 2007. "Context Matters: The Influence of State and Campaign Factors on the Gender Gap in Senate Elections, 1988–2000." *Politics and Gender* 3 (1): 33–53.

Page, Benjamin I., and Robert Y. Shapiro. 1983. "Effects of Public Opinion on Policy." *American Political Science Review* 77 (1): 175–190.

Peffley, Mark A., and Jon Hurwitz. 1985. "A Hierarchical Model of Attitude Constraint." *American Journal of Political Science* 29:871–890.

Peltola, Pia, Melissa A. Milkie, and Stanley Presser. 2004. "The 'Feminist' Mystique: Feminist Identity in Three Generations of Women." *Gender and Society* 18 (1): 122–144.

Pew Research Center. 2002. "Generations Divide over Military Action in Iraq." October 17. Available at http://www.people-press.org/2002/10/17/generations-divide-over-military-action-in-iraq.

———. 2003a. "Conflicted Views of Affirmative Action." May 14. Available at https://www.people-press.org/2003/05/14/conflicted-views-of-affirmative-action.

———. 2003b. "Religious Beliefs Underpin Opposition to Homosexuality." November 18. Available at https://www.people-press.org/2003/11/18/religious-beliefs-underpin-opposition-to-homosexuality.

———. 2012a. "The Gender Gap: Three Decades Old, as Wide as Ever." March 29. Available at http://www.people-press.org/2012/03/29/the-gender-gap-three-decades-old-as-wide-as-ever.

———. 2012b. "More Support for Gun Rights, Gay Marriage than in 2008, 2004." April 25. Available at https://www.people-press.org/2012/04/25/more-support-for-gun-rights-gay-marriage-than-in-2008-or-2004.

———. 2013a. "Growing Support for Gay Marriage: Changed Minds and Changing Demographics." March 20. Available at https://www.people-press.org/2013/03/20/growing-support-for-gay-marriage-changed-minds-and-changing-demographics.

———. 2013b. "In Deficit Debate, Public Resists Cuts in Entitlements and Aid to Poor." December 19. Available at http://www.people-press

.org/2013/12/19/in-deficit-debate-public-resists-cuts-in-entitlements
-and-aid-to-poor.

———. 2013c. "Public Opinion Runs against Syrian Airstrikes." September 3. Available at https://www.people-press.org/2013/09/03/
public-opinion-runs-against-syrian-airstrikes.

———. 2014a. "Bipartisan Support for Obama's Military Campaign
against ISIS." September 15. Available at https://www.people-press
.org/2014/09/15/bipartisan-support-for-obamas-military-campaign
-against-isis.

———. 2014b. "Wide Partisan Differences over the Issues That Matter in 2014." September 12. Available at http://www.people-press.org/
2014/09/12/wide-partisan-differences-over-the-issues-that-matter-in
-2014.

———. 2015a. "Growing Support for Campaign against ISIS—and Possible Use of U.S. Ground Troops." February 24. Available at https://
www.people-press.org/2015/02/24/growing-support-for-campaign
-against-isis-and-possible-use-of-u-s-ground-troops.

———. 2015b. "Less Support for Death Penalty, Especially among Democrats." April 16. Available at http://www.people-press.org/2015/04/
16/less-support-for-death-penalty-especially-among-democrats.

———. 2016a. "Low Approval of Trump's Transition but Outlook
for His Presidency Improves." December 8. Available at http://
www.people-press.org/2016/12/08/3-political-values-government
-regulation-environment-immigration-race-views-of-islam.

———. 2016b. "More Americans Disapprove than Approve of Health
Care Law." April 27. Available at http://www.people-press.org/2016/
04/27/more-americans-disapprove-than-approve-of-health-care-law.

———. 2017. "Public Supports Syria Missile Strikes, but Few See a 'Clear
Plan' for Addressing Situation." April 12. Available at https://www
.people-press.org/2017/04/12/public-supports-syria-missile-strikes
-but-few-see-a-clear-plan-for-addressing-situation.

Piurko, Yuval, Shalom Schwartz, and Eldad Davidov. 2011. "Basic Personal Values and the Meaning of Left-Right Political Orientations in
20 Countries." *Political Psychology* 32 (4): 537–561.

Pollock, Philip H., III, Stuart A. Lilie, and M. Elliot Vittes. 1993. "Hard
Issues, Core Values and Vertical Constraint: The Case of Nuclear
Power." *British Journal of Political Science* 23 (1): 29–50.

Powlick, Philip J. 1991. "The Attitudinal Bases for Responsiveness to
Public Opinion among American Foreign Policy Officials." *Journal
of Conflict Resolution* 35 (4): 611–641.

Pratto, Felicia, Lisa M. Stallworth, Jim Sidanius, and Bret Siers. 1997.
"The Gender Gap in Occupational Role Attainment: A Social Domi-

nance Approach." *Journal of Personality and Social Psychology* 72 (1): 37–53.

Presidential Gender Watch. 2017. "Finding Gender in Election 2016: Lessons from Presidential Gender Watch." Available at http://presidentialgenderwatch.org/wp-content/uploads/2017/05/Finding-Gender-in-Election-2016.pdf.

Pressman, Steven. 1988. "At Home: The Feminization of Poverty: Causes and Remedies." *Challenge* 31 (2): 57–61.

Prince-Gibson, Eetta, and Shalom H. Schwartz. 1998. "Value Priorities and Gender." *Social Psychology Quarterly* 61:49–67.

Quadagno, Jill, and JoEllen Pederson. 2012. "Has Support for Social Security Declined? Attitudes toward the Public Pension Scheme in the USA, 2000 and 2010." *International Journal of Social Welfare* 21 (s1): S88–S100.

Rand, Jennifer. 2017. "Equal Means Equal: Why Women Need the ERA (Now More than Ever)." *Huffington Post*, August 21. Available at https://www.huffingtonpost.com/entry/equal-means-equal-why-women-need-the-era-now-more_us_5992149ee4b0caa1687a62c2.

Ratcliff, Jennifer J., G. Daniel Lassiter, Keith D. Markman, and Celeste J. Snyder. 2006. "Gender Differences in Attitudes toward Gay Men and Lesbians: The Role of Motivation to Respond without Prejudice." *Personality and Social Psychology Bulletin* 32 (10): 1325–1338.

Rathbun, Brian C., Joshua D. Kertzer, Jason Reifler, Paul Goren, and Thomas J. Scotto. 2016. "Taking Foreign Policy Personally: Personal Values and Foreign Policy Attitudes." *International Studies Quarterly* 60 (1): 124–137.

Riffkin, Rebecca. 2015. "Higher Support for Gender Affirmative Action than Race." Gallup, August 26. Available at http://www.gallup.com/poll/184772/higher-support-gender-affirmative-action-race.aspx.

Rodriguez, Victoria. 2019. "23 Girls Get Real about Why They Joined the Women's March." *Seventeen*, January 18. Available at https://www.seventeen.com/life/a15841964/girls-womens-march.

Rohlinger, Deana. 2018. "Three Reasons Why Teachers Are Protesting Now." *News and Observer*, May 4. Available at http://www.newsobserver.com/opinion/op-ed/article210455909.html.

Rokeach, Milton. 1973. *The Nature of Human Values*. New York: Free Press.

Ruddick, Sara. 1980. "Maternal Thinking." *Feminist Studies* 6 (2): 342–367.

Saad, Lydia. 2012. "U.S. Acceptance of Gay/Lesbian Relations Is the New Normal." Gallup, May 14. Available at http://www.gallup.com/poll/154634/Acceptance-Gay-Lesbian-Relations-New-Normal.aspx.

Saad, Lydia, and Jeffrey M. Jones. 2016. "U.S. Concern about Global Warming at Eight-Year High." Gallup, March 16. Available at http://www.gallup.com/poll/190010/concern-global-warming-eight-year-high.aspx.

Sapiro, Virginia. 2002. "It's the Context, Situation, and Question, Stupid: The Gender Basis of Public Opinion." In *Understanding Public Opinion*, 2nd ed., edited by Barbara Norrander and Clyde Wilcox, 21–41. Washington, DC: CQ Press.

———. 2003. "Theorizing Gender in Political Psychology Research." In *Oxford Handbook of Political Psychology*, edited by David O. Sears, Leonie Huddy, and Robert Jervis, 601–634. New York: Oxford University Press.

Sapiro, Virginia, and Pamela Johnston Conover. 1997. "The Variable Gender Basis of Electoral Politics: Gender and Context in the 1992 US Election." *British Journal of Political Science* 27:497–523.

Schlesinger, Mark, and Caroline Heldman. 2001. "Gender Gap or Gender Gaps? New Perspectives on Support for Government Action and Policies." *Journal of Politics* 63 (1): 59–92.

Schnittker, Jason, Jeremy Freese, and Brian Powell. 2003. "Who Are Feminists and What Do They Believe? The Role of Generations." *American Sociological Review* 68 (4): 607–622.

Schuman, Howard, Charlotte Steeh, Lawrence Bobo, and Maria Krysan. 1997. *Racial Attitudes in America: Trends and Interpretations*. Cambridge, MA: Harvard University Press.

Schwartz, Shalom H. 1992. "Universals in the Content and Structure of Values: Theoretical Advances and Empirical Tests in 20 Countries." In *Advances in Experimental Social Psychology*, edited by M. P. Zanna, 1–65. New York: Academic Press.

Schwartz, Shalom H., and Anat Bardi. 2001. "Value Hierarchies across Cultures: Taking a Similarities Perspective." *Journal of Cross-Cultural Psychology* 32 (3): 268–290.

Schwartz, Shalom H., Gian Vittorio Caprara, and Michele Vecchione. 2010. "Basic Personal Values, Core Political Values, and Voting: A Longitudinal Analysis." *Political Psychology* 31 (3): 421–452.

Schwartz, Shalom H., Gila Melech, Arielle Lehmann, Steven Burgess, Mari Harris, and Vicki Owens. 2001. "Extending the Cross-Cultural Validity of the Theory of Basic Human Values with a Different Method of Measurement." *Journal of Cross-Cultural Psychology* 32 (5): 519–542.

Schwartz, Shalom H., and Tammy Rubel. 2005. "Sex Differences in Value Priorities: Cross-Cultural and Multimethod Studies." *Journal of Personality and Social Psychology* 89 (6): 1010–1028.

Scott, Jacqueline. 1989. "Conflicting Beliefs about Abortion: Legal Approval and Moral Doubts." *Social Psychology Quarterly* 52 (4): 319–326.

Sears, David O., and Cary L. Funk. 1990. "Self-Interest in Americans' Political Opinions." In *Beyond Self-Interest*, edited by Jane J. Mansbridge, 147–170. Chicago: University of Chicago Press.

———. 1991. "The Role of Self-Interest in Social and Political Attitudes." In *Advances in Experimental Social Psychology*, edited by M. P. Zanna, 2–91. New York: Academic Press.

Sears, David O., and Leonie Huddy. 1990. "On the Origins of Political Disunity among Women." In *Women, Politics and Change*, edited by Louise A. Tilly and Patricia Gurin, 249–277. New York: Russell Sage Foundation.

Sganga, Nicole. 2017. "Meet the Protesters Flooding Politicians' Town Halls." *CBS News*, February 24. Available at https://www.cbsnews.com/news/meet-the-protesters-flooding-politicians-town-halls.

Shapiro, Robert Y., and Harpreet Mahajan. 1986. "Gender Differences in Policy Preferences: A Summary of Trends from the 1960s to the 1980s." *Public Opinion Quarterly* 50:42–61.

Shirazi, Rez, and Anders Biel. 2005. "Internal-External Causal Attributions and Perceived Government Responsibility for Need Provision: A 14-Culture Study." *Journal of Cross-Cultural Psychology* 36 (1): 96–116.

Sidanius, Jim, Shana Levin, James Liu, and Felicia Pratto. 2000. "Social Dominance Orientation, Anti-egalitarianism and the Political Psychology of Gender: An Extension and Cross-Cultural Replication." *European Journal of Social Psychology* 30 (1): 41–67.

Simien, Evelyn M., and Rosalee A. Clawson. 2004. "The Intersection of Race and Gender: An Examination of Black Feminist Consciousness, Race Consciousness, and Policy Attitudes." *Social Science Quarterly* 85 (3): 793–810.

Sinclair, Harriet. 2017. "Republican Orrin Hatch in Children's Healthcare Debate: Some People Won't Lift a Finger to Help Themselves." *Newsweek*, December 3. Available at http://www.newsweek.com/republican-orrin-hatch-childrens-healthcare-debate-some-people-wont-lift-729712.

Smith, D. Clayton. 2001. "Environmentalism, Feminism, and Gender." *Sociological Inquiry* 71 (3): 314–334.

Smith, Tom W. 1984. "The Polls: Gender and Attitudes toward Violence." *Public Opinion Quarterly* 48 (1): 384–396.

Somma, Mark, and Tolleson-Rinehart, Sue. 1997. "Tracking the Elusive Green Women: Sex, Environmentalism, and Feminism in the United States and Europe." *Political Research Quarterly* 50 (1): 153–169.

Stack, Steven. 2000. "Support for the Death Penalty: A Gender-Specific Model." *Sex Roles* 43 (3–4): 163–179.

Stern, Paul C., Thomas Dietz, and Linda Kalof. 1993. "Value Orientations, Gender, and Environmental Concern." *Environment and Behavior* 25 (3): 322–348.

Steuernagel, Gertrude, David Ahern, and Margaret Conway. 1997. *Women and Political Participation: Culture Change in the Political Arena.* Washington, DC: CQ Press.

Stevens, Heidi. 2017. "What We Can Learn from Women's March Blowback." *Chicago Tribune,* January 24. Available at http://www.chicagotribune.com/lifestyles/stevens/ct-upside-of-womens-march-haters-balancing-0124-20170124-column.html.

Stokes, Bruce. 2013. "Big Gender Gap in Global Public Opinion about Use of Drones." Pew Research Center, July 25. Available at http://www.pewresearch.org/fact-tank/2013/07/25/big-gender-gap-in-global-public-opinion-about-use-of-drones.

Stokes, Bruce, Richard Wike, and Jill Carle. 2015. "Global Concern about Climate Change, Broad Support for Limiting Emissions." Pew Research Center, November 5. Available at https://www.pewresearch.org/global/2015/11/05/global-concern-about-climate-change-broad-support-for-limiting-emissions.

Stoutenborough, James W., Donald P. Haider-Markel, and Mahalley D. Allen. 2006. "Reassessing the Impact of Supreme Court Decisions on Public Opinion: Gay Civil Rights Cases." *Political Research Quarterly* 59 (3): 419–433.

Strickler, Jennifer, and Nicholas L. Danigelis. 2002. "Changing Frameworks in Attitudes toward Abortion." *Sociological Forum* 17 (2): 187–201.

Stuart, Tessa. 2017. "Inside the Historic Women's March on Washington." *Rolling Stone,* January 22. Available at https://www.rollingstone.com/politics/features/inside-the-historic-womens-march-on-washington-w462325.

Swift, Art, and Steve Ander. 2015. "Americans' Views of Gov't Handling of Healthcare Up Sharply." Gallup, May 6. Available at http://www.gallup.com/poll/183014/americans-views-gov-handling-healthcare-sharply.aspx.

Thornton, Michael C., Linda M. Chatters, Robert Joseph Taylor, and Walter R. Allen. 1990. "Sociodemographic and Environmental Correlates of Racial Socialization by Black Parents." *Child Development* 61 (2): 401–409.

Tickner, J. Ann. 1992. *Gender in International Relations.* Vol. 5. New York: Columbia University Press.

Truth, Sojourner. 1887. "Sojourner Truth on the Press." In *History of Woman Suffrage,* vol. 2, *1861–1876,* edited by Elizabeth Cady Stanton, Susan Brownell Anthony, and Matilda Joslyn Gage, 926–928. Rochester, NY: Charles Mann.

Ufheil, Angela. 2018. "Des Moines Women's March Draws Thousands to Iowa's Capitol." *Des Moines Register*, January 20. Available at https://www.desmoinesregister.com/story/news/2018/01/20/des-moines-womens-march-attracts-several-thousand-iowas-capitol-building/1050915001.

Unnever, James D., and Francis T. Cullen. 2007. "The Racial Divide in Support for the Death Penalty: Does White Racism Matter?" *Social Forces* 85 (3): 1281–1301.

Unnever, James D., Francis T. Cullen, and Julian V. Roberts. 2005. "Not Everyone Strongly Supports the Death Penalty: Assessing Weakly-Held Attitudes about Capital Punishment." *American Journal of Criminal Justice* 29 (2): 187–216.

Verba, Sidney, Nancy Burns, and Kay Lehman Schlozman. 1997. "Knowing and Caring about Politics: Gender and Political Engagement." *Journal of Politics* 59 (4): 1051–1072.

Weber, Max. 1965. *Politics as a Vocation*. Minneapolis: Fortress Press.

Weiss, Penny A. 1998. *Conversations with Feminism: Political Theory and Practice*. New York: Rowman and Littlefield.

Welch, Susan. 1975. "Support among Women for the Issues of the Women's Movement." *Sociological Quarterly* 16 (2): 216–227.

Welch, Susan, and John Hibbing. 1992. "Financial Conditions, Gender, and Voting in American National Elections." *Journal of Politics* 54 (1): 197–213.

Whitehead, John T., and Michael B. Blankenship. 2000. "The Gender Gap in Capital Punishment Attitudes: An Analysis of Support and Opposition." *American Journal of Criminal Justice* 25 (1): 1–13.

Wilcox, Clyde, Lara Hewitt, and Dee Allsop. 1996. "The Gender Gap in Attitudes toward the Gulf War: A Cross-National Perspective." *Journal of Peace Research* 33 (1): 67–82.

Wilcox, Clyde, and Robin Wolpert. 2000. "Gay Rights in the Public Sphere: Public Opinion on Gay and Lesbian Equality." In *The Politics of Same-Sex Marriage*, edited by C. A. Rimmerman and C. Wilcox, 409–432. Chicago: University of Chicago Press.

Winter, Nicholas J. G. 2008. *Dangerous Frames: How Ideas about Race and Gender Shape Public Opinion*. Chicago: University of Chicago Press.

Wirls, Daniel. 1986. "Reinterpreting the Gender Gap." *Public Opinion Quarterly* 50 (3): 316–330.

Wolpert, Robin M., and James G. Gimpel. 1998. "Self-Interest, Symbolic Politics, and Public Attitudes toward Gun Control." *Political Behavior* 20 (3): 241–262.

Wood, Wendy, and Alice H. Eagly. 2002. "A Cross-Cultural Analysis of the Behavior of Women and Men: Implications for the Origins of Sex Differences." *Psychological Bulletin* 128 (5): 699–727.

———. 2012. "Biosocial Construction of Sex Differences and Similarities in Behavior." *Advances in Experimental Social Psychology* 46:55–123.

Zainulbhai, Hani. 2015. "Women, More than Men, Say Climate Change Will Harm Them Personally." Pew Research Center, December 2. Available at http://www.pewresearch.org/fact-tank/2015/12/02/women-more-than-men-say-climate-change-will-harm-them-personally.

Zalewski, Marysia. 1994. "The Women/'Women' Question in International Relations." *Millennium* 23:407–423.

Zaller, John. 1992. *The Nature and Origins of Mass Opinion*. New York: Cambridge University Press.

Zelezny, Lynnette C., Poh-Pheng Chua, and Christina Aldrich. 2000. "Elaborating on Gender Differences in Environmentalism." *Journal of Social Issues* 56 (3): 443–457.

# Index

**Mary-Kate Lizotte** is an Associate Professor of Political Science in the Department of Social Sciences at Augusta University.